Rethinking Christian Martyrdom

Critiquing Religion: Discourse, Culture, Power

Series editor: Craig Martin

Critiquing Religion: Discourse, Culture, Power publishes works that historicize both religions and modern discourses on "religion" that treat it as a unique object of study. Using diverse methodologies and social theories, volumes in this series view religions and discourses on religion as commonplace rhetorics, authenticity narratives, or legitimating myths, which function in the creation, maintenance, and contestation of social formations. Works in the series are on the cutting edge of critical scholarship, regarding "religion" as just another cultural tool used to gerrymander social space and distribute power relations in the modern world. *Critiquing Religion: Discourse, Culture, Power* provides a unique home for reflexive, critical work in the field of religious studies.

Christian Tourist Attractions, Mythmaking and Identity Formation
Edited by Erin Roberts and Jennifer Eyl

French Populism and Discourses on Secularism
Per-Erik Nilsson

Reframing the Masters of Suspicion: Marx, Nietzsche, and Freud
Andrew Dole

Religion, Nationalism and Foreign Policy
Filiz Coban Oran

Representing Religion in Fil
Edited by Tenzan Eaghll and Rebekka King

*Spirituality, Corporate Culture, and American Business:
The Neoliberal Ethic and the Spirit of Global Capital*
James Dennis LoRusso

Stereotyping Religion: Critiquing Clichés
Edited by Brad Stoddard and Craig Martin

Rethinking Christian Martyrdom

The Blood or the Seed?

Matt Recla

BLOOMSBURY ACADEMIC
LONDON • NEW YORK • OXFORD • NEW DELHI • SYDNEY

BLOOMSBURY ACADEMIC
Bloomsbury Publishing Plc
50 Bedford Square, London, WC1B 3DP, UK
1385 Broadway, New York, NY 10018, USA
29 Earlsfort Terrace, Dublin 2, Ireland

BLOOMSBURY, BLOOMSBURY ACADEMIC and the Diana logo are trademarks of Bloomsbury Publishing Plc

First published in Great Britain 2023
This paperback edition published 2024

Copyright © Matt Recla, 2023

Matt Recla has asserted his right under the Copyright, Designs and Patents Act, 1988, to be identified as Author of this work.

For legal purposes the Preface on pp. vi–x constitutes an extension of this copyright page.

Cover image © Yi Lu / EyeEm. Getty Images

All rights reserved. No part of this publication may be reproduced or transmitted in any form or by any means, electronic or mechanical, including photocopying, recording, or any information storage or retrieval system, without prior permission in writing from the publishers.

Bloomsbury Publishing Plc does not have any control over, or responsibility for, any third-party websites referred to or in this book. All internet addresses given in this book were correct at the time of going to press. The author and publisher regret any inconvenience caused if addresses have changed or sites have ceased to exist, but can accept no responsibility for any such changes.

A catalogue record for this book is available from the British Library.

Library of Congress Control Number: 2022935013

ISBN: HB: 978-1-3501-8425-1
PB: 978-1-3501-8429-9
ePDF: 978-1-3501-8426-8
eBook: 978-1-3501-8427-5

Series: Critiquing Religion: Discourse, Culture, Power

Typeset by Newgen KnowledgeWorks Pvt. Ltd., Chennai, India

To find out more about our authors and books visit www.bloomsbury.com and sign up for our newsletters

Contents

Preface		vi
1	Why Martyrdom at All?	1
2	"Willing Suicide": Martyrdom as Self-Formation	19
3	"True Because a Man Dies for It": Martyrdom as Institutional Violence	41
4	Blood Is Seed: Martyrdom and the Triumph of Christianity	57
5	"Voluntary" Martyrdom: Avoiding the Stigma of Suicide	93
6	"In Love with Death": Pathology and Identity in Martyrdom	113
7	The Immorality of Religious Martyrdom	139
Conclusion		163
Notes		169
Bibliography		201
Index		213

Preface

I can't remember what first stimulated my interest specifically in the study of Christian martyrdom. Having grown up deeply involved with a nondenominational Christian evangelical church, though, my higher education pursuits always involved religious history. Driven by the inherited presumption that the "original" Christianity was plainly depicted in the gospels, and that the intervening millennia of history were both unimportant and degraded, I was drawn to the first centuries of Christian history. Surely the origins of the tradition held the keys to its truth, certainly more so than subsequent developments.

Although I wouldn't have described it this way at the time, I was motivated to understand Christianity from the outside, since I knew surprisingly little about the history of the tradition. Mine was a largely ahistorical faith lodged in the text of the New Testament and its current interpretation by pastors and exuberant youth group leaders. The Vineyard Movement and the "Toronto Blessing" were having a strong impact in my congregation as I came of age, however, and these movements made frequent reference to the early church to support charismatic practices like prophecies, speaking in tongues, and being "slain in the Spirit." Perhaps all of this contributed to my desire to learn more about the earliest years of the Christianity. I was struck by the phenomenon of Christianity growing from a handful of people to a worldwide tradition—how did it happen, exactly? My insider position led me to believe that the answers came from the tradition itself; essentially, it grew because it was Christian. I was compelled to fill in the details with further study.

My childhood exposure to the phenomenon of martyrdom in Christian history was comparatively limited, save the extensive focus on Jesus himself. Contemporary martyrs, on the other hand, powerfully gripped my attention. Their occurrence reiterated both the persistent power of evil forces—corporal and political as well as spiritual—and the inevitable triumph of Christianity.

In retrospect, these contemporary martyrdoms, whose stories were told by traveling missionaries and reports from organizations such as Voice of the Martyrs, had common features. First, they came from elsewhere. They were not here, in the United States, and that was demonstrated both explicitly and implicitly.[1] A sense of gratitude, and usually a touch of patriotism, seemed to be a perennial component of stories of martyrdom. *We* are blessed because we are not placed in situations where we need to make a choice about martyrdom. Our freedom was presented as a spiritual blessing and the obvious telos of any divinely inspired earthly government. Martyrdom elsewhere was a reaffirmation that martyrdom was not only unnecessary here but also not possible, precisely because unnecessary. Cases of religiously related deaths with domestic ties such as in Jonestown or Waco, those that violated the norm by occurring closer to home, were dismissible because of the heterodox beliefs of those involved, despite their self-identification with Christianity.

Martyrdoms provided a sense of accomplishment that the world was being "won for Christ," given the paradoxical belief that more Christian deaths means more Christian growth. They instilled an urgency to fulfill the "Great Commission," a command given by Jesus to his disciples in the gospels of Matthew and Luke, to "go and make disciples of all nations, baptizing them in the name of the Father and of the Son and of the Holy Spirit, and teaching them to obey everything I have commanded you" (Mt. 28:19-20). The pain and suffering of those persecuted would cease when the nations were converted, and our part was to contribute monetarily to this cause. Those teenagers from our religious community who "answered the call" to engage in missionary work with organizations such as Youth With a Mission were accorded a special status and provided the opportunity to share progress in the Great Commission whenever they returned home.

The second characteristic of the martyrdoms I was exposed to—at least the ones I remember—was an element of significant pain and torture.[2] The vivid retelling of bodily disintegration is familiar to any scholar of Christian martyrdom. Many early Christian martyrdoms gloss over detail of the actual death of the martyr, emphasizing instead the martyr's exchange with the presiding official or the crowd prior to death. To the extent that those stories were told in my church, however, they have long since been crowded out of my mind by bloodier tales, ones that counterintuitively provided, through their excess, a psychological and emotional distancing to accompany the geographic distance of their occurrence.

I remember in particular a tale I heard as a child, likely from a missionary guest speaker, of a Chinese pastor who was incarcerated for his Christian activities. As I recall the story, officials had been attempting by various means to get him to renounce Christ and cease his evangelizing activities. Finally, they brought the pastor's young son together with him for interrogation. The officials informed the pastor that they would cut off his son's fingers before his eyes one by one as long as he continued to refuse to renounce his activities.³ The pastor tearfully prayed and exhorted his son to remain strong as he began to lose his digits. I don't even remember the ultimate outcome; at the very least, I imagine the son would have been horribly dismembered. That was hardly the point. The moral of the story was both to appreciate the privilege of not being tested in such a painful fashion combined with the implication that a Christian ought to be willing to suffer and die rather than deny Christianity, even in word only.

Such tragic and gruesome tales produced a mixture of horror and fascination in me, the confluence of which was remarkably effective in amplifying a profound sense of guilt. I wanted to hear more, to learn of other horrible tales, all the while knowing that I neither desired such opportunities to "prove" myself nor that I should wish such unspeakable things on anyone. Fascination, horror, and consequent self-revulsion were an inseparable conglomeration of feelings, the combination of which left a permanent mark on my memory. I was unaware that I was not alone in my ambivalence toward martyrdom.

During my years of graduate study of religion, I experienced a deconversion from the Christianity that had provided an anchor for my life's narrative up to that point. Deconversion implies a quick transition, which this certainly was not—in retrospect it had been taking place for a period of years as I examined more closely the flaws in my narrative of my life, the areas where it seemed to fail the ideological coherence I thought it had. My genuine love for my beliefs and my curiosity to learn more had made graduate study in the history of Christianity a natural fit, but I grew disenchanted with what I perceived as discrepancies between the teachings of the Christian communities I took part in and the actions of those who participated in them, including myself. The history of Christianity seemed to provide only echoes of the same discrepancies. Though it does not produce the same result for everyone—and though it felt intensely personal and unique at the time—increasing numbers of Americans have had this experience, or something like it, in the last few decades.⁴ It is not without reason that many devout parents warn their children—my warning came from a longtime mentor—that higher education will "shipwreck your faith."⁵

This may be the most important contextual fact about my work ... or it may not. My experience within Christianity was a beneficial one, overall. If I judged the tradition solely by its impact on me, the good outweighed the bad, I think. So it is not out of some personal animosity that I critique the tradition in which I spent nearly the first three decades of my life. At the same time, the bulk of my scholarly work has been animated at least in part by a deeply held (and at times acutely felt) sense that there is something deceptive about the Christian tradition, that it does more harm than good. Over time, and subsequent to my deconversion, I came to realize this deception is not unique to the Christian tradition but is a tendency of all institutions that exert control over our lives, that *are* our lives: to become an unquestioned good.

Even after finding this commonality, though, and despite my now outsider status, I've continued to focus particularly on the Christian tradition for a couple reasons. The first is personal and practical: it is what I grew up with and where my academic expertise lies. These are sunk costs I have been unable to leave behind. The second is particular to the field of religious studies and may be more the case with Christianity. Studying "religion" with a focus on Christianity is an interesting locus that carries with it the burdens of the history of Western education and its inextricability from theology. A theological approach to academic study remains overt and unapologetic in many areas of the study of religion, and there is certainly a place for that. In many conversations and conference presentations over the years, however, I discovered a quasi-theological approach to Christianity as well, one that bracketed, but left implicit, theological truths, thus positioning itself to have listeners in multiple audiences. Certainly one can study religion without being religious, I suppose, but it seems exceedingly rare that one would study a particular religious tradition without any stake in the game. From one perspective, that common fact neutralizes the impact of any particular position. We're all coming from somewhere, right? The Christian tradition is so embedded into the fabric of education, the study of religion, and even Western culture more broadly, however, that our scrutiny should extend further. Combined with the particular American institution of the First Amendment, the embeddedness of Christian ideas allows them to be broadly accepted with minimal question, because they have always been there.

Part of me regrets the felt need for self-disclosure, for contextualization, in order to help the reader situate the text before them. What I appreciate most about key thinkers employed in the field of religious studies, from Durkheim, Weber, and Heidegger to Foucault and Derrida, and within the history of Christianity, from Gibbon to Frend, is that they were unburdened—on the page at least—with this need. Their ideas were bold and unapologetic, holding themselves wide open to critique, perhaps having bitten off more than they could successfully chew. Much scholarship now critiques this seeming hubris as we parse their ideas according to their authors' identities, for this is the fundamental truth of the moment. I will discuss this thoroughly in the context of martyrdom, but "identity" is present in martyrdom because it is present in all historical, psychological, and social analysis. We parse our reality according to our race, ethnicity, ability, religious affiliation, politics, and more. We provide each other a willing means of dismissal. We can thus be comfortable we are not making ourselves too vulnerable, but we can also be left wondering if we are saying anything at all. Are ideas all wholly contained within identities? Though it will not reach near the impact of the aforementioned "greats," my writing has been inspired by their spirit, if appropriately chastened by the current need to know (and share) my place.

Finally, if I'm being honest, some part of the Christian narrative, or at least my interpretation of it, still resonates with me. From an experiential perspective, I'm as convinced now that there is no supernatural "Other" as I once was convinced that there was. Nonetheless, I am drawn to an ideal of socioeconomic leveling in the here and now, to the idea that we can overcome our worst tendencies to divide and conquer in order to maximize life for all living. In nostalgic moments, I wish as many do that it would come in the form of a supernatural savior. On reflection, however, I place hope in an existential authenticity and liberal ideals, slow-moving though they may be, as our best hope for redemption.

Though I have been developing many of the ideas in this text for years, the beginning of my concerted efforts to assemble them here coincided nearly exactly with the beginning of the country's shutdown due to Covid-19 in March 2020. Researching and writing is often a solitary affair, but the events of the last few years have increased this feeling. Nonetheless, I am grateful to the space and support offered by family and friends to complete this work. Thanks in particular to Hannah, Harland, Joe, and Juli Recla for their longtime and unwavering love and support. Thanks also to John Bieter, Riley Caldwell-O'Keefe, Beth DePalma Digeser, Hal Drake, Josh Harris, Doug Hezeltine, Ryan Myers, Charles Odahl, Brad Onishi, John Soboslai, Christine Thomas, and Shelton Woods. Not all of them would agree with my approach or my conclusions, but I have valued their friendship, mentorship, and relationship all the same.

1

Why Martyrdom at All?

The Martyrdom of John Allen Chau

In November of 2018, 26-year-old American John Allen Chau died at the hands of the Sentinelese, inhabitants of a remote island off the coast of India that is largely isolated from the modern world. With the help of fishermen from a neighboring island, Chau had landed alone on the island of North Sentinel—avoiding the coastal patrols designed to keep ships away from its shores—in order to introduce Christianity to its inhabitants, as he described in detail in his journals. The fishermen who transported him to the island reported seeing the Sentinelese dragging his body across the beach, presumably for burial, the following day. For a short time, Chau's death garnered significant international media attention. He was derided as foolish, deluded, and selfish by some in the media.[1] Family and some close friends lamented his death as unnecessary, but others who knew him (and many who didn't) acclaimed him as a martyr.[2] How should we understand his demise?

Unless we identify with Christianity like Chau, there is a different value in asking whether he is a martyr. It cedes the possible ground for a neutral discussion and veers into ideological territory. More specifically, asking this question is to participate in, and as a result provide support for, a Christian interpretive heuristic. While understandable, given the considerable cultural linkage between Christianity and martyrdom, it affords the tradition the ability to set the parameters for understanding the phenomenon and should give pause to those attempting to understand martyrdom outside a theological lens.

It is not only Christians who have an impulse to know whether Chau was a martyr, however. Why? On the simplest level, Chau's death seems to fit the martyr type, and we want to know whether our assumption is correct. This speaks to the prominence of Christian ideology in Western history and its continued functional value for many. We might argue instead that "martyr" represents a category that has cross-ideological value. In that case, we might compare and contrast different interpretations of martyrdom from religious and political traditions to find underlying commonalities. The problem here is that attributions of martyrdom are always contested, both within and across traditions, so finding consistent criteria is difficult.[3] Criteria governing martyrdom, regardless of tradition, are dynamic.

Though contested in scholarship, and while its application in the particular case is also contested in the public sphere, the definition of martyrdom is seemingly uncontroversial. It commonly denotes persons killed because of their beliefs, and it is usually assumed those beliefs are religious in nature. To put it another way, one might say martyrs die for something bigger than themselves.[4] Given that he was a Christian killed by the North Sentinelese, and given that his clear intent was to "share Christianity" with them, Chau seems to fit the definition. However, this common definition says both too much and too little. It is claiming too much to say that Chau was killed because of his beliefs. He did not know the language, and he was killed within hours of landing on the island. His reasons for landing remained unknown to the Sentinelese. It would also be inaccurate to say he died for his beliefs, which also implies his killers knew of his Christianity. On the other hand, "his beliefs" is not saying quite enough. They were not, after all, an either random or unique set of ideas; they represent a specific understanding of Christianity. Additionally, to assume that the martyr dies for "something bigger"—more important—than himself is (in most cases at least) to oversimplify what is a complex context into a simple binary.

This common definition owes its perspective to the communities that claim the martyr.[5] Identifying the martyr from this perspective, in many cases, requires untestable questions, such as whether the martyr was directed by the divine. While these questions are critical to the phenomenon of religious martyrdom, they are a poor starting place because of their theological assumptions. I will suggest that we begin with an alternate definition of martyrdom: *willing suicide with ideological support*. This is not an insider definition and it may seem unpleasant or controversial, for reasons I will discuss. It also avoids the inaccuracies mentioned above. "Willing" makes clear that intent is inherent to martyrdom. A person who is not willing to commit or encourage their own destruction cannot be a martyr. Note that willingness is not claiming that, given ideal circumstances, the person would still choose death. It is to say that given their real or perceived circumstances, they are willing to kill themselves. In his seminal work on suicide, Emile Durkheim defines it as "all cases of death resulting directly or indirectly from a positive or negative act of the victim himself, which he knows will produce this result."⁶ "Suicide" in my definition of martyrdom conveys more precisely the sense of willingness that "dying" does not—allowing oneself to be destroyed. It also allows for the possibility that the martyr may actively participate in their destruction in a way that would normally be described as "killing." "Ideology" conveys more than "belief(s)" in suggesting a system that is shared by others. Though I will primarily examine martyrdom in Christianity, "ideology" also provides space for other religious traditions as well as nonreligious institutions. "With ideological support" suggests something different than "for an ideology," however. "For an ideology," for example, would still be a concession to the institution that assumes the willing suicide's intentions are identical with it. This is not something we can know to be true, and assuming it is the case adds several attendant challenges. However, it is the case that the institution provides both general support for the idea of martyrdom (and sometimes support in the specific case) as well as naming and supporting the so-named martyr after death. This is the primary criterion that differentiates the martyr from the willing suicide.

So was John Allen Chau a Christian martyr? The phenomenon of martyrdom has been a central element in Christianity since its beginnings, and given the institution's global influence today, it is no surprise that martyrdom became the question around which his history and death were primarily discussed. Chau was raised in a family with considerable roots in Christianity; he attended the same evangelical university, Oral Roberts, that his parents and siblings did. He engaged in evangelization efforts with multiple Christian organizations across many different countries before his final journey.⁷ These social milieux did not predetermine his end—indeed, the vast majority with Chau's circumstances would not seriously consider following in his footsteps—but they provided the environment within which he made his fateful decision.

Chau was also clearly aware of the possibility of becoming a martyr. Though his death would be contingent on his actions, he saw it as entirely up to God. He wrote in his journal, "If you want me to get actually shot, or even killed with an arrow then so be it. I think I could be more useful alive though, but to you, God, I give all the glory of whatever happens. I DON'T WANT to die."⁸ Clearly, though he was conflicted, if staying alive was the most important thing on Chau's mind, he would not have set foot on the island shortly after writing these lines. Durkheim suggests that "life is none the less abandoned because one desires it at the moment of renouncing it."⁹ Chau's conviction that God wanted—whether having directly communicated with Chau or through the command of the "Great Commission"[10]—him to share Christianity with the Sentinelese islanders outweighed his fear for his own life.

Despite this seeming evidence in his favor, Christians do not agree unequivocally that Chau was a martyr. Eliza Griswold notes that many missionaries she spoke with after Chau's death are concerned about the amount of attention paid to his case. "For many Christians, it was difficult to weigh the morality of his actions."[11] Others looked on his death more favorably. One missionary and college professor told Griswold, "Often, we look at stories when missionaries are killed, we see a drastic increase in interest … Do we feel that God would call someone to a mission field knowing that they'd be martyred and knowing that there will be a greater interest in mission and in God being known among the nations?"[12] The question is left unanswered, but he and others seem to conclude—though they may be unwilling to say so plainly—that insofar the martyr's death promotes others to become missionaries, it is a positive outcome. Indeed, a *Fox News* follow-up a year after Chau's death is titled "US missionary killed by remote island tribe inspires others to join mission field," based on the claims of the missionary organization Chau had been involved in before his death.[13]

Disagreement over the legitimacy of a given martyrdom is not uncommon within a tradition. This has been the case with Christian martyrs throughout history as well as martyrs in and around all other ideologies as well. Nonetheless, there is a more fundamental question we can ask: What does martyrdom *do* for those involved with the phenomenon? Insofar as debates over martyrdom continue to exist, they do because the term retains some functional value. Why might categorizing a death as martyrdom be functional?

Existence is the foundational prerequisite for humanness, and we are psychologically and biologically "hardwired" for self-preservation.[14] As a result, we are fascinated by the counterintuitive, willing self-destruction the martyr enacts. We seek an explanation, an excuse for this willing suicide, which is really a justification for our own continued striving for existence. This justification is fragile because unverifiable, but to the extent it is successful it is extremely powerful, grounded as it is on the firmest ground of existence: human life. This existential fact provides the basis for martyrdom's efficaciousness—an exception to the rule—and allows us to examine its functionality for more specific participants.

With a base level of functionality established, we need to distinguish the functionality for the various parties involved. First and most important, what does martyrdom do for the martyr? This question has been largely neglected in scholarship because it has primarily examined martyrdom within specific institutional contexts. Since the Christian martyr dies for Christianity, the justification must be found within its dogmas, right? Here we find most commonly that she sacrifices herself for the cause, for her God, for her eternal existence. But this can only be the understanding of those who remain, which may include the would-be martyr, but not the martyr. The martyr is forever hidden behind the impenetrable barrier of death. Prior to this, however, it is clear that the community that claims the martyr is not the hermeneutic key to understanding martyrdom. The history of Christianity provides some context for understanding Christian martyrdom, but little about understanding the broader phenomenon. Wrestling with what willing suicide does for the subsequently titled martyr will form the basis of my approach to rethinking martyrdom.

A second question, then, is what martyrdom does for those who remain. Chau's death draws our attention because it combines two important factors. First, it reminds us of our own mortality, as all deaths have the potential to do. But in that Chau's death was intentional, it also suggests possible answers to questions of meaning. Chau was aware of the deadly risks of his actions and choose to act anyway. This counterintuitive act might suggest (though it needn't) that he knew something we don't or found value somewhere we have not.[15] Cases like Chau's are rare in that they highlight the inescapable phenomenon of death *and* conspicuously locate meaning there. Further, these cases draw upon these two elements simultaneously—at least as we encounter them—and this is fascinating because we seem to instinctively conceive of death and meaning as polar opposites. As noted in the previous paragraph, death is the limit, the end, of the possibility of meaning; as a result, it is something that we tend to avoid, both in practice and in anticipation. When ultimate meaning is seemingly found *in* (or through, or beyond) death, then, we question with excited hope that traditional juxtaposition of death and meaning. Chau—despite considerable fear, which he expressed in his journals in the days leading up to his demise—valued the possibility of sharing Christianity with the Sentinelese islanders above his continued existence. As distant observers, we are irresistibly drawn to question whether Chau's death points to an objective meaning, to a greater purpose. After all, if there *is* objective meaning—if Chau was right, and if his purpose could apply to me—I want to know it as well. This is the promise of martyrdom. It steps into the void and responds to the question of meaning with an unequivocal "here!" But where is "here," exactly?

This is where academic scholarship on Christian martyrdom has been focused; "here" may be supernatural, but it is represented by the Christian institution. Institutions are defined as "multi-faceted, durable social structures made up of symbolic elements, social activities, and material resources," which "provide meaning and stability to social life."[16] Christian martyrdom, following this definition, would be one among many symbolic elements that provide meaning for social life. Since that meaning resides in the Christian institution, it may be simpler to say that Christian martyrdom validates Christianness. Over time, this description has moved from being simply functional to being essential, at least for many scholars: martyrdom *is* an identity discourse. While the use of martyrdom as one means to talk about community identity should not be overlooked—perhaps particularly in the case of Christianity—it by no means explains the willing suicide, the process of claiming that willing suicide for the institution as martyrdom, or the unique way this process unfolded for the institution of Christianity. Christian martyrdom as identity discourse enters the discussion with all these layers established. If Christian martyrdom is Christian identity discourse, then martyrdom ceases to be an independent phenomenon and becomes a function of Christian belief. Martyrdom is by no means unique to Christianity; neither is it ubiquitous within Christianity, so equating martyrdom to Christian identity discourse serves the function of describing and/or reinscribing Christian ideology.

That Christian martyrdom contributes to a discourse about Christianness is both true and a facile observation. Everything labeled Christian participates in Christian meaning-making in some way—this is tautological. The comparatively unexplored question is *how* martyrdom contributes to Christian discourse. I argue that Christian martyrs provide sustenance for the Christian narrative in a fairly straightforward fashion. The blood, the flesh, the life force of the willing suicide are consumed by the Christian institution, which chews up and then regurgitates the Christian martyr to be swallowed again by its adherents as meaning-making discourse. For these adherents, the Christian martyr legitimates the Christian narrative that justifies their continued source of meaning, and thereby their existence.

This explanation of martyrdom's function may—like the definition above—initially seem unpalatable, or perhaps uncharitable. I think this is in large part because Christianity is so inextricably interwoven into the Western tradition. The advantage of this explanation is that it points out the missing element in current discussions of Christian martyrdom: the death. No matter how one speaks of John Allen Chau, the starting point of the discussion is that he is dead. There is no question of his contribution to Christian identity formation without this prior fact. That Chau went to his death intentionally, albeit with understandable trepidation, is without question, and that he understood his potential death in Christian terms is also indubitable. However, it is also abundantly clear that the vast majority of those who identify as Christians do not intend to be and will never be martyrs. This gap is not successfully bridged by equating martyrdom to a Christian identity discourse.

It is important to emphasize that martyrdom tells us nothing about the truth of a given institution. It provides a poignant illustration of several universal human phenomena: (1) how we are purpose-seeking creatures, (2) how we are willing to trade the lives of others for the security of purpose, and how, given that fact, (3) institutions support the destruction of certain lives for their survival and promotion. In addition to these sociocultural and phenomenological facts, we can add another: the particular lives that we trade, that we kill for meaning, are not random. They are vulnerable lives. Self-selected though they may be, they are potentially compromised lives that institutions leverage for their self-perpetuation. After all, as mentioned above, not all adherents to an ideology that promotes martyrdom become themselves martyrs; thus, there are other psychosocial considerations for understanding martyrdom. There have been numerous explanations for this discrepancy. Previous generations of modern scholarship placed the blame for the martyr's death primarily on the martyr herself. More recently the aforementioned "identity" approach to martyrdom has attempted to redeem Christian martyrs from the blame for their own deaths but has missed in this process that while "blaming the victim" is an unhelpful scholarly approach, reabsorbing martyrdom into the institutional community overlooks clear differences between martyrs and non-martyrs. Intentionally or not, it perpetuates the predominant institutional narrative that death validates institutional truth. An important question, then, is *who* is more likely to become a martyr, and why? While the full answer is not yet known, we will explore the extent to which psychosocial factors hold answers that theological and sociocultural ones lack. Why did John Chau make the deadly calculation when so many others do not?

As noted above, some of Chau's fellow Christians are able to reconcile his death through a theological lens: Chau's death was a transaction with the divine, and one that energizes Christians, which potentially brings more into the fold, securing and validating the institution's meaning-making ability. Why, then, would some other Christians be reticent to acclaim Chau as a martyr? Christianity exists as an institution in cooperation and competition with all others. Individuals participate in a number of intersecting and overlapping cultural institutions, and while this introduces complexity and at times contradiction, it also avoids an unhealthy overreliance on any particular institution. For example, since Chau seems to have broken the law in order to land on the island of North Sentinel,[17] this puts the institution of Christianity in competition with the institution of law. Acclaiming Chau as a martyr may imply approval of breaking the law, in this case a law banning outside contact with the Sentinelese for the protection of all involved. The illegality of his actions was at least a minor concern for Chau himself but outweighed by other convictions. Those who remain clearly weigh their institutional obligations, and tactical approaches to those obligations, differently.

Institutional tension was no different in the ancient past, and many of the earliest Christian martyrdoms were no less controversial. The passage of time and the establishment of a hegemonic Western Christian institution have rendered the ideal martyr one-dimensional and uncomplicated, have made the martyr simply "Christian." And this is the best outcome for institutional power, that it operates uncontroversially, that it is not seen as arbitrary or partisan.[18] When it strikes us that a particular martyrdom is complicated and controversial, we take it to be different from the norm, but all instances of martyrdom are complicated in this way because there is no necessary correlation between willing suicide and the institution. That link must be intentionally forged and frequently maintained.

Most Christians who expressed reservations did so not based on Chau as an individual but to the extent that the particulars of Chau's case would hurt rather than harm the goal of spreading Christianity. Was martyrdom in Chau's individual interest, though? Though he was conflicted and had to talk himself out of his fear of death, he calculated it was. His family disagreed. According to John's father, a psychiatrist, "John was an 'innocent child' … who died from an 'extreme' vision of Christianity taken to its logical conclusion." Another pastor and former friend suggested that Chau's death reveals problems with "evangelical culture."[19] The subsequent media attention from Chau's death, and the consequent arrest of the fishermen who helped Chau to the island, led the spouse of one of the fishermen to comment, "He has filled my family with sorrow for our whole life."[20] The young man's death was not seen as beneficial to those closest to the events.

Chau's father's comment about "extreme" Christianity is worth further consideration. The father likely concludes that a Christianity that asks the individual to seriously risk death is extreme. Is he correct? Is this extreme undertaking ever justifiable, and by whom? If the Christian worldview is taken in isolation, it seems that there might be few, if any, mitigating factors in spreading the gospel, especially if God commands one to do so. While this may seem artificial, it also seems to be a fundamental characteristic of martyrs like Chau. Chau's father pragmatically takes into account other institutions (family, work, etc.), but there is a sense in which it is unjustified to do so. His understandably is a justificatory mechanism based on a sincere sorrow to reconcile tragedy with his own continuing Christian belief. Clearly from Chau's father's perspective, Chau did not hear from God and/or his understanding of Christianity is wrong. At the very least, however, we can say that Chau's interpretation appears an equally viable one in Christian terms.

What about for us, people who aren't connected to Chau and do not necessarily share his beliefs? What are the costs and benefits of Chau's martyr status? Perhaps we too might decide that Chau's understanding of Christianity was an abnormal one and thus dismiss Chau as deluded, as others did. Some confined this delusion to Chau himself, and others extended it to his Christianity as well. Today perhaps fewer than ever are likely to acclaim Chau's death as a good thing for the world or for Christianity; the type of Christianity practiced in contemporary culture does not require or desire death. This would necessitate believing that Chau was mistaken and/or that his version of Christianity is a misinterpretation of Christianity. The functional result is that the Christian institution bears no responsibility for Chau's death. This understanding is mistaken.

Even those who are outsiders to a particular institution should not regard the phenomenon of martyrdom with indifference. Individual existence precedes institutional essences such that no individual belongs to a single institutional structure.[21] For the fully competent individual, the value of the choice to suicide should remain paramount. Yet we can see the contradictions here in that suicide is generally prohibited and nearly universally stigmatized, while institutionally supported and promoted suicide is acceptable as martyrdom. This does not mean it is preferable or should be accepted. Rather, a conviction to martyrdom lies on morally questionable ground.

Chau's actions were clearly abnormal. I do not say this to slight him, nor does it function here as a way to dismiss the act of martyrdom as "crazy." Quite the opposite. Taking the manifestation of abnormality seriously in the case of martyrdom allows us to parse the confluence of individual and social factors that lead to willing suicide with ideological support. It need not be controversial to suggest it is abnormal to put oneself in mortal peril—Chau's actions are not unique, but they are certainly uncommon. But his fateful action did not arise in the moment, either. Chau was described as a thrill seeker who was compelled by extreme stories of missionary work and outdoor adventure from an early age.[22] Thrill seeking is certainly not qualitatively abnormal but it can also lead to disregard for self-harm at extremes.[23] Further, Chau seems to have been single-mindedly focused on reaching the Sentinelese from the time he first read about them in high school. He avoided romantic relationships, "believing it irresponsible given the risks of his mission." A friend from his missionary language school recalled that Chau's decision "was a sacred trust for him that no amount of reasoning would wrest from his grasp."[24]

Whatever the contours of Chau's differences, they manifested in an atypical calculation that resulted in his early demise. If martyrdom is not guided by a divine hand, would-be martyrs self-select with the assistance of inculcated institutional propaganda. It is not the case that martyrdom built the Christian institution, but through manipulation of our nature, and with our willing cooperation in exchange for meaning, martyrdom provides Christianity ongoing institutional support. Its mitigation as an institutional phenomenon would be a step in the right direction, indicating one more area of resistance to infusing institutional narratives with meaning built on human death.

Chapter Outline

There have seemingly always been a small but steady number of individuals willing to be martyrs, staking meaning on—or trading meaning for—their own flesh and blood. Within the study of religion, there has been a dearth of explanations for this phenomenon that are not supportive of or deferent to an institutional explanation: martyrs died because of and for the institution. Christianity explains both the "why" and the "what for" of the Christian martyr, as does Islam for Islamic martyrs, Judaism for Jewish martyrs, and so on. The insufficiency of this conclusion is obvious, and it extends beyond mere oversimplification. Clearly if the *telos* of the religion was martyrdom, it would not be a living institution. While the traits of a particular religion may be a part of the explanation for martyrdom, then, they cannot be the whole of it. Thus, we are returned to the same question: why martyrdom? I will suggest where the answers plausibly lie, and I will critique the moral implications of the way martyrdom has been utilized within traditions and studied by scholars. I will do this primarily through examining the Christian tradition.

This first part of the text, Chapters 2 through 4, retheorizes the martyr and martyrdom from phenomenological, existential, and institutional perspectives.

In Chapter 2, I begin the reconstruction of the why of martyrdom by exploring how and why it is phenomenologically rooted not in institutional affiliation but in our human anxiety about death. I use the early work of Martin Heidegger in his *Being and Time* to establish this existential basis for martyrdom. I will argue that martyr is phenomenologically first the willing suicide, and this suicide is one among many possible manifestations of human anxiety about death. It is, however, a unique one in that it exhausts all the possibilities of existence at once, and this is why suicide is—counterintuitively—so fascinating to those of us who live on. I argue that the initial appeal of the martyr is prompted in part by understanding the martyr's death as a potential substitution for our own. Establishing willing suicide as the root of martyrdom prepares the ground for explaining martyrdom from first-person and third-person perspectives. While the phenomenological anxiety about death is the same for both martyr and non-martyr, the response could not be more different in impact. On its own, the import of this chapter is to suggest that our fascination for martyrdom is rooted not first in its ostensible ideological connections but in its appearance as a paradoxical solution for the problem of death.

The persistence of martyrdom can be seen more easily by first establishing this phenomenological and existential common root. The death of another cannot once and for all substitute for one's own anxiety over death; it requires additional and ongoing cultural and institutional support (e.g., prohibitions against suicide, the establishment of power over death as the sole prerogative of the state, as well as the social community of those who identify as Christian). Even seemingly indirect supports such as socioeconomic security necessarily contribute to the perceived efficaciousness of this substitution, and psychological abnormalities may mediate it. However, insofar as the martyr is seen wholly as proceeding from and justificatory of the institution, other supports remain largely invisible. In Chapter 3, I outline the common institutional necessity that underlies how willing suicide becomes martyrdom: control of violence. I will argue that willing suicide is necessarily autonomous and anti-institutional and therefore must be controlled to make meaning. One potential product of institutional control of the willing suicide is the creation of the martyr. This product is not unique to, but is perhaps more characteristic of, religious institutions. Successfully controlled, the martyr facilitates the perpetuation of the given institution and thereby its purpose-giving and death-substituting functions for its living adherents. The vast majority of humanity has not been and will not be a martyr; for those who remain, these aforementioned few become "sacrifices" in the truest sense—via institutions, we create meaning with their deaths. An important takeaway from this chapter, furthering the argument that specific ideology does not explain martyrdom, is the conclusion that the control of violence underlying martyrdom is a common institutional function and not exclusive to religious traditions.

Nonetheless, originating as it does in the narrative of a martyr's death, and because it has been a hegemonic force throughout much of history, Christianity provides an effective institution to examine both the "why" and the function of martyrdom. Beyond the willing suicide of the progenitor, however, martyrdom traditionally plays a crucial role in the story of Christian triumph—the growth of the tradition from minority cult to institutional sovereign. In Chapter 4, I will argue against the grain of the Christian narrative, suggesting that martyrdom's importance to the Christian tradition is not that it contributed to Christian triumph but that it served as a retroactive symbol of and justification for the institution's transformation to sovereignty. I'll explore the church history of the fourth-century Bishop Eusebius of Caesarea as the first comprehensive manifestation of this narrative. This suggests there is no inherent linkage between Christianity and martyrdom. The important point instead is that the Christian institution, like all sovereign institutions, capitalizes upon human death to justify and perpetuate its sovereignty.

It is worth noting here that for scholars of the ancient Christian world, texts are an invaluable resource. However, if it is the case that martyr texts are a record of the writer's thoughts about martyrdom than the martyr herself, expecting these sources to tell us all we can know about martyrdom is limiting.[25] Though most scholars do not believe the text to be a straightforward representation of reality, the scholarly trend of interpreting martyrdom as an identity discourse furthers reliance on the text and removes the burden of trying to understand martyrdom from the perspective of the agent. Instead, the martyr is removed and the text stands in for a Christian community, and thereby a Christian identity. It is equally possible, however, that the martyr story is not representative of the martyr's impetus for martyrdom. Indeed, it cannot be to the extent that martyrdom is institutionally valuable. The identity approach implies that the martyr's understanding—insofar that the martyr exists at all—is identical to the writers and the Christianity they represent. This is because of a comparative lack of alternative material to text and Christian doctrine, but it may also result from lack of impetus to explore outside well-worn disciplinary approaches.

I do not suggest ignoring the text. We cannot ignore such a rich source of information, but we also should not assume it represents the sum of available information. A willingness to consider research from philosophical, psychological, anthropological, and even neurobiological sources will naturally extend the parameters of potential evidence. I thus use Christian texts without the concomitant assumption that textual interpretation represents the only or best approach to early Christianity. In emphasizing other types of data, rather, I am attempting to fill in clear gaps in our understanding as well as challenging the assumption that Christianity (or any institutional tradition) must be understood on its own terms. This sui generis approach tends toward an unquestioning assumption of theological priorities and paradigms, though it pays lip service toward a rediversification of approaches in the study of religion.

Chapters 5 and 6 examine trends in scholarship around Christian martyrdom in comparison with the theoretical and textual perspectives proffered in prior chapters. In Chapter 5, I examine a particular, important aspect of the institutional control of martyrdom: the stigmatization of suicide. Building on the preceding chapters I suggest that the stigmatization of suicide is practically grounded not in any inherent immorality of the act but in the explored institutional need to control violence. While this makes sense structurally, the negative moral valuation of suicide exists in tension with the phenomenon of martyrdom, since the latter is grounded in the former. In order to distance martyrdom from suicide and maintain the control of violence, arbitrary criteria for distinction must be consistently reinforced. I explore several of these criteria that are collectively embodied in the concept of "voluntary martyrdom" and argue that while they do not mark any real distinction of martyrdom from suicide, they do indicate the point past which the willing suicide can no longer render value for the institution. In other words, the voluntary martyr symbolizes uncertainty at the margins of violence that is redemptive for the institution, and that which cannot be assimilated. There are no salient qualitative distinctions of martyrdom from suicide; martyrdom is an ideological instantiation of suicide.

In Chapter 6, I critique the prevailing recent approach to examining early Christian martyrdom (and consequently Christian martyrdom more broadly) as an identity discourse. I contextualize this approach as following a general trend in the social sciences from the mid-twentieth century forward that understands human social life as primarily bounded by identities. I will argue that martyrdom-as-identity represents (among other things) an overcorrection to a perceived tendency to dismiss martyrdom because it is pathological. Based on the previous chapter, I suggest that a step forward in understanding the phenomenon of martyrdom may indeed lie in considering psychological abnormality while at the same time cautioning that this approach entails neither a callous dismissal of martyrs nor an exoneration of institutional responsibility for the perpetuation of martyrdom. I will also contend that an overreliance on the concept of identity has rendered it practically meaningless in the study of early Christianity, and particularly in the case of martyrdom as I have explained it, since identity presupposes a living human to identify with. The function of this exploration of martyrdom as identity, I conclude, is less to critically examine martyrdom than to reaffirm Cristian institutional uniqueness. Recognizing the limits of this approach allows us to refocus on the driving "why" of martyrdom.

Chapter 7 explores the moral implications both of the traditional understanding of martyrdom and the way it has been studied over the previous few decades. A critique of the notion of martyrdom itself is perhaps where my approach differs most from previous approaches. That martyrdom, which involves persecution, violence, suffering, and death, has moral implications should be obvious, yet those implications are rarely explored. I will be clear, however, about my moral perspective and the assumptions that undergird it, so far as I see them.

I begin with the phenomenological observation that the individual human agent is unavoidably saddled with the burden of choice, and this on the basis of self-consciousness. This self-consciousness is shaped in social contexts, often in ways more profound than the individual is willing to admit. Nonetheless, choice of comportment is always available in whatever expansive or limited range of existence an individual experiences. This is particularly evident in the case of willing suicide, which involves a conscious choice to eliminate the possibility of all future choice. Though a theological understanding of martyrdom would not deny the agency of the martyr, the agency of the "true martyr" is made fully commensurate with the divine will and thus effectively erased. Identity approaches instead subsume the agent in the social identity of the Christian, which has a similar practical impact. We must reckon with the phenomenon of martyrdom on individual as well as institutional levels.

I'm ethically attentive to what might be identified as a utilitarian perspective. Far more than a simple tally of bodies, as it is often mischaracterized by critics, this approach advocates the solution that results in the greatest net happiness or the least net suffering for all involved. While this is much more difficult to identify in practice than in theory, it is not impossible to get quite close. The question this approach asks of institutions that promote martyrdom might be as follows: are the deaths of martyrs justified in light of broader institutional, ideological, or political goals? In other words, do the benefits to the remaining community of the deaths of certain individuals, measured in religious and nonreligious aspects, outweigh the harms both to the agent and to others? The institutional answer is "yes," but unless we are to justify any amount of violence for the perpetuation of the institution, we should uncover the method of justification for such a response. It is precisely the recognition of choice, set against the backdrop of institutional influence, that leads me to hold the martyr responsible for her choices but make the institution bear the moral weight of setting the practical parameters of those choices for its own self-perpetuation. Any existing religious institution, like any institution, is governed not by consistent moral logic but by self-perpetuation.

Following this general framing, I argue that institutional promotion of martyrdom is immoral. In making this argument, I build upon the arguments of Hector Avalos, who contends that religious violence, justified as it must be on unverifiable premise, is immoral.[26] Martyrdom is one of many manifestations of religious violence. The promotion of religious martyrdom is thus immoral, for it is the promotion of violence without empirical warrant. This aligns with the utilitarian ethical approach noted above because no justification for action can be calculated in the favor of institutional values that cannot be assessed. The invaluable institution has no plausible moral limits, which is why any amount of violence can be perpetuated in its name unless external ethical parameters are established. This critique of martyrdom is not only a critique of religious institutions, of course, but one way into a broader cultural critique of how we establish value in cultural institutions and, ultimately, imbue our own existence with meaning.

Responding to an Expected Critique

A final response to a possible critique may be appropriate here. Because I return the physical death to its central role in constituting the martyr, one might conclude I am uncritically accepting the stories of Christian martyrdom, assuming they must have taken place, and in the ways described. This is not the case, nor is it necessary for my approach.

The majority of historical writing on Christian martyrdom up to the modern era was theologically motivated and uncritically accepting of the fidelity of martyrdom texts to real events. Edward Gibbon's work—though not the first to critique the presentation or use of martyrdom by the Christian institution—provides a convenient turning point toward a critique of martyrdom, and much subsequent historical work has been dedicated to verifying the authenticity of martyrdom accounts.[27] The result, over several centuries, has been a drastic reduction in the "usable" content of the field. Herbert Musurillo's accounts of early Christian martyrdoms, for example, contain only a slim number of total cases.[28]

Of course, this only represents the accounts for which positive corroborating evidence has been found of their validity. It does not mean that all other accounts have been dismissed; in many cases, there is simply a lack of evidence either way. Nonetheless, this is a dramatic decrease from the innumerable masses of martyrs imagined by Christendom. Fortunately for early Christian martyrdom scholars, tools such as discourse analysis and "identity" provide mechanisms to reincorporate dismissed stories of Christian martyrdom as components of "Christian identity" (or later "identities" as part of "Christianities"). In part as a result, taking actual death seriously in understanding martyrdom may appear as a regression to abandoned paradigms.

Yet, to recenter death as a crucial component for understanding martyrdom is not to make a truth claim about a particular early Christian martyrdom story. One can hold a healthy dose of skepticism about Christian martyrdom accounts and believe that death is crucial for the most accurate understanding of the institutional phenomenon. I agree with contemporary scholarly understanding that doubts the validity of a good number of martyrdom accounts in their extant form; it is fairly easy to see attestations of "myriad" or "innumerable" deaths as biased assessments.[29] On the other hand, I doubt that the majority of specific martyrdom accounts were fabricated whole cloth. Even if one were to dismiss the entirety of early Christian accounts of martyrdom, and perhaps even the death of the progenitor, as farce, one must yet reckon with willing suicides such as John Chau and Charles Moore (discussed in Chapter 5), who used their understanding of Christianity to make meaning with ideological support.

The emphasis on death—particularly as willing suicide—and the critique of an exclusive identity approach to martyrdom is uncomfortable because it decenters theological, or ideological, sui generis approaches to understanding religious martyrdom. That is, the prevailing approach to martyrdom validates—or at best leaves open—the understanding that martyrdom is both uniquely rooted in identification with a religious institution and is on behalf of that institution. My approach, in contrast, decenters reverence for the particular institution and questions the value of exchanging human life for institutional support.

In acknowledging this manipulation of death as a common fact of institutional life, I am not supporting it; on the contrary, it represents the final inability for any institutional-cultural narrative to be successfully totalizing. It may be that, in the end, we feel even sacrifice for the preservation of meta-institutions—institutions such as democracy that have historically preserved the coexistence of otherwise totalizing institutions—is unjustifiable.[30] I fear, though, that sacrifice is unavoidable until such undetermined point that we find more reliable ways to counteract our biological tendency to prioritize me over us, and us over them. From an individual perspective, the phenomena represented by "martyrdom" might be seen to do this in the crudest of ways: giving up "me" for "us." Under the surface, however, it is a gamble undertaken because "us" has convinced "me" that I gain most from self-destruction, despite the lack of empirical evidence. From an institutional perspective, the instrumentality of the transaction is blatantly obvious. The death of a few of us is necessary in order to sustain the fiction that the rest of us (vis-à-vis them) can live by. This fiction certainly is sustained by the institution's perceived value, which might well die without it; thus, any and all efforts must be made to keep that perceived value high, providing material benefits when necessary and intangible benefits wherever possible. This is the core of institutionality: it is sustained, as are we who constitute it, by self-interest.

2

"Willing Suicide":
Martyrdom as Self-Formation

Like dying for a cause, or dying for something bigger, another common description of martyrdom is self-sacrifice, and this description has multiple inextricable significations: the ritual act of killing (and willingly being killed), the living thing killed, and the justified, symbolic exchange of this valuable and present thing for something more valuable but less (immediately) present.[1] There are historical, theological, social, and psychological reasons for the characterization of martyrdom as sacrifice. The paradigmatic martyr in the history of the Western world is the early Christian martyr, who died nearly two millennia ago in a time when Christianity was a cult within the Roman Empire. The survival and growth of Christianity is attributed in no small part to Christian martyrs; it is thus easy to conclude that martyrs died for the political and ideological victory of Christianity. Theologically, the martyr reflects the sacrifice of Christ, who both was sacrificed (Rom. 3:25) and who sacrificed himself (Heb. 9:26) to atone for human wrongdoing. These two biblical references display the necessary, willing comportment of two agents toward the sacrifice: the sacrificer and the sacrificed. Christian martyrs imitate the sacrifice of Christ historically and theologically, following the example of the original Christian martyr, by seemingly paradoxically being sacrificed *and* by sacrificing themselves. The martyrs' sacrifice, like that of Christ, is *for* Christianity in an abstract sense, and it is also *for* others, providing an intermediary between the mortal and the divine. Even stripped of these specific theological connotations, in a social sense martyrdom is said to reflect a "selfless" death for others, a death that benefits a community. The death reaffirms the cause, the identity, that the community shared with the martyr. The sense of connection with the martyr functions on an individual psychological level as well. We who remain living are attracted to the martyr and perceive that attraction as grounded, at least in part, by some fundamental truth their action points to.

Though this understanding of martyrdom as sacrifice is rooted in the value of life (and the concomitant aversion to death), then, it is articulated by specific historical and theological circumstances. Outside an acceptance of the Christian theological premises that motivate this understanding, we are unable to answer the "why" of the martyr. If we do not have recourse to divine influence, what made (and makes) the martyr different from the non-martyr?[2] Can the difference(s) be identified quantitatively or qualitatively? If, for example, the martyr is motivated by a desire for justice, the afterlife, or a love of God to sacrifice him or herself, one might either presume that the non-martyr is void of these desires—which seems unlikely—or that the martyr simply possesses a greater desire for love, justice, and so on, than the non-martyr. If the martyr possesses more of a particular quality that enables martyrdom, how much more? Is there a certain quantity that activates martyrdom? In other words, is it possible to identify a measurable difference between the martyr and those who remain?

In order to demonstrate the need for identifying the difference of the martyr, it may be helpful here to provide a representative example of past attempts to identify the impetus of the martyr. In "The Motivation of Martyrs: A Philosophical Perspective," Jay Newman contends that our praise of martyrs is empty if not accompanied by some understanding of why they martyred themselves.[3] He dismisses psychological drives as a sufficient explanation for the martyr's action, in part because such a theory seems to negate intentionality. Why should we praise the martyrs, he asks, if their motivations were subconscious or accidental?[4] Newman also dodges the common charge of selfishness, arguing that self-interest and care for others are not mutually exclusive. "I see no reason for not saying," he concludes, "… that in sacrificing his life the martyr acted in his own interest as well as in the interests of others."[5] After allowing the possibility of self-interest, Newman outlines (and rejects) four potential self-serving motivations for the martyr, answering potential critics with a rhetorical flourish:

> Perhaps the martyr can actually see things which we cannot, things to which we are just blind. For it is not simply a case of our rejecting his course and his rejecting ours; *he has known our course and lived by it*, but we shall have never lived by his.[6]

The action of the martyr is motivated by a source that is inaccessible to most. Here Newman implies a qualitative quasi-theological difference between martyr and non-martyr. A mere three sentences later, however, he suggests that the reason we praise the martyr is not for his self-interest but his support of others' interests. "It is his love for his fellow man," he contends, "that enables him to regard doing something for his fellow man as leading him to self-fulfillment."[7] Love for others helps the potential martyr realize that a seemingly self-interested action is also an others-interested action. After creating space for the martyr's interest, Newman gives love the power to reconfigure self-interest as self-sacrifice. It is left to the reader to ponder how martyrdom is in the best interest of those the martyr loves. Yet, as it turns out, the love is not ultimately directed toward others anyway, but God. "It is that the martyr sees his interests as being those of God—justice, dignity, love itself—and his act is seen by him to fit in with some sort of universal plan, universal order."[8] Thus, while recognizing the seeming difference of the martyr's interest from our own, in aligning with God's interest, Newman strips the martyr of agency. His "philosophical perspective" is given a theological release valve.

The problem is not just that Newman's approach, like those he is reacting to, is deterministic. Rather, the difficulty is that no measurable distinction differentiates martyr and non-martyr in his analysis. Newman incorporates a model of love without any justification. He takes for granted that the martyr participates in a model of loving self-sacrifice. This is, of course, only defensible by recourse to the death of Christ, which is understood as a "death for," in this case for humanity. Without this theological understanding, there is no apparent connection between death and the interests of others.

Readings of martyrdom as self-sacrifice are based upon on an ex post facto construction that attempts to account for an aberrant or anomalous activity, not for the benefit of the agent but for those remaining. A measurable difference would provide firmer ground both for assessing the martyr's motivation and understanding the relationship of martyr to non-martyr. It is not difficult to uncover, because it is right before our eyes. The clear demonstrable difference between the martyr and the non-martyr is death.

The Centrality of Death

There are perhaps several reasons why death is not often explored as the difference between the martyr and those who remain. The first is that death appears so ubiquitous as to be banal. Millions die without being attributed the title of martyr; this gives the appearance that the death is not a significant locus for analysis. Further, despite the fact that death is the sine qua non of the martyr, it seems morbid to discuss it. Our modern sensibilities may be offended by the explicit, gruesome, and often fanciful accounts of Christian martyrdom.

Behind these reasons, however, lies a fundamental aversion to death. Though the death of the martyr stares us in the face, we defer instead to abstract notions of sacrifice.

When referring to death, I am not referring to the suffering that heralds its imminence in martyr accounts. In some accounts, the level of pain involved is intended as the marker of a true martyr's death (as well as their response to pain or, more frequently, lack thereof).[9] This is exemplified in the remembrance and frequent dramatization of the crucifixion of Jesus.[10] Rather, death here is the other of life, the end of existence. When it is typically discussed, it is understandably not death itself that is described but those moments that immediately precede it. These indeed are important but should not be mistaken for the death itself.

If death itself is ultimately inscrutable, though, what is its use for our exploration? In keeping death as the ubiquitous, yet definitive foundation of the distinction between martyr and non-martyr, in systematically making this conscious and explicit, we establish an alternative, atheological means to comprehend the phenomenon subsequently labeled martyrdom. It is the common ground on which the actions of the martyr, the nonaction of the non-martyr, the relationship of the non-martyr to the martyr, and the relationship between the martyr and the institution stand. The power of the martyr is universal in nature but necessarily individual in execution. Recognizing this connected distinction is key to understanding martyrdom's appeal. However, not just any death will do. We are interested in intentional death. Intentionality distinguishes this category from innumerable deaths that might be attributed to accidental or "natural" causes and provides the "for" that allows the introduction of ideology.

There are two questions that will help reorient toward this approach. The first is what martyrdom means to the martyr. It is an error to presume that we know the intentions of early Christian martyrs because they were Christian. It is no more necessarily explanatory that they were "early Christian," as if the combination of history and religious identity constitutes an isolable difference common to "them," yet different from either their contemporaries or from "us." If we set aside the presumption that a religious (or religio-historical) identity label gives us unique insight into the difference of the martyr, though, what is left? In some cases we have record of the purported words of the would-be martyr, and these give a unique perspective, but their value is also limited in their obvious tendency toward ideological framing.[11] If these Christian martyrs all imply Christianity as motivating their anticipated martyrdom, we should consider the potency of this framing for these agents while acknowledging its limitations in establishing the uniqueness of the martyr. Can we identify what martyrdom means to the martyr beyond the limited cases where we have their words?

An approach that minimizes the importance of the details of the specific case might seem to be at odds with one that purports to account for intentionality, which is presumed individualized. This critique is made from the perspective of traditional interpretation of individual martyrdoms through an institutional lens. Every individual case is isolated from an already-having-been constructed group and analyzed vis-à-vis that group, reaffirming its cohesiveness of the same group while giving the appearance of individuality. In this paradigm the martyr dies first and foremost as a *Christian* martyr. However, if religious identity alone is insufficient to produce martyrdom, and we don't know for certain what factor or combination of factors are sufficient to produce that result, we begin our analysis at the simplest commonality. Death is both universally experienced and radically individuating in its anticipation.

When asking what martyrdom means to the martyr, then, we are asking why one dies intentionally. The second question to reorient our analysis of martyrdom follows upon the first. If martyrdom is first intentional death, how can the underlying phenomenon be more accurately described? As I will explore, it is the inextricability of death's radical openness—its potentiality—and its finality that contributes to its appeal. Consequently, martyrdom is not first a sacrifice, a loss of self; it is an active formation through the exhaustion of potentiality in death.

Active formation over and against the implications of self-sacrifice is important. One of the normative ways to privilege Christian martyrdoms—distinguishing those deaths that are deserving of remembrance from those that are not—is with the implicit or explicit attribution of passivity. The "true" martyrdom is linked with a seeming absence of aggressiveness or violence. This has ideological utility; the overt presence of the agent's intentionality threatens the value of the death for institutional reproduction. It does so in part because of the anti-institutional nature of suicide and the historical stigmatization of the phenomenon as a result, as I'll explore in Chapter 5. However, characteristics such as passive or violent are also arbitrary distinctions.

The distinction between self-forming and self-sacrificing is clearly irrelevant for the being of those dead who have been labeled as martyrs, but it is critical for the understanding of those who remain, both those few who will and those who will never be considered martyrs. This distinction impacts not only our understanding of early Christian history but also our understanding of institutional structure and function; most importantly, though, it engages our understanding of our being. From an individual perspective, the notion of considered self-sacrifice is insurmountably problematic. We seem cognitively unable to justify any action when calculated as a net loss in our well-being. Insofar as self-sacrifice is understood as a net loss—if that is what is intended by "giving ourselves up for something greater"—it is practicably impossible.[12] Of course people may believe they are taking such an altruistic action, but it typically removes something from the equation, as we saw in Newman's analysis above. In the case of martyrdom, the institutional framework eliminates the calculation of the will of the agent as a variable insofar as it expresses any variation from an institutional identity. This reinforces the importance of the social institution.

What actually takes place is that to the extent one embodies the identity, the values of the institution, those become intertwined with the self. This is not to say that the self and social identity or the institution become one and indistinguishable, though this certainly has theological resonance. It is to say that to varying degrees one can comport the self to mirror perceived institutional values, and one is motivated to do so based on past experience of or future promise of the net benefits derived from such an exchange. If there is perceived to be a net loss, it is unsustainable because it increases rather than decreases existential anxiety. To that extent the institution would appear as a problem to be solved rather than a solution to a problem.

What this means is that from the individual perspective there is only self-formation, not self-sacrifice. To put this another way, even self-sacrifice is self-formation. It is important to point this out because from a social perspective, if we perpetuate the notion that the individual must understand the embrace of death as a self-sacrifice, we reinforce a cycle of support for the institution based on individual death. If, on the other hand, we recognize the embrace of death, regardless of its cultural context, as an exhaustion of death's potentiality in an intentional act, we can distinguish different operations taking place on individual and group levels.

As we will discuss, a complete picture of death must include both its finality and potentiality. In self-sacrifice the finality of death is certainly implicated but not necessarily its potentiality; in self-formation through death, both finality and potentiality culminate. It is important to note here the potential of reexamining psychological perspectives on martyrdom, however, because they have been largely neglected in recent scholarship on Christian martyrdom. An identity-discourse characterization of martyrdom excludes individual psychological variables as they interact with social boundaries. Instead, as befitting an institutional perspective, martyrdom is entirely a function of the identity for which the sacrifice was made. The introduction of the agent, which is also necessary for true incorporation of the notion of willingness, necessitates recognizing the insufficiency of ideological identity alone to predict martyrdom. The perspective of the martyr is not contained by "Christian"—this should be obvious. Even assuming this identity plays a significant role—and sometimes it does not—it cannot differentiate the dead from the living. Identity discourse in this way is institutional reproduction.

We need a different term to distinguish our understanding of "martyr" from its foundation, which is ontological rather than socio-institutional. Unfortunately, there is no single word in the English language that captures the nuance I am trying to convey, so we will have to be satisfied with two: "willing suicide." This phrase is admittedly peculiar as well as disdainful to some and thus deserves further explanation.

Suicide of course needs the fullest justification, laden as it is with centuries of dynamic legal and moral meaning, much of it condemnatory. The backdrop of this scene is the perceived necessity for an institutional monopoly on violence—thus the distinctions of killing, martyrdom, suicide, manslaughter, and so on, from natural or accidental death. Martyrdom is usually seen as an act that is qualitatively different from suicide on the basis of its "for," the particular divine or institutional purpose for which it is intended. While there is an institutional transformation that takes place to turn the suicide into the martyr, there is no qualitative difference in the dying itself; the transformation is post-mortem. The martyr is not qualitatively different from the suicide, in other words; she is a subcategory of the suicide.

Suicide has a negative valence, while martyrdom remains laudable in theory if not in practice. I use the term, then, not only because it is more accurate, as I will explain, but also because it challenges conceptions that suicide is inherently immoral, and martyrdom inherently moral.[13] Suicide as I'm using it—and as it should be used, I argue—has no inherent moral value. It could be judged "good" or "bad" based on case-dependent criteria but is not automatically so. I will discuss these ideas further in Chapter 5.

There are many phrases that describe what we call suicide, roughly divided between those that emphasize the self-killing element and those that emphasize the willing or voluntary dying element.[14] We need to maintain both these elements, because suicide partakes in both.[15] "Willing suicide" does this, I propose. "Willing" can be read as an adjective or a verb, depending on the usage. In adjectival usage, it clarifies the nature of suicidal intent. As a verb form, it allows for application to indirect forms of suicide, such as "suicide-by-cop."

Willing in this latter case suggests that the agent willed her own killing, even if the act was not completed by her own hand. "Suicide" additionally carries the necessary implication of violence that "death" and "dying" lack.

Studies of martyrdom have traditionally been preoccupied with historical-critical modes of discourse. From the Enlightenment era, the scholarly study of Christian martyr acts has increasingly centered around whether such tales have a historical basis and how close the story adheres to historical events.[16] The late twentieth century experienced a change in which individual martyr tales have been looked at, not for their historical correlation but what they say about those who wrote them down and their original audiences.[17] They grew and lived in different times and places, different contexts, and taken separately, rather than used for broad generalization, they help paint a diverse picture of early Christian practice. In the last two or three decades, there have even been studies done on individual martyrs from psychological and feminist perspectives, as well as others, designed to return agency to those whose tales are told.[18] In the postmodern, contextual methodology of study, though, something has been lost, a perspective that would give us insight into the fundamental question: Why martyrdom? The theological answers to this question are insufficient. It does little work to explain martyrdom as part of what it means to be Christian when the vast majority of all Christians have not been martyrs and, when given the opportunity, have naturally chosen flight or evasion as life-prolonging responses. Even if it is the case that martyrdom represents a truer form of Christianity—which few Christians would argue—this still tells us little about any commonalities among those who pursue it "for" any number of institutions.[19] While the willing suicide with ideological support may prove comparatively rare, it points to a more comprehensive understanding of the potential "why."

Being-Towards-Death and the "Why" of the Willing Suicide

Martin Heidegger's *Being and Time* provides a helpful resource for reassessment of the "why" of the willing suicide. Though the text is difficult, it is unique in its patient—to the point sometimes of being painful—exposition of the nature of humanity, and it provides a foundation upon which significant phenomenological and existential work has been built. Before diving directly into Heidegger's understanding of death and its possible insight into the why of willing suicide, it is helpful to provide some context for how death fits into his project.

Heidegger's ambitious goal is to uncover, insofar as possible, the nature of being.[20] What is it to say something "is?" To ask this question, we are already invoking a unique characteristic of humanness: "Being is an *issue* for it."[21] To mark this uniqueness, he labels humanness "Dasein" (being-there). Dasein has a foot in the realm of existence, as all entities do, but another in ontology, in the ability to question being. For this reason, Dasein cannot understand itself (i.e., what is Dasein?) simply by examining the world. "We have no right to resort to dogmatic constructions and to apply just any idea of Being and actuality to [Dasein], no matter how 'self-evident' that idea may be."[22] However, Dasein tends to fall back on exactly this, understanding itself through the world, through institutions, through tradition. This is because the "horizon" of Dasein's understanding of its being is time, and thus Dasein is in part its past, its history. Heidegger explains the results of this mode of understanding:

> When tradition thus becomes master, it does so in such a way that what it "transmits" is made so inaccessible ... that it rather becomes concealed. Tradition takes what has come down to us and delivers it over to self-evidence; it blocks our access to those primordial "sources" from which the categories and concepts handed down to us have been in part quite genuinely drawn. Indeed it makes us forget that they have had such an origin, and makes us suppose that the necessity of going back to these sources is something which we need not even understand.[23]

What is particularly important for us is that death, the limit of Dasein's time horizon, is among the primary "sources" obscured by tradition. Although practically we acknowledge death as ubiquitous and unavoidable, it is "life"—particularly institutional life—through which being is usually founded. Yet life, as Heidegger explains, already presupposes being and will thus not help us in understanding it.[24] Rather, "because Dasein is in each case essentially its own possibility, it *can*, in its very Being, 'choose' itself and win itself; it can also lose itself and never win; or only 'seem' to do so."[25] In other words, Dasein is always faced with a choice in comporting itself toward an end: "Dasein has assigned itself to an 'in-order-to' ... in terms of a potentiality-for-Being for the sake of which it itself is—one which it may have seized upon either explicitly or tacitly, and which may be either authentic or inauthentic."[26]

In Dasein's "everydayness," its existential condition, it is constituted by the element of care.[27] This care includes what Heidegger calls solicitude (*Fürsorge*) with other Dasein. Solicitude is critical because here Dasein's potentiality-for-Being is traditionally taken over by Others, by the incorporeal "they-self," an inauthentic self.[28] Care reveals itself in anxiety, which accompanies mere being in the world.[29] This anxiety makes Dasein aware of its radical individualization, providing possibility, potentiality, for inauthentic response (e.g., fear)[30] or authentic response. We are anxious because we are already in the world, but we are anxious about our potentiality of Being, the innumerable ways in which we can comport ourselves.[31] This is what it means to say that being is an issue for Dasein, and it sets the stage for further discussion of death's relation to being.

Death, both as pragmatically understood and Heidegger outlines, is an end.[32] Having been biologically brought into the world through birth, death stands as the final limit *and* possibility for being complete. Death, as the latter end of Dasein's time, is always the implicit limit against which authentic and inauthentic potential is gauged. Yet "as long as Dasein *is* as an entity, it has never reached its 'wholeness.' But if it gains such 'wholeness,' this gain becomes the utter loss of Being-in-the-world. In such a case, it can never again be experienced *as an entity.*"[33] Death can and should be seen as both limit and possibility, but it is colloquially recognized as the former, a limit managed by tradition and not willingly to be crossed. The willing suicide, on the contrary, actively addresses the possibility of death in its finitude.

There are always elaborate means of social tranquilization of Dasein's being-towards-death. The evasion of death, however, is an inauthentic comportment toward being. The ground for an authentic being-towards-death is thus implied. To return to our martyr, though, we have already been given a preliminary answer to the first question, which was "what the martyrdom means to the martyr" or "why intentional death." Death for the willing suicide is potentiality-for-being-a-whole, which is perceived by the willing suicide as authentic.[34] Of course, this is a possibility for all of us, but it is not actively recognized as such.

Recall a scene from any epic war movie where the commander rallies his troops before battle. The soldiers feel the immediacy of death acutely as they prepare to place themselves in harm's way. A clash of paradigms is evident as two matrices collide, one that sees death as the limit to completeness and one that sees it as possibility. In such a scenario, the leader knows that encouraging the soldiers that they might not die, while certainly possible, is unlikely to lessen anxiety and increase the chances of their committed engagement in battle. Rather, it is in this moment that death is confronted directly; what is not possible is to prevent death but to manage how one comports oneself toward it. Courage, bravery, and honor are all invoked as qualities against which the possibility of exhausting possibility is measured. The speech, the calm before the storm, also represents the volitional element as constitutive of all who take part in a struggle in which the outcome is radically uncertain.[35] This scenario provides a rough analogue to the individuating process that takes place for the willing suicide. There is a strict delimitation of possibilities but trending in an opposite direction from what normally occurs, hurtling toward death rather than fleeing from it. In other words, a reversal takes place through which the best avenue toward fulfillment of potentiality becomes accelerating, rather than diverting, one's approach toward death.

One might argue that this understanding of death's inevitability is not significantly different in everyday life than in battle, albeit felt more acutely in the latter. Of course, death is inevitable! This ready admission and dismissal, though, reflects the lack of felt proximity from which it is uttered. "Death is unavoidable," one says, mumbling under one's breath, "… but not for me."[36] This delimitation, this "leveling of possibilities," communicates that death is unlikely, working cooperatively with cultural and institutional narratives.

From the analogy above, the difference of being-towards-death as it manifests in the willing suicide and in others appears quantitative rather than qualitative. This lessens the perceived difference between everyday Dasein and the willing suicide. The willing suicide faced the same existential possibilities as all Dasein. To put it another way, because the existential difference between the willing suicide, having been completed, is incommensurable with we who remain, we assume that there must have been an incommensurability before death, and this turns out not to be the case. When the willing suicide is given an ideological "for," however, the situation is often reversed. That is, the Christian may feel commensurability with the Christian martyr on the basis of Christianity, but this is derivative of the commonality of being-towards-death. The comportment of the willing suicide represents a direct confrontation of the latter horizon of potentiality that grounds all Dasein, while that of everyday Dasein is an evasion. The martyr provides a particularly helpful example of the willing suicide here because the rituals that celebrate and perpetuate the death of the martyr provide considerable evidence that we who remain know it is the case that the martyr, from an existential perspective, is qualitatively different. She serves as a substitute for assuming wholly one's own potentiality.

Authenticity and the Martyr

The institutional reinterpretation of certain willing suicides as martyrs has at least two potential aims. The first and most common, seemingly paradoxically, is as an impetus to life. Death, when understood only through its finality, opposes life. As noted in the previous chapter, we have a fundamental desire for self-preservation. In part for this reason, the willing suicide intuitively appears aberrant. A social institution—Heidegger's "tradition"—that can harness the potentiality of death can provide a welcome evasion of death for those who remain. If successful, it "explains" the death of the willing suicide as martyr and justifies avoidance of being-towards-death for the rest of us. A second possible aim of this institutional reinterpretation is identification of a model to be replicated.[37] This is obviously much rarer in its appearance. In both cases, however, death is redirected. As Heidegger explains, "*No one can take the Other's dying away from him.* Of course someone can 'go to his death for another'. But that always means to sacrifice oneself for the Other '*in some definite affair*'. Such 'dying for' can never signify that the Other has thus had his death taken away in even the slightest degree."[38] The attempt to appropriate the willing suicide as martyr amounts to an *un*willingness to face our own death.

Heidegger does not address martyrdom as such in *Being and Time*. We have already seen that the understanding of being through tradition is a means to avoid the anxiety of being, including that of its limit in death. He does elaborate on the paradoxical nature of death, having been completed. Being-towards-death, until one's death, represents possibility. Yet upon death, Dasein has reached its limit and lost, rather than fulfilled, all possibility. The condition for possibility is being; existentially speaking, death ends rather than fulfills possibility.[39]

> Manifestly Being-towards-death … cannot have the character of concernfully Being out to get itself actualized. For one thing, death as possible is not something possible which is ready-to-hand or present-at-hand, but a possibility of *Dasein's* Being. To concern oneself with actualizing what is thus possible would have to signify bringing about one's demise. But if this were done, Dasein would deprive itself of the very ground for an existing Being-towards-death.[40]

This passage seems to indicate that willing suicide is an inauthentic being-towards-death because it actualizes the potential being-towards-death. This appears to have much in common with the fragile (and in practice readily permeable) boundary between death as a means and as an end in discussions of martyrdom.

Although reaching a seemingly similar conclusion to Christian institutional paradigms about martyrdom, this ontological deconstruction is in fact opposite. Note that distinction between the willing suicide and Christian martyrdom in the institutional paradigm might be explained on the grounds of "selfishness," in juxtaposition to an appropriate institutional and theological end such as Jesus Christ. As we will explore in more detail, however, these criteria for authenticity are institutionally bounded, despite their seeming obviousness. Designation of acceptable or unacceptable martyrdoms, whether through analysis of character, speech, attitude, and/or historical context, serves to qualify for martyrdom those willing suicides that are assimilable to the institution and disqualify those who are not. Certain martyrs and martyrologies, from an institutional perspective, have a higher cost-benefit ratio than others.[41] This process of legitimization, concurrent with the stigmatization of suicide, has provided fodder for much of the study of Christian martyrdom. Along with determining the historical accuracy of martyrdoms in the ecclesiastical record, each has been measured against a theological ideal. This is not Heidegger's aim. Historical and theological questions are not questions of being.

Heidegger is rather reemphasizing one of the constitutive elements of Dasein. This is care, manifest as anxiety, which can serve as an impetus toward authentic or inauthentic being. It is in turning to the world, to entities within the world, that Dasein becomes inauthentic. Simply, an entity cannot bring about a resolution of the question of being. Indeed, the larger point is that a "resolution" of the question of being is not what is called for in an authentic being-towards-death. Again, as Heidegger notes, "To concern oneself with actualizing what is thus possible would have to signify bringing about one's demise. But if this were done, Dasein would deprive itself of the very ground for an existing Being-towards-death."[42] The actualization of being-towards-death closes off the possibility of any being-towards-death.

Authentic being-towards-death is, in a word, anticipation. Anticipation can be conceived not as an actualization but as a radical openness toward the potentiality of being. Death provides the most radical individualization of this potentiality, what Heidegger calls one's "*ownmost* potentiality-for-Being."[43] It thus cannot be an embracing, an actualization of any of the grasped possibilities for potentiality of being. "Anticipation [of death] discloses to existence that its uttermost possibility lies in giving itself up, and thus it shatters all one's tenaciousness to whatever existence one has reached."[44] The willing suicide, in its resolution of anticipation, is an inauthentic response to the question of being.

There is a step from this ontological abstraction to our particular application: the Christian martyr resolves the question of being inauthentically. This partially addresses the second question for this chapter, which is how martyrdom can more accurately be described. In part, this is through a move from martyrdom, a foundationally social description, to willing suicide, an individual one. However, from an ontological perspective, martyrdom, as willing suicide recaptured by ideology, is an attempt at reaching wholeness, at resolving the question of being, and one which is inauthentic.

There is a point, then, on which we can agree with the contention that religious martyrdom is sacrifice, which suggests a fundamental and irreversible loss of self. My protest against this contention is not that it is in all senses inaccurate; rather, it is that the position is exclusively social in origin, thereby disenfranchising the individual perspective and preventing the grounding of death in an ontological question of being. Willing suicide for entities (including objects, institutions, ideologies, etc.), actualized as it must be against existential phenomena, fails at its goal of becoming whole.

It is important to note that to identify the inauthenticity of the willing suicide, and consequently of the martyr, is not necessarily to assume that the intention—the "for"—of the willing suicide is commensurate with the institution. Volition is unable to be identified with precision, often even by the agent himself.[45] This can readily be seen in any activity where the agent remains to tell the tale;[46] the perceived discrepancies between the actions of the agent at the time in question and the subsequent explanation given of his motivation reveals not only the gap between signifier and signified but also the alienation of the self even from its own intention.

In individually or institutionally viewing the martyr as martyr, existing Dasein moves farther away from authenticity and answering the question of being. The "sacrifice" of the martyr, understood this way, is indeed a loss of self for the martyr, but not only for the martyr. Sacrificing the martyr constitutes a loss of self, an evasion of being, for all who situate themselves in respect to the martyr. It is succumbing to the traditions that occlude an authentic being-towards-death. Although this recognition alone significantly alters the traditional understanding of martyrdom as self-sacrifice, we must still explore the components of the martyr's death comparatively through a division of perspectives in order to more fully elucidate the link between the willing suicide and the martyr.

Further establishing Heidegger's authentic being-towards-death in its place in the question of being, the impetus for the philosopher's work, may go some way to justify the importance of claims about authenticity. The thrust of his explication of being-towards-death is directly antithetical to social explanation. Dasein as Dasein is already in a world among entities. Dasein does not structurally think first, in a Cartesian manner, to create the world around him, but already *is*. This is in fact what is at issue, what is the cause of his anxiety, a constitutive part of being. Being-towards-death, not exclusively, but perhaps most simply and effectively, serves to call Dasein from wallowing in certainty. Heidegger introduces "conscience" as the calling toward one's potentiality.[47] The delimiter of death gives Dasein leverage, so to speak, to hold itself in the call of conscience, what Heidegger describes as "resoluteness."[48] Conscience here is not a calling away from the world but the basis for any authentic commitment to it. Authentic Dasein is not determined by entities within the world, though it is always already in a world.

The resoluteness in which death plays a pivotal role thus is clarified, but for what? Being-towards-death is not an ontological end in itself; why be resolute? Heidegger's aim is to introduce a state of potentiality-for-being-a-whole, wholeness.[49] But at this point there is something of a crisis. The question becomes how to consider together anticipation, an authentic being-towards-death, and resoluteness, an authentic potentiality-for-being. Heidegger asks,

> What if resoluteness ... should bring itself into authenticity only when it projects itself not upon any random possibilities which just lie closest, but upon that uttermost possibility [death] which lies ahead of every factual potentiality-for-Being of Dasein ... What if it is only in the anticipation of death that resoluteness, as Dasein's *authentic* truth, has reached the *authentic certainty* which *belongs* to it?[50]

Death is the only certain delimiter of being for Dasein, and for this reason it unifies; yet it also radically individuates because it cannot be taken on by an other. It also cannot be actualized through entities but must constantly be held open.[51] The phenomena of both individual and social existence are bounded by being-towards-death.

Heidegger's discussion does not illuminate anything that is not already implicitly known.[52] He allows us to highlight the commensurability of the martyr and non-martyr; they are ontologically identical. However, this paradigm shift toward an explicit awareness of the grounding of death is radical in that it serves to relativize all subsequent structural certainties, even those such as Christianity that systematically build upon the universality of death. At the point where we might seem ontologically closest to uncovering an authentic comportment of Being in martyrdom, we are practically farthest away because through martyrdom death is instantiated for an institutional entity rather than a constitutive part of being.

Martyrdom to the would-be martyr, then, represents the same existential phenomenon as it does to the non-martyr—an actualization, however misplaced, of being-towards-death. The preceding analysis prepares the way for a more detailed analysis of the second question we proposed, which is how the martyr might be more accurately described. I have suggested that, over and against the traditional reading of Christian martyrdom as an instantiation of nonviolent self-sacrifice, we should not read the martyr first as martyr, which reflects a social transformation. Rather the martyr is first the willing suicide, an intentional self-killer in a violent act of self-formation. The consideration of intentionality and violence is also important because the classification of authentic deaths as in a strange way nonvolitional is prompted by the perceived necessity—driven in part by the ideal of the early Christian martyr—for authentic death to be nonviolent. That is, violence, not having been adequately described or delimited, is given a negative moral value; it is thus disallowed from tainting beneficial deaths, which are correspondingly labeled nonviolent in nature in order to leave space for divine will. This reinforces the inaccurate juxtaposition of martyrdom and suicide.

Answers have been provided, at least in a preliminary way, to the primary questions posed earlier. Martyrdom to the martyr is an attempt at the finalization of being, an attempt to approach wholeness. As such, I contend that the martyr be first described as the willing suicide in order to center analysis around the individual components of death and intentionality. While exposing a distinction, however, this also indicates that the separation of martyr and non-martyr is less than might be perceived. There is a qualitative difference between the martyr and those who remain, but the ontological condition of being-towards-death is common. The willing suicide resolves that condition permanently, and the permanence of that resolution precipitates our fascination.

The Denial of Death and Terror Management

Though rewarding, Heidegger's writing is notoriously inaccessible. Writing nearly half a century later, Ernest Becker approaches similar themes from the intersection of psychoanalysis and existentialism. His approach is helpful to add, and not only because it is more accessible. He considers in detail the result of the human orientation toward death from anthropological and psychological perspectives, concluding that the cultural systems we establish in order to reconcile our discomfort with our unique position introduce a significant amount of evil into the world, perhaps in many cases more than the benefits such systems provide. I'll return to the social implications of Becker's argument in the next chapter, but first he establishes humankind's existential orientation.

Even more than for Heidegger, death for Becker is the hermeneutic key for understanding humanity. As he suggests, "the idea of death, the fear of it, haunts the human animal like nothing else; it is a mainspring of human activity—activity designed largely to avoid the fatality of death, to overcome it by denying in some way that it is the final destiny for man."[53] The human response to this fear is to create a form of immortality. Insofar as this creation is successful, it creates an imperfect answer to the existential paradox: a finite body with a mind able to imagine the infinite.

From an evolutionary perspective, a healthy fear of death serves as a robust indicator of the instinct for self-preservation.[54] Yet this fear cannot grow unchecked; it has to be managed in order to function, and the diversity of social culture and individual character reflects the variety of means humans use to manage their fear more or less effectively. I will return in subsequent chapters to the construction of the "normal" and "abnormal," but what we call "normal" denotes long-term management of the fear of death so as to prolong life and hopefully make it tolerable in the process. This normalization has significant overlap with Heidegger's "they-self," the leveling of the self according to culture and tradition.

The martyr serves an interesting function in this paradigm. Becker affirms that "we admire most the courage to face death; we give such valor our highest and most constant admiration; it moves us deeply in our hearts because we have doubts about how brave we ourselves would be."[55] Our admiration is no doubt a function of the act's biological contrariness, but it is also appealing because it appears a courageous solution most of us will never try: the willing exhaustion of the finite for infinite, risking of course the loss of both but perhaps truly gaining infinitude. To the extent this may be done, however, its evidence is beyond mortality and thus beyond our ability to verify. In that sense we who remain gain nothing. For the rest of us, "character" provides an imperfect solution to the existential paradox—one finds a way in the world by limiting one's infinite horizons appropriately based on cultural narratives, trading unlimited potentiality for prescribed meanings. Our feelings for the martyr are complicated, as we saw in the case of John Chau, for we also have a conflicting allegiance to the institutions that daily validate our character. These institutions also dictate the terms of death, rarely if ever ceding to individual will. As Becker states, "Society wants to be the one to decide how people are to transcend death;

it will tolerate the *causa sui* project only if it fits into the standard social project. Otherwise there is the alarm of 'Anarchy!'"[56]

This principle, the natural expansiveness of institutional control, explains and precedes any and all laws against violence, including the act of suicide. This helps explain why it is, if martyrdom is so fundamental to Christianity, that there have been so few martyrs. Particularly in the modern world, most of us do not have our "eggs in one basket," and willing suicide requires a level of autonomy or alienation, a level of separateness from dominant cultural narratives that we simply do not have.[57] The willing suicide is understandable in one sense, refusing the compromise with the body that life entails. Yet it is from another angle quite abnormal that this individual is unable to broker a compromise that keeps him alive, unable to countenance the possibility that the narrative that justifies death is unproven. He gambles that "proof" lies beyond, or in the very act of finalization, and hastens to that end.

Authentic Dasein lives somewhere between "they-self" and the actualization of being-towards-death. Becker is unconvinced that a healthy compromise can be found for most. The "normal" dooms us to a life that is not really ours, and those that refuse compromise with society verge on madness. Like the proto-existentialist Kierkegaard that he admires, Becker ultimately gestures toward faith, a faith that posits a resolution for the existential paradox in a Creator. Yet though he seems reluctant to fall back on familiar paradigms, he is unable to articulate this resolution without the contours of traditional religion.[58] Though assuring the reader he is not writing an apology, he cannot identify a better answer to the question of the ideal illusion, consoling himself in any case that "all men are here to use themselves up and the problem of ideal illusion doesn't spare any man of that. It only addresses the question of the best quality of work and life that men can achieve."[59]

To end this chapter, it is worth considering whether Heidegger's existential phenomenology or Becker's existential psychoanalytic description of humanity can be empirically tested. While a plausible explanation of our relationship to death, is it verifiable? Terror Management Theory (TMT) is a significant body of research that attempts to do just this. Pioneered by psychologists building on Becker's work, TMT argues that all our individual and social actions take place against the backdrop of our "terror" about our own demise.[60] Our concern about our finitude prompts significant actions to allay that concern. There are now decades of research establishing a relationship between mortality salience and group-reinforcing responses to cultural preferences, even controlling for many other potential variables. After reminders of death, "we react generously to anyone and anything that reinforces our cherished beliefs, and reject anyone and anything that calls those beliefs into question."[61]

Insofar as they are successful, narratives or endeavors that respond to the terror of death allow the individual to thrive on individual and group levels. TMT's response is different than the Heideggerian one; it suggests that knowledge of our "terror" allows us to construct the most effective narrative we can to combat it. This is the ideal. Heidegger seems to suggest something further: we abandon any narrative that allows psychological or cultural return to the "they-self" and embrace the reality of our death completely. An authentic response is one that fully owns the potentiality and finality of my own death; anything less is inauthentic. TMT doesn't seem to disallow an authentic response, but it doesn't seem to require one either: a functional response is the primary goal.[62] TMT theorists are in this sense less pessimistic than Becker himself.

In response to TMT, some psychologists have argued that the terror of death is unlikely to have developed from an evolutionary perspective, because terror of death in and of itself would seem to be contrary to a biological imperative to thrive.[63] TMT proponents argue that the terror of death emerges as the byproduct of brain developments that allowed human communication and social interaction to increase chances for survival.[64] Theory of mind, the ability to conceive of others, intuit their similarities and differences, and communicate with them, necessarily entails a conception of the self as well, and that conception of the self is set against the observed backdrop of death. In the TMT paradigm, fear of death is the inevitable product of self-consciousness, and the evolutionary adaption is the ability to buttress against the terror of death in such a way for the individual and group to thrive.

TMT doesn't necessarily provide additional support for an understanding of martyrdom. According to TMT, martyrdom could be one of many possible narratives in response to the terror of death, but is it a viable one? There is some additional research support for the idea that people respond to the terror of death by reinforcing their preexisting narratives,[65] but if this is a general human condition, and provides us with a likely but not necessary response (i.e., doubling down on one's own worldview(s)), this gives us minimal insight into the impetus for martyrdom. In fact, even if religion is seen through an existential and/or TMT paradigm—in the former usually functioning to the detriment of humanity and in the latter possibly functioning to its benefit—martyrdom might be seen as itself a vestigial byproduct of the adaptive function of religion, and one that thwarts its general tendency. Other evolutionary theorists have posited, however, the selective role of self-sacrifice to the possible detriment of the individual but for the ultimate benefit of the group, and this aligns in part with a Christian institutional perspective.[66]

TMT does give some possible connection points. First, it provides additional support for the important idea that martyr and non-martyr start from the same existential foundation. That is, we do not need a theological explanation in order to account for a particular attitude with regard to death, whether that be one of implicit (or explicit) avoidance or whole-hearted embrace. According to both Heideggerian ontology and TMT, the martyr and the non-martyr start from the same place.

Additionally, although it seems initially counterintuitive, there seems to be no reason not to establish embracing death as one possible response to the terror of death. This is to say nothing of its comparative value, but to say it is one among—and not antithetical to—other narratives constructed in response to the terror of death. If it is a plausible narrative, though, we are returned to the question of what factors might determine whether this narrative rises to the top. We see historically and statistically that it is a comparatively rare response. It undoubtedly needs institutional support—this is what transforms the willing suicide to martyr—but institutional support alone is clearly insufficient, and perhaps even a very weak influence, as the vast majority of people, even in times of extreme duress, do not willingly suicide.

For critics of TMT, fear of death is not the only—nor perhaps the most important—existential condition to which we respond, and this is particularly important considering that social scientific research has been unable to substantiate a widespread fear of death in a number of studies. Other scholars have identified meaninglessness, guilt, isolation, and identity as drivers of culture and meaning-making.[67] A potential takeaway here is that martyrdom need not necessarily be based on the counterintuitive embracing of death in the face of the terror of death. A strong case can be made for willing suicide, even in the face of considerable pain, as a quest for meaning, as a response to the guilt within a religious system, or as a means of overcoming societal isolation and reinforcing social identity.[68] Death according to this paradigm is a byproduct of a meaning-making project and not the ultimate aim. It seems clear that a monocausal explanation of fear of death lacks sufficient support, though fear of death may be one of many factors contributing to the embrace of religion. In such a case, even to the extent that it is present, the fear of death is something categorically different than the experience of death, and thus fear of death has no necessary conflict with embracing death, which can clearly be accomplished in the seeming absence of fear, as testified in martyr stories and other cultural accounts.

Another important aspect of the literature on death anxiety is the idea that religion itself is but one of the cultural mechanisms that can be deployed to respond to existential (or terror management) concerns. Other cultural institutions can serve a similar function if they are sincerely believed by the agent. In subsequent chapters, I will suggest that the propensity for martyrdom, on a social level, has a relationship with the quality and quantity of potential meaning-making frameworks that the agent has available.[69] As noted above, it is a question of the extent to which your eggs are in one basket.[70] Cultural meaning-making systems highlight different human domains but are not mutually exclusive. A religious domain could be augmented by a socioeconomic domain, which could be supplemented by a political domain. If one has "credit" or "standing" in multiple domains, there are many places to which one can turn if a single domain is challenged. In such cases, the domain in question can be repaired and restored, or even abandoned in some cases, without irreversible loss to the individual, because substantive sources for meaning-making are still operative. However, if all meaning-making capacity is concentrated in one domain, there are no alternative means for restoring loss of significance or addressing anxiety when that framework is challenged, whether directly or indirectly. In such cases, an especially zealous response—one that promotes dogged certainty, dedication, and/or conflict—may mitigate that anxiety.[71]

It may be that certain religious frameworks are distinguished by promising literal immortality along with the possibility of symbolic immortality (through material artifacts and in the memory of others). This would seem to be particularly important to explore in relation to willing suicide, because insofar as one is immortal, temporal death would seem less significant. This sentiment indeed is echoed throughout Christian literature (1 Cor. 15:55), and regardless of its objective reality, a sincere belief in literal immortality can both resolve existential anxiety and be supremely motivating. However, none of these factors discussed—belief in literal immortality, meaning-making potential concentrated in one domain, particular manifestations of death anxiety—appear singly or in combination to uniquely differentiate the martyr from the non-martyr. Only in death is difference expressed.

I've attempted to show that martyrdom as self-sacrifice is a sociocultural interpretation that is not commensurable with the more foundational existential one: willing suicide as self-formation. This paradigm shift allows us to see that our fascination with martyrdom is not necessarily connected to the ideology with which the martyr is associated but the meaning-making power of death. This is the difference of martyr from nonmartyr. I turn to how that power is harnessed for institutional support in the following chapter.

3

"True Because a Man Dies for It": Martyrdom as Institutional Violence

In the previous chapter, I redescribed the martyr as first the "willing suicide," symbolizing the shift from a social understanding to an individual, existential one and emphasizing the self-formation, rather than self-sacrifice, of the violent and intentional death. In this chapter, I will suggest that the specification of the willing suicide as martyr, the transition from willing suicide to "willing suicide with ideological support," can be categorized as a process of institutionalization. This process is proactive and not reactive. While I have argued for examining the willing suicide prior to martyrdom, this should not be understood in a chronological sense. It is not as if the institution repeatedly comes upon the willing suicide after death and opportunistically creates a martyr. In nearly all cases—though notably not the crucial few upon which most other martyrdoms are institutionally patterned in religious traditions—an ideology needs to have been established, one that the willing suicide can be "for." While I will discuss the specific institutional content of the willing suicide's development within Christianity in the next chapter, however, I'll first identify common institutional operations.

Specifically, I'll argue first that violence has no innate moral value; second, that the institution *qua* sovereign institution must control violence; third, that willing suicide, because uncontrolled, appears as extra- or anti-institutional violence and as such must be reconciled to the institution; and fourth, that the reconciled violence is given the name martyrdom. Given the transgressive phenomenon of willing suicide and the raw potency of human violence, it behooves any institution to establish a mechanism to recapture as much of that violence as possible—individual death for institutional life. Martyrdom represents a potent and efficient recapture of violence—potent because willing suicide is individually fascinating and efficient because the self-referentiality of the willing suicide has no obvious signification and can thus be wholly redirected toward the institution. This operation continues to function effectively, however, only insofar as we do not realize that as "a thing is not necessarily true because a man dies for it."[1]

A reconsideration of our understanding of violence highlights the source of offense at rooting martyrdom in the willing suicide. Violence has no inherent moral value, and its social investment with the character of a universal moral violation simply indicates the reinforcement of institutional norms.[2] Violence denotes physical force intended to hurt or kill. In relation to the law, the term often denotes illegitimate rather than legitimate (institutionally sanctioned) force. This approach reframes forms of what would otherwise be seen as violence, such as execution or collateral damage. Martyrdom, I argue, is a lesser recognized form of this institutional violence—while the willing suicide is violence in its raw, personal form, reclassification as martyrdom symbolizes the act having been co-opted into (and having proceeded from) the institutional realm.[3] I will ultimately argue that this reclassification is unjustified, but it is not unjustified because all violence is unjustifiable. Rather, this institutional appropriation of violence is unjustified because it is used to proactively legitimate the institution.

Georges Bataille provides an effective framing for understanding the fluidity of violence in its original form and its lawful guise. Bataille contends that violence is in fundamental opposition to work, to societal productivity, to community.[4] He begins—as with Heidegger—with the notion that man is "discontinuous," feeling completely alone though surrounded by others. "We are attempting to communicate, but no communication between us can abolish our fundamental difference. If you die, it is not my death. You and I are *discontinuous* beings."[5] At the same time we feel aware of a "lost continuity"[6] or the possibility of creating continuity. Death, Bataille contends, is the ultimate representation of this continuity: "Death means continuity of being."[7] Note here the correspondence with the being-towards-death and the being-a-whole of Heidegger as well as Becker's description of the finitude of the body and the perceived infinitude of the mind. The end of violence in this formulation is the continuity that is represented finally in death. The social challenge is that individual violence disrupts societal function, the world of work. Bataille describes the tension that results well: "Continuity is what we are after, but generally only if that continuity which the death of discontinuous beings can alone establish is not the victor in the long run. What we desire is to bring into a world founded on discontinuity all the continuity such a world can sustain."[8] To limit disruption, then, violence becomes subject to regulation. One might say prohibition, but violence is never completely prohibited; rather, the arenas in which its use is acceptable and the agents who may exercise it are circumscribed. This regulation acts in a legal and punitive form, but it also is inculcated in a moral form in, for example, the nearly universal prohibition against murder, so defined as to distinguish from institutional and acceptable forms of killing.[9] Violence thus manifests as a transgression, and transgression obtains an immoral value. However, it is not violence itself that is wrong, but transgressing institutional regulation, because it indicates autonomy, the presence of competing forms of regulation.

If violence itself is not morally weighted, neither, at least initially, is its prohibition. As Bataille indicates, the sphere of work is diametrically opposed to violence in that it requires regulation, the blunting of excess. The deregulation of all forms of violence is the return to a state of nature, a disavowal of that which differentiates humanity.[10] The fact, then, that the circumscription of violence is socially necessary assigns moral culpability neither to the agent nor the institution. Awareness of the necessity of regulating violence is critical not because of the inherent immorality of violence but because it is precisely the necessity—the ubiquity of violence and its institutional monopolization—that leads to its selective transformation. If violence appears to be a phenomenon in one instance and not in another, its appearance becomes synonymous with moral culpability. If, on the contrary, violence is exposed in all its manifestations, it appears initially as a neutral construct and forces a more critical analysis of the genesis and telos of transgressive acts.

Bataille's genealogy of violence sees its circumscription as a necessary requirement for a functioning society. Making violence subject to regulation is the creation of society. There is another angle from which to view the social structuring of violence, through the lens of that which regulates it. This returns us to the sovereign, whether embodied in the individual or the institution. By institution, I am referencing a purposive social organization. Not all institutions are sovereign, which indicates supreme (or at least viability for supreme) authority in a given domain, but we are focusing particularly on the sovereign institution as it is the one that needs—for society and for itself—to control violence. Violence, or the threat of violence, represents the constitution and evidence of the sovereign institution.[11]

The power of violence lies in its fundamentality for humanity—it threatens existence. Violence, however, powerful though it is, has no necessary institutional correlation; using the language of semiotics, it is the ultimate signifier without a "signified." The sovereign institution, on the other hand, is a signified with no necessary signifiers. There is nothing that proves sovereignty; there are only arbitrary signifiers to which people assent (or do not). The control of violence is the control of the most powerful signifier and its signification—what violence means and when. Sovereign institutions thus must attempt to monopolize violence, because insofar as violence continues to signify other purposes, it weakens the potency of its signification for any single purpose. I say that sovereigns must *attempt* to monopolize violence, suggesting they may not always succeed but will seek to reconcile unsanctioned violence with greater sanctioned violence and will continue to do until either violence is reconciled or the sovereign institution is no longer.

Dimitris Vardoulakis provides a helpful categorization of scholarly work on sovereignty into two types of theories.[12] The epochal approach, which sees types of sovereignty developing chronologically, is most identifiable in the work of Michel Foucault. Jacques Derrida and Giorgio Agamben have instead understood a logic of sovereignty that is recognizable across time. Subsequent works have attempted to mediate these approaches, identifying historical developments of sovereign power that yet retain common features. The drawback to all of these mediations, according to Vardoulakis, is that they posit a utopian future somehow without sovereignty, without the justification of violence. Though understandable, he argues that this is not a sustainable way forward. The future elimination of violence—particularly through violence—has no historical precedent and thus appears less viable than identifying the most successful form of managing it. Using Walter Benjamin's "Critique of Violence" for inspiration, Vardoulakis proposes his own typology of sovereign power defined by a mean-ends relation. Ancient forms of sovereignty, which he claims historically culminated in Christianity, privilege ends over means. All are "us," so long as they are Christian, and ultimately violent means are justified against "them" so that they will end up as "us." Modern forms of sovereignty reverse that order, focusing on lawfulness within the predetermined context of the nation-state, the symbolic boundaries of which define who is a "neighbor." The postmodern form of sovereignty, biopolitics, "blurs the distinction between means and ends." Everyone polices everyone, including themselves, and whether or not one lives up to the norms in a given area determines whether one is "us" or "them."[13] These forms are not mutually exclusive, importantly, for they share a central logic: justification of violence—specifically, by identifying an "other," someone who is not the neighbor, by clarifying an "us" and a "them" against whom violence is justified.[14]

The obvious question that arises, which most examinations of sovereignty have as their explicit or implicit aim, is whether it is possible to think of a politics without the justification of violence at its center. This is not a question of the elimination of violence but its minimization. This question suggests another provocative one for consideration on the individual level. To put it in terms we discussed in the previous chapter, is it possible to live within institutions and maintain an authentic being-towards-death, one that refuses to substantiate meaning with violent death, whether of self or other? Vardoulakis offers what he terms "democratic judgment" as a viable option, a politics that is constantly questioning the justification of violence and dejustifying it where possible.[15] It is from this perspective—one that questions the justification of violence—that I describe the transition from willing suicide to martyrdom as an example of the institutionalization of violence. After all, it is not as if violence is justified for its own sake—excess is justified as necessary on the basis of exceptional circumstances.[16] The goal, again, is not construed as a permanent dejustification of violence, an eternal separation of sovereignty from democracy. As Vardoulakis suggests, "If it is in practice impossible to separate democracy from sovereignty, then there is all the more reason to remain vigilant and proactive in exercising judgments."[17]

Insofar as violence is controlled by the sovereign institution, it becomes, in a sense, something else. Violence is the raw force upon which sovereignty is justified, so its deployment by the sovereign institution is always *justified* violence, which can go by a variety of other names but is rarely identified simply as violence from the perspective of the institution. It takes names more suited to its justified or justifiable status. This leads to the second point, which is that willing suicide is an example of—perhaps *the* example of—anti-institutional violence. Violence against an institution that is precipitated by an alternative institution abides by the recognizable logic of controlling violence and is resisted by traditional means. The violence of the willing suicide is in a unique category and must be sanctioned. This is the case for at least two reasons. The first is that this form of intentional violence involves the fewest possible number of people. All other forms of human-on-human violence involve, at least potentially, the intentionality of multiple agents and thus entail multiple safeguards against violating institutional norms around violence (prohibitions against murder, assault, etc.). A second reason is that willing suicide is counterintuitive. It undermines our general expectation of self-preservation. This contributes to the fascination around it, as we have discussed, as well as to a heightened sense of it being a fundamental taboo. Other forms of violence take for granted the need for self-preservation—indeed, they may be seen as the motivation for the violence in the first place. Further, when violence contravenes institutional norms in these cases, there is the possibility of reconciliation to sovereign authority through punishment. Willing suicide as a form of violence is perfectly situated to expose the frail foundation of sovereignty, which is built on the monopolization of violence. Willing suicide shows clearly that sovereignty relies on the ongoing assent of every individual agent subject to sovereign authority. At any moment, any individual can wield violence just as sovereign authority can, and the willing suicide exposes the fact that it is not primarily respect for sovereignty that prevents them from doing so but something internal to the agent herself. Because of this, and although laws against suicide are ineffective deterrents, sovereign institutions establish prohibitions against suicide. The general effectiveness of this particular prohibition is exemplified by the traditionally unquestioned categorical separation of martyrdom from suicide.

Punishment is a common name under which sovereign violence can be exercised in response to violation of institutional norms. Though not always directly, these violations themselves may take the form of violence. Punishment reconciles the violation (and in many cases the violator) with sovereign authority; if the original offense was violent in nature, punishment was also traditionally enacted using violence. To the extent that this is not the case today, it is because the sovereign institution's control of violence is evidenced elsewhere.[18]

Our historical understanding of Christian martyrdom is birthed out of violence as punishment. To be more specific, the phenomenon labeled martyrdom represents the intersection of two institutions, institutions with different purposes and thus different criteria for the justification of violence. For the sovereign institution, so-called martyrdom is execution, the justification for which is active refusal to submit to sovereign authority. This refusal is either the self-generation and symbol of autonomy or the attempted signification of another sovereign. In either case, the act of violence named "sanction," "punishment," or "execution" reconciles the violation to sovereign authority. All is right again. From the perspective of the opposing institution, whose existence is justified on the basis of another purpose, the violence of the so-called execution must be differently named. Without the sovereign authority to commit violence, this diffuse and comparatively unregulated institution seeks instead to redefine it, to redirect its signification.

There is something unique here, however, that differentiates the act designated as martyrdom and makes its redefinition from violation possible. The effectiveness of punishment is predicated on the expectation that people will seek to avoid suffering and preserve existence when it is threatened. To the extent that this is not the case for the individual, violence loses its ability to signify the sovereign who wields it. In this light, the uniqueness of martyrdom is perhaps that it represents a clever (and retroactive) institutional way of turning anti-institutional violence on its head: when you kill yourself, you are not expressing anti-institutional, autonomous violence; you are instead *proving* the sovereignty of another institution. This transition relies on the fact that violence is a raw signifier with no signified and the sovereign institution is a signified with no signifier. The transition from willing suicide to "willing suicide with ideological support"—martyrdom—is thus essentially a process of (re)institutionalization. Insofar as we derive meaning from institutional narrative, we assent to the institution's sovereign ability to exchange death for life.[19]

It is important to remember that we are not observing the juxtaposition of violence to nonviolence here but a question of whether and what violence signifies. The casting of an institutional clash as an exclusive opposition of violence versus nonviolence is simply another means of justification. The American civil rights movement in the 1960s provides an insightful corollary. When the broader American public watched acts of violence meted out by white cops and vigilantes on Afro-American bodies, they did not disavow violence.[20] Rather, enough people—or the "right" people—no longer accepted the justification of violence in those circumstances.[21] To the extent that the victims did not retaliate, it is not as if bystanders witnessed nonviolence or the extreme imbalance of the state's violence against the individual body for the first time. This is the regular operation of violence. Given a complex context of circumstances, the violence was instead unable to sustain its prior link of signification. Yet it did not simply go away—it came to signify the validity of another institution.[22] Perhaps more accurately, the sovereign institution was compelled in a limited sense to transform in order to accommodate forms of activity previously recognized as illegitimate and sanctionable. The function of violence to protect and legitimize the institution did not change; its sphere of exercise merely shifted. If one takes away from this example that violence is "wrong" in some absolute sense, one misses its ongoing institutional operation. One can—and should—argue for the "rightness" of a particular cause, but the violence is only a signifier.

With this critique of the violence/nonviolence binary, I can articulate more clearly a point I made in opening this chapter: martyrdom creates martyrs, not the other way around. The willing suicide is the individual foundation for the martyr, but the individual, prior to death, is also influenced by the norms of the institution, which supply and encourage the suicide's "for." This means the institution is not just a beneficiary of, but also a participant in, the process. As such, we need to critically examine its ends and its costs.

Martyrdom, then, is birthed from punishment and—at least for Christianity—maintains its historical definition vis-à-vis punishment, which is the signification of the sovereign institution. The idea of punishment always remains accessible in a supernatural sense. Even where the religious institution is sovereign, diabolical forces embodied in human actors can still do interpretive work. In the case of John Chau, the North Sentinelese would be unlikely to be cast as evil in any intentional sense. In such cases, the idea of punishment—or attempted punishment, anyway—could remain as part of the grand Christian narrative of a struggle between good and evil.

However, the power of martyrdom's meaning is derived from the signifying power of the specific type of violence—willing suicide—now controlled by the sovereign institution that renamed it. What I have suggested is that we are introducing a third perspective that allows us to critique the other two. The first perspective understands violence as punishment, as execution. The second, competing perspective understands violence as nonviolence, as martyrdom. The third perspective refuses the sovereign definitions of the first two, returning this form of violence to its fundamental components: willing self-killing or willing suicide. This perspective is pre-institutional; it is a refusal of institutionalization. Yet it cannot last, because the agent of its refusal can no longer act.

I have described the well-known need for sovereign institutions to monopolize the use of violence, suggested that willing suicide is anti-institutional violence, and argued that the successful recapture of that violence for the institution is indicative of the willing suicide becoming martyrdom. A question that remains is that of function. How does this recapture serve the institution? As a competing institution within the domain of a sovereign institution, insofar as the lesser institution wants to claim the willing suicide, they do so rhetorically. The sovereign institution sees execution, the competing one sees spiritual triumph. As we will see in the next chapter, the retrospective narrative of early Christian martyrdom was one of counterintuitive triumph through the willing death of its adherents. Generally speaking however, it is helpful to identify the institutional benefit of such a narrative as well as reiterate how this benefit functions on the level of the individual.

Bringing More Evil into the World

Ernest Becker, whose work we discussed in the previous chapter, elucidates both institutional and individual benefits of meaning-making narratives and roots them in the same source that creates the willing suicide and the martyr: the fear of death. Becker wrote a second book intended as a companion text to his Pulitzer Prize–winning volume *Denial of Death*. This posthumously published text *Escape from Evil* picks up the same themes of death's inevitability and examines them from a primarily institutional perspective. Building on his first work, Becker claims that disease and death are the two primary "evils" for the human organism. Situated as we are within a finite body, but with the evolutionarily developed capacity to imagine ourselves beyond it, we rely on this latter capacity to organize socially toward the end of quieting our fears about finitude. Socialization itself quiets the fears of death to a certain extent, and the collective, immortality projects of these social organizations do so even more effectively. Disease and death are still present, however, for these immortality projects are constructed as they must be against the fear of death and not death itself. Arbitrary as they are, these projects are neither self-sustaining nor particularly resilient. They continue to function only insofar as we embody them. It is worth quoting Becker at length here:

> Since men must now hold for dear life onto the self-transcending meanings of the society in which they live, onto the immortality symbols which guarantee them indefinite duration of some kind, a new kind of instability and anxiety are created. And this anxiety is precisely what spills over into the affairs of men. *In seeking to avoid evil, man is responsible for bringing more evil* into the world ... It is man's ingenuity, rather than his animal nature, that has given his fellow creatures such a bitter earthly fate.[23]

Immortality projects, in other words, are not without costs. Institutions—purpose-driven social organizations—create and maintain these immortality projects. They are not designed to support or facilitate a variety of different projects; they have developed, rather, around the support of a narrower set of practices, relationships, values, and beliefs, the conglomeration of which is established over and against the innumerable other configurations of purposes.[24] They are not self-critical, then; they are self-promoting. To the extent that we rely on them, the threat of their loss is a threat to our purpose, our meaning, our primary barriers against the fear of death. In the italicized phrase above, Becker is exposing the fundamental trade of death for life. Though our primordial aim is avoidance of the fear of death, we are willing to trade the lives of others to secure our immortality projects. This is another way of illustrating Heidegger's suggestion in the previous chapter that death is always ultimately our own. The death of another is, in the final instance, not as important as our own, and as a result we can increase others' fear of death—as well as increase deaths themselves—in the quest to mitigate fear of our own. This can be incidental, or it can be quite intentional. It sets up a paradoxical situation, Becker suggests, following Otto Rank, in which we preserve our immortality over our lives.[25]

I suggest a modification to Rank's formulation, at least in the vast majority of cases. We are willing to preserve our immortality over *their* lives. The paradox does not normally extend to the individual level, and we will repeatedly return to the idea that even the most elaborate institutions are unable to persuade the vast majority of people to value their own immortality over their own lives when the latter is brought into sharp focus. Martyrdom appears within this paradigm as a rarity, a manner of heroism (in Becker's formulation) that relatively few will choose, and its rarity is connected to its institutional value. Rather than keeping one's head down, it is instead maximizing vulnerability in order to seize immortality all at once. It garners admiration, stirring us on an existential level. On a social level, its rarity provides us (who remain) another opportunity to both assure ourselves that we are "on the right track" and console ourselves that less risky ways will perhaps eventually get us to the same destination. As Becker describes, "This is the basic role and function of the hero in society: he is the one who gambles with his very life and successfully defies death, and men follow him and eventually worship his memory because he embodies the triumph over what they fear most, extinction and death."[26]

The willing suicide does not of course defy death in any straightforward way, and this contributes to her paradoxical appeal. She defies death by embracing it, and we cannot know whether the desired result was achieved. On an individual level, the death is left as a compelling question mark. This is where an institution opportunistically enters: it transforms the act of violence into something mundane and functional. The defiance of death becomes support for a system that men can worship. Society is made up of such hero systems, systems of meaning-making, and, as Becker concludes, the primary task of studying these systems is to assess "how high are the costs of this lie."[27]

Becker is highlighting, then, at least two fundamental ways we might critically assess a given institution. One is according to the effectiveness of its immortality project. Another is the extent to which that project, whether due to its internal construction or historical circumstance, relies on the perpetuation of violence and death to maintain itself. Generally speaking, the more clearly violence is exposed as a primary means of securing and maintaining an immortality project, the more questionable that project becomes, predicated as it is on the exchange of some lives for others.

By "exposed" here, I mean something akin to Vardoulakis's concept of "dejustification." Violence is revealed in its raw unjustified—and vis-à-vis the sovereign institution, unjustifiable—form. Given the cultural diversity of humankind, this would seem to rightsize all immortality projects to a regional or local level; to put it another way, we *should* be fairly skeptical of any universalizing immortality project. Yet our fear of death is so central that we are taken in, time and again, by the sense that *this* project is different, and as such we willingly participate in obscuring to ourselves the sustenance of violence by which it is fed.

To a certain extent, obscuring institutional violence is a standard feature of sovereign power. As noted above, sovereign violence is never pursued for its own sake. It is seen as an exception, and its execution is toward a professed aim of order, of safety, of peace—"a perpetual and universal peace outside of history."[28] As Vardoulakis importantly notes, this peace need not be evident in society in order for its imperatives to be operative. Violence is thus required when order is disrupted and thereby safety and peace—its presence or simply its possibility—threatened. There is a tendency, then, to focus myopically on the professed aim with little regard to the scope and nature of the violence utilized to achieve it. Like Vardoulakis, Becker turns to a democratic system to combat this tendency.

> Democracy does encroach on utopia a little bit, because it already addresses itself to the problem of mystification by free flow of self-criticism. We could carry the utopian musings a bit further and say that the gauge of a truly free society would be the extent to which it admitted its own central fear of death and questioned its own system of heroic transcendence—and this is precisely what democracy is doing much of the time.[29]

The traditional method of institutional operation is precisely the opposite of Becker's formulation. As the title of Becker's book suggests and as Heidegger describes, the individual in conjunction with the institution denies his fear of death by placing mostly unquestioned trust in one—and if possible, more than one—institutional means of heroic transcendence. Becker thus allows us to put a finer point on martyrdom's function for institution and individual. The violent death of the willing suicide becomes life for the sovereign institution, and the institution itself functions to provide narratives of meaning for its adherents. Martyrs can serve in this role directly—as "heroes"—and indirectly as legitimacy for the institution (and its narratives).

Implications for Religion and (Non)violence

The potential impact of this argument for the contentious discussion of religion and violence is not insignificant. The traditional approach to Christian martyrdom places all the violence on one side. It divides martyrdom events into persecutors and persecuted, guilty and innocent, perpetrator and victim. Insofar as it is successful, the martyr narrative renders violence on one level inscrutable. Why was such violence enacted against an innocent party? It is unjustifiable and diabolical. As noted above, this paradigm shift creates potential space for a new justifiable sovereign institution.

If the narrative includes the willing participation of the so-called victim, however, this shifts the balance of violence, creating a more complicated scenario. There is no longer a clear victim or a clear display of innocence. And if the death of this agent is fodder for her community, this suggests a need for the assessment of the costs and benefits of such a process. And if the victim's community not only opportunistically benefits from the death of one of its own but also supports and encourages the willing suicide in indirect or direct fashion, it becomes clear to see that our understanding of martyrdom is grossly inaccurate—we have it backward. It is not unreasonable violence enacted unjustifiably against an innocent victim but part of a calculated institutional practice of fabricating viability with the blood of its own adherents.

Another practical implication of this argument is that violence is not only ubiquitous within institutions of religion but also—like other institutions—a necessary part of their functionality. Religious institutions justify violence using the same structures as so-called secular institutions do, but religious ones "are able to feed many more premises into those structures," namely supernatural ones.[30] This understanding affords both a fresh look at martyr discourse and a position from which to critique the oft-attempted separation of violence from religion in modern scholarship.

Present-day religious discourse—particularly in post-9/11 America—is polarized around the issue of violence. Nearly all the military conflicts of the last century have been given religious justification, either contemporaneous with or after the events in question, and even recent natural disasters have been attributed to the wrath of God.[31] In reaction to the at times overly simplistic correlation between religion and violence (particularly when this paradoxically and tragically provokes acts of violence against others for their perceived religious identity),[32] twenty-first century scholars have often gone to great lengths to sever the link between religion and violence. One example is Karen Armstrong, a former nun and prolific scholar of religion. In 2009, she founded a movement called the "Charter of Compassion," based on a manifesto that contends compassion is the core of all the world's religious traditions, and that violence has no place in religion. The movement's charter, which people from around the world were encouraged to sign online, indicates the ideological separation of religion and violence:

> We therefore call upon all men and women ... to return to the ancient principle that any interpretation of scripture that breeds violence, hatred or disdain is illegitimate ... It is also necessary in both public and private life to refrain consistently and empathically from inflicting pain. To act or speak violently out of spite, chauvinism, or self-interest, to impoverish, exploit or deny basic rights to anybody, and to incite hatred by denigrating others—even our enemies—is a denial of our common humanity.[33]

The charter implies that religion can and should be separated from violence in order to continue to contribute to a global future. Despite a reference to "ancient principle," the charter reveals an idealistic anachronism, suggesting an accepted "basic" set of rights for all persons. Even bolder, however, is the statement that all textual interpretations that produce violence are illegitimate. In one fell swoop, most of the Western religious tradition, indeed world history, is excised. The intent to mitigate unnecessary violence—and I will suggest in Chapter 7 that all religious violence falls into this category—is admirable, but the charter's apparent means is to naïvely overlook the violence advocated in the religious texts of many traditions and promote a myth of pure origins. Even if one agrees that this is a necessary tactic to combat religious violence, it remains to be explored just why, if it is not integral to religion, violence has dogged its steps from the earliest times into the present.

Armstrong herself subsequently devoted a book to this topic. In *Fields of Blood* she makes several connected arguments to enact a separation between religion and violence. The first is that the definition of religion is notoriously slippery and thus difficult to connect in any concrete way to violence.[34] The second, connected argument is that the distinction of religion as a discrete cultural sphere, separate from other areas such as politics, is a modern phenomenon.[35] The implication is that there was nothing identifiable as "religion" to blame for violence until the post-Reformation era, and thus it is anachronistic to single out religion for blame for violence. This line of argumentation cuts both ways, however, which makes it more difficult for the majority of her chronological exploration of religious traditions and their interactions with the broader civilizations in which they participate.

Armstrong's thesis is that religions arose as a way to explain and compensate for the inevitable inequalities in society.[36] In other words, the blame for inequalities, which often lead to violence, lies with civilization itself; religion often "endorsed structural and martial violence, but it also regularly called it into question."[37] Insofar as it is designed to combat the argument that religion is responsible for all (or nearly all) violence, and that if only we got rid of religion, violence would go away as well, Armstrong's argument is effective. As she notes, "We see the impossibility of describing any religious tradition as a single unchanging essence that will always inspire violence."[38] Her nuanced approach to ancient religion and the development of religious traditions within their cultural milieux is warranted and welcome. The results are complicated, however, because it is difficult to convincingly diffuse religion into its cultural environment to shield it from blame for violence only to single it out for praise in relation to positive social change.

Even were it the case that we could in every case historically identify religion proceeding from, and intended as a counter to, the injustices built into civilization, we would still want to explore the implications of (whatever we identify as) religion in violence moving forward from that point. The question remains the same: where and to what extent does religion, do religious institutions, contribute to violence, and is that violence on balance part of a positive contribution to society?

The attempt to distance religion from violence, part perhaps of a broader tendency to paint "religion" (or at least some religion) as a societal good, can prevent thorough exploration and recognition of unwarranted violence within religious traditions. Wellman and Tokuno suggest that "religious conflict is predictable and should be expected … because religion is often an independent cultural force in society, it has the tendency to become a threat to other cultural and political powers. Religious violence may not be inevitable … but it should surprise no one."[39] As I have argued, the phenomenon of martyrdom needs to be considered in this exploration of violence, particularly within the Christian tradition where—at least in the abstract—martyrdom is considered an unadulterated good. There are of course studies, primarily from religious insiders, that apologetically examine contemporary religious martyrdoms.[40] There are also straightforward historical compilations of martyr tales.[41] However, few treatments attempt to connect the institution of martyrdom within religion to greater issues of religious violence in the present.[42] The implication seems to be that martyrdom is retained within religious traditions simply because it is tradition, not because the liturgical performance of violence, the recreation and celebration of martyrdom, retains a critical institutional function.

I have suggested that this hallowed form of religious violence is unexplored in part because we are implicated in sovereign institutional norms for discourse on violence. It is not simply unwillingness to countenance the strong presence of violence within religion; for Christianity in its hegemonic position, the interpretation of religious violence as a corruption, as "bad religion," is beneficial for an institutional monopoly on violence. The willing suicide, transformed into the laudable death of the martyr, provides an impetus for life in present tradition. In the following chapter, we will explore the roots of this development in the Christian tradition.

4

Blood Is Seed: Martyrdom and the Triumph of Christianity

It would be difficult to find a scholarly work on early Christian martyrdom that does not include the apologist Tertullian's famous phrase: "We spring up in greater numbers the more we are mown down by you. The blood of the Christians is seed."[1] Though written at the opening of the third century, the phrase has been taken as emblematic of the eventual triumph of Christianity over Rome, both by ancient and modern scholars. Of course Tertullian could not have foreseen—and did not consider possible—Christianity's eventual relationship with the state established through the help of the sympathetic Roman Emperor Constantine over a century later. The ready application of this phrase as a hermeneutic key for the growth of Christianity is thus ironic, particularly because its author represented what would become a decidedly heterodox perspective on martyrdom.

There is, however, a way in which martyrdom did become the seed for the growth of the church, but it was not through blood, at least not directly. It was through narrativization, through historicization. The fact that the first three centuries of Christian history are read through the lens of persecution and triumph misleadingly suggests a mutually recognized war between "Rome" and Christians. In the beginning, Rome was winning and it looked as if Christianity would suffer defeat; yet as Tertullian predicted, increased defeat paradoxically caused increased growth until the pagan Roman Empire was vastly outnumbered by the overwhelmingly Christian populace. Through such a lens Eusebius of Caesarea, the fourth-century bishop and church historian, authored the still-prevailing means of explaining the early Christian relationship with the state. The representation of the Christian kingdom as not (or not only) a spiritual but a temporal goal achieved under Constantine is perhaps unsurprising, but it was not an inevitable outcome of a burgeoning growth process.

In the previous two chapters, I described martyrdom as first "willing suicide" and suggested that this autonomous act of violence, due to its inherently anti-institutional nature, must be controlled by the sovereign institution and thus can be used to its benefit. In this chapter, I will illustrate this argument using the development of martyrdom in early Christianity, with the *Ecclesiastical History* of the fourth-century CE Bishop Eusebius as a guide. The point here, reading against the Eusebian account, is to suggest that Christianity did not "triumph" because of martyrdom; martyrdom was instead one piece of the Eusebian narrative retroactively engineered to justify Christian success. The significance of this paradigm shift is not just a matter of historical accuracy. The story itself is inextricably tied to notions that "true" martyrdom is Christian and orthodox, which serves of course to perpetuate Christianity as a sovereign institution. As I implied in the previous chapters, martyrdom is not inherent to (nor uniquely good within) Christianity; rather, the control of violence is inherent to the sovereign institution. Political victory helped imperial Christians certify a transformation of martyrdom from a rare and radical act of self-formation to an affirmation of imperial Christianity.

Within the prototypical Eusebian narrative, I will expand on the martyrdom of Polycarp and the martyrs of Lyons and Vienne, for several reasons. These martyrdoms figure largely in Eusebius's account, they are well-known and oft-referenced, and they contain identifiable features that demonstrate the utility of the martyrdoms to their multiple audiences. Filling a critical gap in Eusebius's chronology, I will also juxtapose two significant Christian figures in the early third century, Tertullian of Carthage and Clement of Alexandria, the first of whom ironically would come to represent extremism or heresy – the latter, orthodoxy. A discussion of Cyprian of Carthage's interactions with martyrs a brief half-century later displays the increased tension that the autonomy of the willing suicide implies for the church when not fully controlled as martyrdom. The chapter will end by bringing Eusebius's account up to his own day to suggest that the consolidation of the Roman Empire under the Emperor Constantine allowed proto-orthodox Christianity the power to certify and enforce the transformation from willing suicide to martyrdom.

Through the late twentieth century, scholarship on early Christianity has followed the Eusebian narrative. In his well-known *Martyrdom and Persecution in the Early Church*, W. H. C. Frend reveals both the centrality of tradition to conceptualizing the early Christian martyr and his own location within that tradition. He gushes in his praise: "Their constancy and steadfast devotion were truly amazing. No passage of time, no change of circumstances can dim their glory. Even in our own day ... the examples of these men and women live on, a memorial to the impact which Christianity made on the civilization of the Roman Empire."[2] This brief passage provides interstices through which to interrogate the dominant interpretation of early Christian martyrdom—the apparently transcendent laudability of the martyrs, the unquestioned presumption of the indispensability of martyrdom for Christian growth, and the attribution of one of Christianity's greatest impacts on society to violent and antagonistic death. T. D. Barnes is more critical of Eusebius than Frend, suggesting that Eusebius is unreliable for understanding persecution of Christians before the mid-third century.[3] Though Barnes acknowledges the sporadic nature of persecution in the period, he still concludes that "though an individual Christian might never himself be persecuted or harassed, the church became and remained a church of martyrs."[4]

Within this paradigm, the so-called "Great Persecution" of Christians in the early fourth century was a temporary delay to an inevitable outcome.[5] Frend concludes that "the pagan world had had enough, enough of bloodshed, enough of the butchers' shop in service to the gods ... As the killing went on, so more turned to Christ. Persecution even quickened the pace of conversions."[6] The presumption of Christian triumph necessitates a measure of incredulity over the idea that Rome seemed to be unaware of their impending defeat at the hands of growing Christianity. If martyrdom was a seed for growth, the question runs, why would government play so readily into the hands of zealous Christians? Perhaps the most obvious answer is the most accurate. Perhaps the deaths of Christians were insignificant to the empire—there is little evidence to suggest Christian death contributed to Christian growth beyond retrospectively and rhetorically.

The Eusebian Narrative

Eusebius's history is certainly not limited to discussions of martyrdom. His primary goal is to validate the fourth-century status quo under the first Christian emperor by creating a narrative of the previous three centuries that posited a Christian Roman Empire as its natural and divinely inspired outcome. While Eusebius may have been wary of the application of fate to his history, the natural tendency of his narrativization of Christian history at least conveyed his feeling that the weight of "the accidents of history" had positively led to the final defeat of the enemies of Christianity by Constantine.[7] Among the contributing factors to this victory, if one reckons by the amount of space given to it in his history, martyrdom is one of the most significant. To understand the legacy of interpretation Eusebius has left behind, it is helpful to survey the uses to which martyrdom is put in his *Ecclesiastical History*.[8]

He gives numerous purposes for writing his history, among them to record those who struggled through blood and trials against attacks on the divine Word. In the first two centuries, however, his number of martyrs are relatively few and read as a "who's who" of early Christianity. The death of Jesus is markedly absent, but in describing Stephen as the protomartyr,[9] he notes that he was "first after the Lord … to gain the crown" (*HE* 2.1.1). The first martyr to receive extended treatment is James, the brother of Jesus. James is given public opportunity to renounce Christ; he responds instead confirming salvation found in him. Hegesippus, Eusebius's source, writes that "on account of these words some believed that Jesus is the Christ" (2.23.9). Subsequently, he is thrown from the temple and stoned.

Paul and Peter—disciples of Jesus—are naturally numbered among the martyrs, and the remaining relatives of Jesus are also called martyrs for assuaging the emperor Domitian's fear of revolt by assuring the emperor that Christ's kingdom was heavenly rather than earthly (3.20.6). Symeon, however, the second bishop of Jerusalem, was said to have suffered death by crucifixion under Trajan (3.32). Immediately following this, Eusebius claims that martyrdoms had grown so great as to warrant the oft-cited query from Pliny the Younger to the emperor Trajan as to how to try Christians. The effect of the emperor's response, according to the bishop, was to reduce somewhat the threat of persecution (3.33.2).

There are two elements here that illustrate the draw of the martyrs for Eusebius. First, as he will do increasingly throughout his history, he makes grand statements about the growing influence of Christianity. The bishop concluded that Christianity had grown steadily up to his time. This thesis seemed to explain the query of Pliny, a provincial governor whose letters to the emperor Hadrian in the early second century inquiring about how to treat Christians are often seen as evidence of Christianity's rapid growth. Why else would the governor write to the emperor if he were not overwhelmed by the influence of Christians?[10] Eusebius takes the additional step of suggesting that the "witness" of Christians was primarily in their deaths. "Plinius Secundus, one of the most distinguished governors, was disturbed at the multitude of martyrs, and reported to the Emperor about the multitude of those put to death over the faith" (3.33.1). It is notable that Pliny's letter itself does not explicitly refer to execution but punishment of recalcitrant Christians (*Letters* 10.96.3).[11] The very purpose of his letter is to find out what the extent of punishment should be, and it seems unlikely he pursued any course of action aggressively before getting a response.[12] He does note in closing his letter the importance of his query because of the "number of persons involved. For many of every age and of every rank and of both sexes have been already and will be brought to trial" (10.96.9). However, he concludes with a note of confidence that the majority will be able to be reformed. In contrast, Eusebius uses the exchange to reinforce the "natural" opposition to Christian growth.[13]

A similar dynamic to the third-century persecution under the Emperor Decius can be observed in smaller form. Under pressure, while there were a number of obstinate Christians, the majority were not willing to be martyrs. Eusebius is able to exploit the lack of concrete instances in the favor of Christian growth. The point here is not to deny Christian growth; Pliny's letter is evidence enough of governmental concern. Rather, it is to mitigate Eusebius's triumphalist generalization that the multitude were martyrs.

Book Three of the *Ecclesiastical History* relates the death of Bishop Ignatius. Eusebius treats his account briefly (*HE* 3.36), and little is known of him beyond his martyrdom, which is foreshadowed through a series of letters he wrote to various churches along the route from his bishopric in Antioch to a presumed death in Rome. There is little application of Ignatius's death within his own writing to the church at large, certainly in comparison to the martyrdom of his contemporary Polycarp. Further, Ignatius's zeal for a bloody fate suggests notions of a "death wish" or psychosis.[14] There is an excess in the bishop's writing that challenges any smooth recapture for martyrdom. He seeks above all identification with Christ, but it is only through death that it can be found. He is used cautiously within Christian scholarship, for "he glows with the fire and impetuosity … which carries him beyond the bounds of sobriety."[15] It is as much by virtue of his position as his unorthodox enactment of the martyr that he is primarily remembered, and justified by his alignment with the narrative of the triumphant church.

Book Four recounts in detail the death of Polycarp as well giving background to the cause of Justin Martyr's death. In retelling the martyrdom of Polycarp, Eusebius does reference a paragraph from the martyrdom, which tells of other martyrs having preceded the bishop, for his own martyrdom was said to be a symbolic end to the persecution (4.15.3). However, it is not until Book Five, with the martyrdoms of Christians in Lyons and Vienne, that significant martyrs come from a class other than the clergy or significant church figures. This suggests several possibilities. One is that there were few martyrdoms to report. If persecution was sporadic, and if what sporadic persecution there was was limited effectively to movement leaders, then there were simply limited records to choose from, and the bishop included all that he could. Yet he certainly had more accounts, those that he mentions in passing, such as that of Carpus, Papylus, and Agonathice (4.15.48). He also refers the reader to his collection of ancient martyrdoms, and that would seem to be the reason he does not expand a brief mention of the martyrdom of Pionius (4.15.46–47). So it is possible that the few martyrdoms in the first five books of his work are due to their placement elsewhere. It appears, however, that he knew of others, like the aforementioned, and chose not to recount their tales anywhere.[16]

This suggests another possibility, that the prevalence of upper-class martyrdoms in Eusebius's history is reflective of those that were useful for his purposes. On the surface, this seems overwhelmingly obvious. After all, even before promising to recount the deeds of martyrs, Eusebius proclaims as his first goal to record the succession of the apostles and those in leadership who distinguished themselves (1.1.1). Stephen, James, Peter and Paul, Symeon, Ignatius, Polycarp, and Justin Martyr were all church leaders. Their martyrdoms all also had in common that they adhered to the "true" martyrdom type that would be developed by Clement of Alexandria, as will be discussed below. They had none of the questionable elements that would make later church leaders uncomfortable. Agonathice, on the other hand, "volunteers" herself as a martyr by throwing herself on the stake that was burning fellow Christians Carpus and Papylus.[17] While martyrdoms contemporary with Eusebius contained questionable elements, those in the distant past—*because* in the past—were models, obedient to both God and church. Further, they were of a stature worth remembering by name.

The benefit to pointing out the selective nature of Eusebius may seem counterproductive. It might appear to indicate that there were many more martyrdoms which the bishop excluded, and this is indeed the effect of the Eusebian narrative upon the triumphant church. The reader concludes that there were many martyrs, and that they adhered roughly to the model of the few stories told in detail. However, equally possible and more plausible is that there were fewer unnamed martyrs than commonly believed, and that their embodiment is not just the "orthodox" bishop but also the heterodox volunteer.

Imitation and Veneration in the Martyrdom of Polycarp

Eusebius's history thus describes martyrdom as widely observed, yet as exemplified it is the bastion of a select few. His ideal martyr is not so by choosing but by being chosen. While martyrdom became a significant factor in the growth of Christianity through its post-Constantinian transformation from individual death to institutional life, this transformation had been germinating for centuries. As I noted in the previous chapter, execution by the sovereign institution is simply violence if left unjustified; in the hands of the competing institution it becomes proof, both of the diabolical nature of the Roman institution and of the truth of Christianity. The well-known martyrdom of Polycarp is a prime case to observe these operations in action.

The record of the bishop's martyrdom takes the form of a letter from the church in Smyrna to that of Philomelium as well as the entire church everywhere (4.15.3).[18] The first four chapters serve as prefatory material for the story of Polycarp's martyrdom, but they contain in themselves a model for martyrdom. The first chapter establishes Polycarp's death as the epitome of a "true" martyr. The second chapter blesses those who have been martyred according to the will of God and anonymously describes in gory detail the pains of their struggles, passages that Eusebius did not fail to reproduce. Their perseverance has been rewarded with eternal life. The third chapter singles out Germanicus as an example of these martyrs, a young boy who was fearlessly determined to be martyred. Contrasted to him in the fourth chapter is Quintus, whose initial zeal in turning himself in to the authorities quickly became fear when threatened with the beasts. He sacrificed. The moral of the story, say the Smyrneans, is not to be a volunteer martyr.

The first chapter is worth citation in full, for its manifest and latent messages:

> We are writing to you, dear brothers, the story of the martyrs and of blessed Polycarp who put a stop to the persecution by his own martyrdom as though he were putting a seal upon it. For nearly all that had happened before took place that the Lord might show us from heaven a "gospel-martyr." Just as the Lord did, he too waited that he might be delivered up, that we might become his imitators, *not thinking of ourselves alone. but of our neighbors as well* [Phil. 2:4; italics mine]. For it is a mark of true and solid love to desire not only one's own salvation but also that of all the brothers. (5.1029.1)[19]

These prefatory remarks are unique for the transformative operation they trace. The martyrs are nameless, excepting Germanicus and Quintus. Polycarp, the known bishop, is said to have stopped the persecution with his death.[20] This cessation, while perhaps an actual one, was an ideological one as well. Polycarp had provided for the Smyrneans an example for emulation, a theoretical model to which the church must give assent. Considered in the larger context of the first four chapters, which will be discussed below, there is also introduced a note of apology here. Polycarp is providing a restitution, a community redemption, with his blood covering over the perceived failures of other witnesses. This is confirmed in the next sentence, which justifies with the bishop's death "nearly all" that had happened previously. Like Tertullian's later statement, the sentence intends to be comforting, implying that despite the perceived pains and setbacks in the past, the death of the bishop is a reminder that it was all a divine setup. If everything is from God, and everything from God is good, then the events to which the Smyrneans allude are beneficial to Christians. Polycarp, in contrast to his predecessors, is a true martyr.

The manifest reason Polycarp was a quintessential witness is answered in the next sentence. He waited to become a martyr, as did the Lord. Polycarp's witness was *imitatio Christi*, in imitation of Christ. He redeemed the past failures of fellow Christians and established a model for the community to follow. That model is not rooted in the death, for it only provides evidence of this witness. The model, according to the Smyrneans, is anchored by the waiting. The opening reference to cessation of persecution makes more sense in this light. If there is no immediate threat of death, then they, in waiting, are *imitatio Christi* as well. The past deaths of the martyrs could be glorified in the comparatively secure present.[21]

The latter half of the sentence, a reference to a passage from Paul's letter to the Philippians, reveals a serious concern for the Christian community. Those who wait have been set in contrast to the zealous martyrs, who gave themselves up to the authorities. The manifest spiritual concern masks a more pressing practical one. Those thinking of only themselves will fail and in failure lose their salvation through idolatrous sacrifice. Those additionally thinking of their neighbors will wait to earn their salvation. The waiting will ensure success in suffering. The practical concern may have been that those who offered themselves up to Roman officials for punishment or martyrdom drew unnecessary attention to the existence of a Christian community.[22] Exposing them to imperial scrutiny would certainly test the wills of many Christians who might be found unstable, as the governor Pliny's testing had shown. The exemplum of the witness as the one who waits preserves the future of the community while preserving the solidarity generated by "successful" martyrs.

Germanicus is singled out as evidence of a minor redemption from among, presumably, the lay community. The devil's intent was to get Christians through torture to sacrifice, "but thanks to God, for he did not overpower all" (5.1032.3). But most of them he did, as Quintus illustrates. One wonders whether

Germanicus was not a volunteer as well, for although he is noted as a success, he is not cited as an example. His "waiting" was not recorded; instead, he spurned the attempted dissuasion from the governing official and was said to have pulled a wild beast on himself.

Quintus, on the other hand, was an outsider for more than just his apostasy. He was a foreigner, a recent emigrant from Phrygia, as the Smyrneans make careful note in introducing his character. Further, in contrast to the selfish type portrayed in the first chapter, he was not only thinking himself either; he convinced others to be volunteers. While it is not explicitly stated that his converts also followed in his capitulation to the governor's persuasion to sacrifice, it is likely that, in absence of their mention, most if not all did. The Smyrnean conclusion is a justification for their stance against volunteers: "This is not the teaching of the Gospel" (5.1032.4). And, more than likely, you will not succeed. And, if you do not succeed, you put the lie to the inherent connection between martyrdom and the truth of Christianity.

From a safe interval of distance and time, the Smyrneans can glorify the example of Polycarp to neighboring communities. It is uncertain what caused the period of persecution in Smyrna, in which the crowd of pagans and Jews as well as the governor were said to have been complicit. In any case, the persecution was revelatory to the community in many ways. First, it showed that there were some Christians who were willing suicides, desirous to imitate Christ in death.[23] However, and more devastatingly, it showed that one's Christianity, one's *willingness* to imitate Christ, indicated prior to being mortally tested, was not a guarantee of success. The hope of success, it seemed, was greatly outweighed by the costs of failure, both to the individual and, more critically, the community. In the case of those witnesses who had succeeded, such as Germanicus and Polycarp, it could be said that their deaths took place "in accordance with God's will" (5.1029.2). The actions of the failed martyrs, however, could not be rectified according to the same argument. Such failure could not be God's desire, could it? If the relationship was shifted, however, such a paradigm could readily account for both successful and failed martyrdoms. Failed witness could not bear the weight of divine will, but the successful death could be attributed to divine favor, while the unsuccessful attempt could be evidence of its lack. This, then, was one of two major prongs in the Smyrnean campaign, to neutralize the uncertainty and harness the resolved potential (in the Heideggerian sense of the potentiality of death) of the deaths of the past. Both successful and failed witnesses, voluntary and involuntary, could be harnessed, albeit in different ways, to gain such results.

Another goal of the Smyrneans seems to have been to manage the ideology of martyrdom in the present, which they accomplished in promoting imitation of Christ as waiting rather than dying. This model, however, needed promotion, and the propagation of Polycarp's death provided a means. The Smyrneans thought a certain imitation was to be found in the repetition of Polycarp's story. "We are writing to you, dear brothers, the story of the martyrs and of blessed Polycarp ... [who] waited that he might be delivered up, *that we might become his imitators*." As the passage continues, the mark of true love is to desire the salvation of "all the brothers" (5.1029.1). It appears that a manifestation of the desire for universal Christian salvation was perpetuation of Polycarp's tale. In the wake of persecution, repetition of his story controlled the martyr's death, perpetuating *Christian* life. For the redactor, this also brought the hope of salvation.

This new *imitatio* is reiterated in the closing of Polycarp's story. The Smyrneans note that although Polycarp was the twelfth of martyrs from the area, he alone was the remembered model. Musurillo translates the following: "He was not only a great teacher but also a conspicuous martyr, whose testimony, following the Gospel of Christ, everyone desires to imitate" (5.1044.19). It is notable that Musurillo's translation preserves the essence of the transformation of the death begun by the Smyrneans themselves. The writers certainly intended in numbering twelve martyrs that those had not only given verbal witness but also had been executed. Polycarp himself is named a "conspicuous martyr"; however, Musurillo translated his martyrdom as "testimony" (*martúrion*) that others wish to imitate. There is indeed variance in the usage of the term, and this tension was already present among the Smyrneans. In a time of "waiting," with a heightened perception of the threat of death, the desire for witness could be construed, for some, as commensurate with death itself. In times of peace, however, without the perceived threat of death, the death of the martyr is conceived as wholly imitable in testimony alone, and with the same hope of reward.

In a longer recension, a later redactor wrote the legacy of transmission of Polycarp's tale. One Pionius writes that he recorded an earlier copy that emanated originally from a disciple of Polycarp. He searched for the copy after receiving a vision from the martyr himself and "collected the material ... that the Lord Jesus Christ might also gather me together with his elect into his heavenly kingdom" (5.1045.22). By Pionius's day, he understood that an appropriate, acceptable, and desirable means of *imitatio Christi* was veneration. In preserving and promoting the memory of Polycarp, Pionius too benefited from its original salvific result. While the tendency had not been quite so overt with the Smyrneans, the subtle transformation of imitation, the slowly increasing control over willing suicide to shape the martyr, had begun to appear.

The Martyrs of Lyons and Vienne

The first martyrdom recorded by Eusebius in which all the martyrs were not significant figures in the church is the well-known martyrs of Lyons and Vienne (5.1.1). Again Eusebius remarks that he has recorded the martyrdom in full in his no-longer-extant *Acts of the Martyrs*. The fact that he reproduces the majority of the extant account here begs the question of his methods of selection. In any case, his is the only preserved account of this martyrdom. The traditional title of the martyrdom in later works—"The Letter of the Churches of Vienne and Lyons on the Martyrdom of the Holy Bishop Pothinus and the Others"—is indicative of the focus of the tale, however.[24] The account names six martyrs, although it implies many more, both named and nameless. Only two of the named held positions in the church, one of whom was the aged bishop of Lyons. The rest were slaves, children, and novices in the church. The uniqueness of the account among other extant stories indicates that this was indeed an extraordinary occurrence of martyrdom. Even aside from considerations of interpolation before Eusebius, the account is detailed and graphic, much more so than that of Polycarp. As with his discussion of Pliny, though, Eusebius intends to indicate that these persecutions occurred throughout the empire (5.2.1). Prefacing the account, he remarks that "to judge from the events in one nation, myriads were distinguished by martyrdom" (5.0.1). Yet, as he continues, this account is singular in having been recorded and surviving the chronological interval of the third century. "It is truly worthy of unceasing remembrance" (5.0.1). The bishop explains the account's inclusion:

> Our record of those who order their lives according to God will inscribe on everlasting monuments ... the struggles of the athletes of piety and their valour which braved so much, trophies won from demons, and victories against unseen adversaries, and the crowns at the end of it all ... It will proclaim [them] for everlasting remembrance. (5.0.4)

The reader is to understand both that the struggles of the Lyons martyrs represent those of Christians everywhere at the time and also to realize the uniqueness of their struggle in the singularity of their account. Eusebius accomplishes this in several ways. First, he maintains and reaffirms the "diabolization" of the original account. No names of persecutors are transcribed; though the reigning emperor Marcus Aurelius is mentioned, aside from the governor we have only demonic agents combating the Christians.[25] This lies in contrast to the account of Polycarp, in which names are prevalent and an otherworldly adversary makes almost no appearance. Second and more importantly, Eusebius's usage seamlessly utilizes the martyrs to exemplify all Christians. He memorializes "those who order their lives according to God," making the acts of these men and women stand in for those of all Christians in time of persecution. The bishop claims his record simply inscribes on preexistent monuments the deeds of the martyrs, but it rather monumentalizes the martyrs themselves, making them the epitome of success in the struggle against the devil.[26] Just as Constantine was cast by Eusebius into an epochal role in the victory of the church, the bloody martyr stands in for Christianity itself.

The account of the martyrdom itself is reproduced with little editorializing. The bishop even includes the overlooked comment that upon testing, about ten of the Christians "failed," more than the number glorified in the account (5.1.11). Following the account of their deaths, Eusebius appends a commentary on the character of the martyrs, who refused the title of martyrs, taking rather the name of confessors (*homologoi*). Eusebius intends that these humble and forbearing martyrs be juxtaposed with the recalcitrant heterodox Donatist and Novatian martyrs of his own day, but the passage also reveals the slippage of martyrdom away from identification with death. Transported into the fourth century, the martyrs of Lyons and Vienne might themselves have been Donatists, unable to brook the dilution of death in the face of apostasy on a massive scale. That intransigence was no longer fashionable in the Christian Roman era. The Lyons confessors apparently attributed the title of martyr to Christ and those who had already died but not themselves (5.2.3–4). For their part, the Lyons community attributed to them the power, if not the title, of martyr.

The Lyons community says that the martyrs "made defence for all men; they released all and bound none" (5.2.5). This both reveals that their impending deaths put them in a position of authority and implies that they willingly agreed to stand in for the community as a whole. If the martyrs prayed for their accusers, just as the protomartyr Stephen had, "how much more for the brethren?" (5.2.5). The Smyrneans had been able, with their transmission of the martyrdom of Polycarp, to transform imitation of Christ from dying to waiting. In a similar fashion, the Lyons community addresses the uncertainty of their continued existence after the trying persecution by spreading to Asia Minor the stories of their martyrs, whose forbearance was validated by death. The dichotomization of martyrs and non-martyrs, of dead and alive, was subsumed by that of Christian versus pagan, God versus the enemy. This textual monumentalization was certified by Eusebius who reproduced the story of forbearance on a much broader scale. Through his narrativization, the martyrs can be seen to have achieved their aim in a Christian empire.

According to the bishop, the community at Lyons composed its narrative of the martyrs in part to combat the Montanist controversy that had arisen in Phrygia (5.14.1). Their "firm and orthodox" opinion was sent to Asia Minor to help clear up the controversy (5.3.4). Their assistance consisted, at least for Eusebius, in helping to establish "true" martyrs over and against false ones. The difference between a more conservative and a radical interpretation can be viewed here. While the latter was confident in asserting that the death, in and of itself, was proof of Christianity, the proto-orthodox were more wary. Over a century later, it was obvious to Eusebius that recognizing Christian martyrs required ecclesiastical discernment.

Following the martyrdom, the bishop records the work of Apollinarius of Hierapolis who had written to counter the influence of Montanism, a Christian sect that gained significant influence and caused serious controversy in the late second century. After recording the general rise-and-fall narrative of the group, Apollinarius responds to Montanist claims that their prophets too were martyred. He contends quite simply that none was persecuted by Jews or dispatched unlawfully. "Was there any notable one of them crucified for the Name? No, there wasn't" (5.16.12). Instead, the bishop relates, the two Montanist prophetesses were said to have committed suicide while another of their founding members was raised to the sky in a trance and then cast down and died (5.16.13–14). These Montanists did not seem to have died of natural causes, and it was critical to manage the narrative of their deaths. Apollinarius's obvious claim to true Christianity and clear distinction between that and Montanism precluded justification of their beliefs by their deaths. Hierarchy was established in order to control the power of the autonomy of willing suicide. Montanists were not persecuted by Jews, as they claimed, and their deaths by the state were lawful.[27] When they had been defeated in all other points of argument (which Eusebius does not detail), Montanists fell back on a body count (5.16.20).[28] Apollinarius recognizes the importance of the deaths and cannot deny them but rather controls them by discrediting them.

Eusebius includes an example (presumably of many) of one Alexander who was hailed as a martyr by the Montanists but convicted as a robber by the Ephesian governor (5.18.9). Perhaps more important for Eusebius was Apollinarius's conclusive claim, responding to the Montanist claim that a high quantity of martyrs was proof of truth: "This appears to be actually farther from the truth than anything. For some of the other heresies have innumerable martyrs, but I do not suppose that we shall accept them for that reason, nor admit that they have the truth" (5.16.20–21). The death became insufficient—or rather super-sufficient—proof of Christian identity when the tensions within became greater than those without.

Tertullian and Clement: Mediating the Willing Suicide

The following sixth book of Eusebius's *Ecclesiastical History* covers in a relatively short space the entire first half of the third century. It is predominantly focused on the theologian Origen and is geographically concentrated in the eastern half of the empire. He describes the number of martyrs as countless (6.2.3), and he lists nine martyrs under the Severan persecution in Alexandria, the primary purpose of which was to illustrate the influence of Origen upon each of them (6.4). Indeed, Eusebius describes in detail the absolute disregard for his safety with which Origen worked among the martyrs and the persecuted, indicating that the only explanation for his survival was divine favor (6.3.4).[29] Eusebius gives in the second half of the book significant space to the vehemence of the Alexandrian persecution as narrated by Dionysius. The latter notes some concern over the management of martyrdom, to which I will return. In contrast, Eusebius makes no mention of the Latin apologist, Tertullian, whose writing on martyrdom reflects a zealous belief at odds with the peaceful Christian empire of a century later.

G. W. Bowersock's approach to two antitypical views of martyrdom, represented effectively by Tertullian and Clement of Alexandria at the turn of the third century, provides one model to fill in this scanty period in the Eusebian record. In a chapter articulating the relationship between martyrdom and suicide, Bowersock addresses the "enthusiasm for death" commonly attributed to the martyrs.[30] Following the traditional narrative, he represents "suicidal" martyrdom, that of Tertullian, as external to normative "Christian" concepts of martyrdom. He traces the Latin apologist's conception of death instead to Roman culture, embodied in the deaths of Seneca, Cato, and others.[31] Clement of Alexandria's more moderate position, which accepted death for Christianity but never volunteered it—in the manner of Polycarp—is traced to Plato.[32] So, Bowersock sees the approaches of Tertullian and Clement as Roman and Greek/Christian, respectively. They are more often represented as heretical—in

Tertullian's case, Montanist—and orthodox. Yet the positions of these men might also productively be analyzed in terms of authority. Clement was the bishop of Alexandria and officially represented not only himself but also the burgeoning church. Tertullian, on the other hand, even before becoming more explicitly Montanist in tone, ever only represented a minority of Christians and had no significant official standing in the church. This fact is underrepresented in analyses of their perspectives.

The fourth book of Clement of Alexandria's *Stromateis* deals with martyrdom in some detail, representing one of the first Christian attempts to systematically control willing suicide for Christianity.[33] First, he reorients the death of the body as a necessary capstone to lifelong striving. Quoting the apostle Paul's claim in his letter to the Romans that the wages of sin are death (6:23), Clement argues that death is the association of the body with sin, and conversely, life is the project of separating the soul from the body. Commitment to this project prepares the "gnostic"—the one who strives for true knowledge of God—for death when it arrives (4.3).

Death as Clement describes it is a calling, an invitation one must receive before responding, but when received is answered readily (4.4). This is reminiscent of the Smyrnean contrast between Polycarp, the chosen one, and the failed, volitional martyrs in his tale. Clement invokes a long list of the accomplishments of the martyr. He proves his faithfulness to God, he thwarts the devil, he confirms the steadfastness that Christ inspires, he displays the truth of words by deeds, demonstrating God's power. He also shames the unbeliever through his shedding of blood (4.4). Clement then arrives at the key for his mediation: "We call martyrdom perfection, not because the man comes to the end of his life as others, but because he has exhibited the perfect work of love" (4.4).[34] It is not death itself that is significant but a proper preparation, an indifference to death. Thus, "each soul which has lived purely in the knowledge of God, which has obeyed the commandments, is a witness both by life and word, in whatever way it may be released from the body, shedding faith as blood along its whole life till its departure" (4.4). The gnostic, then, is a martyr regardless of the manner of death. This is contrasted to "simple martyrdom," consisting only of the violent death.

This seemingly subtle expansion of martyrdom prepares Clement to address a more extreme argument of the "heretics" that one who suffers death as a result of confession is a self-murderer. The true martyrdom, they argue, is knowing that which is of God, a sentiment with which Clement must necessarily and carefully agree. Overzealous martyrs demonstrate by their deaths that they do not belong to "us," despite perhaps sharing the Christian name. How do we know they are not "faithful martyrs?" Because they have not known the true god. What evidence do we have that they have not known the true god? They gave themselves up to an empty death. Clement gives the parallel example of the self-immolating Indian gymnosophist as a vacuous public display.

Bowersock argues that Clement is attempting to return martyrdom to its original sense of bearing witness.[35] Behind the bishop's apparent desire for accuracy, though, is an attempt to monopolize martyrdom for the Christian institution. The weight of Clement's argument resides in the parenthetical comment that those whom the heretics critique are not part of the church, which Clement himself confidently represents. While the heretic claims that the fault of the martyr lies in the death, Clement suggests that his crime, instead, is not being "ours." In other words, while for Clement's interlocutors, actions determine membership, for the bishop it is membership that certifies actions (which only then define membership).

The remainder of Clement's fourth book continues to develop a nuanced understanding of true martyrdom. Outward expression must necessarily accompany inward disposition, but the former is by no means a guarantee of the latter. A confession of Christ may be wrought out of fear, or the hope of reward, but for Clement the only worthy cause is love, knowledge itself (4.22). His argument on this point is not distinguishable from the Valentinians he criticizes, who appear to oppose martyrdom because a confession with the voice does not ensure that the martyr has previously confessed in deed. Threading the needle, Clement argues that the death that follows confession cuts away previous acquiescence to worldly desire (4.9). He clarifies: "Those who witness in their life by deed, and at the tribunal by word, whether entertaining hope or surmising fear, are better than those who confess salvation by their mouth alone. But if one ascend also to love, he is a really blessed and true martyr, having confessed perfectly both to the commandments and to God, by the Lord" (4.9). By casting the broadest possible net, Clement attempts to ensure that the sole source of legitimization of martyrdom is the quest for knowledge. He contends that the power of death is not to be cast out, as the Valentinians were suggesting, but controlled for beneficial Christian use.[36]

One thousand miles to the west, another man was actively writing defenses of Christianity. He did not speak as bishop, however, but as layman, and thus his expression provides a helpful contrast. T. D. Barnes concludes, "Tertullian was the first great teacher of unimpeachable doctrinal orthodoxy who dared to enunciate an unpalatable truth: the church is not a conclave of bishops, but the manifestation of the Holy Spirit."[37] The idea of the martyr was the clearest example of the church Tertullian envisioned.[38]

Tertullian's first significant work regarding martyrdom, *Address to the Martyrs*, was apparently addressed to Christians awaiting trial.[39] The fourth chapter forms the core of this work, in which he draws upon well-known historical examples in order to encourage (or shame) the martyrs into pressing toward the goal. The core of examples were ones that were used in a previous work, *To the Nations*, and would be used in a slightly different form in his later *Apology*. Martyrs ought to be steeled by the fact that many pagans have gone to painful deaths for a cause without complaint.[40] He lists Lucretia, Mucius Scaevola, and Peregrinus—well-known Roman figures—among ten individual examples, culminating in a challenge that if pagan men and women can undergo such a contest for glory, "those sufferings of yours which lead to the attainment of celestial glory and divine reward are unworthy of mention" (4.9). He concludes, "Who, then, is not bound to undergo most willingly as much for the real as others do for the false?" (4.9).

This short exhortation lacks the qualifications and contingencies present in the fourth book of the *Stromateis*. Clement's martyrdom appears as a transaction completed primarily between the divine and the martyr, with the persecutor as an incidental partner; *gnosis*, which constitutes true martyrdom, is on another plane. Tertullian's conception of martyrdom is already more visceral, his models corporeal. The otherworldly for Tertullian is the future reward. All of this naturally places a greater importance on the act of martyrdom, the death itself, as a prerequisite.

In contrast to *Address to the Martyrs*, the jurist's *Scorpiace* is rife with biblical examples and scriptural references to advocate martyrdom. This text is an extended apology for martyrdom against primarily the Valentinians, who believed the martyr's death not only unnecessary but contrary to the new covenant with the Christian, announced by Jesus (9.1). Tertullian's argument depends on establishing that God is ultimately the author of martyrdom, having created its possibility by prohibiting idolatry (4.1).[41] Presaging what would turn out to be a beautiful defense of continued persecution against Christians deemed heretical in the post-Constantinian era, Tertullian not only suggests compulsion rather than enticement of heretics but also adds the justification, necessary for his argument against Valentinians, that God abolishes death with death, torture with torture (5.9). In defense of his view, he recites a litany of violence against God's people, from the death of Abel to Daniel (8). Contrary to when he is later arguing against flight in persecution, Tertullian reads Jesus's revelation of bringing a sword rather than peace literally (10.17). To this he adds justification from 1 Peter, 1 John, and Revelation that persecution, suffering, and death are to be welcomed and not avoided (12).

Having outlined the apostles' willing acceptance of the unjust persecutions of rulers, Tertullian states hypothetically that if Christians were to go astray in their reading of the Scriptures, as Valentinians suggested, it would be from eagerness to live (15.1). However, he concludes, they do not go astray because the sufferings of the apostles as well as the mandate to follow them are clear. The desire to live remains an accusation that Tertullian can in turn throw against his opponents as well as against his more conservative and forbearing brethren in the aftermath of persecution. He exploits the ambiguity of life; true life entails physical death. It is ironic that despite representing a comparatively extreme position on martyrdom, Tertullian's view embodies, perhaps even more than Clement's, the transformation that the church was able to achieve with the post-Constantinian narrativization of martyrdom. Death is equated with life to comfort the living who fear death. The proliferation of Tertullian's work may be evidence of the success of such a contradiction.

His most well-known work, the *Apology*, treats the similar theme of a willingness and desire for death. The majority of the work is an attack on the fallacious logic of Roman religion and Rome's motivation for Christian persecution. Tertullian systematically turns the perceived accusations, such as that Christians worship an ass or the cross, against the accusers (16). The rhetoric is heavily weighted toward expressing that the very tactics Rome uses to mete out justice are not only mandated by God but achieve precisely the opposite effect, expanding rather than prohibiting Christianity. References to the deaths of Christians crescendo as the apology nears the end. He contends that martyrdom is not out of weakness. Christians, "who are so willing to be slaughtered," could easily be slaughterers if it were not prohibited, as they fill the empire (37.5). In the end, Tertullian provides a succinct presentation of the Christian martyrs' usurpation of Roman authority. He says to Rome,

> As if all the authority you have over us is not of our choice! Undoubtedly, I am a Christian if I wish to be. Consequently, then, you will condemn me if I wish to be condemned. In truth, if that power you have over me, you do not have unless I am willing, then you have power by my will, not your authority. (49.4–5)

This statement is more revealing of both the nexus of power in the martyr and its contentiousness than his more famous phrase. If the Christian martyr's blood is for the church, it reveals little of the willing suicide. It is a statement of the non-martyr. Here Tertullian comes closer to conveying the agency of the willing suicide. It rests on no institutional authority. His Christianity is voluntary. "I am a Christian" is undoubtedly affiliation with the group of believers, but will is the gateway through which affiliation passes. Its proof is the exhaustion of all potentiality in death; its reappropriation by and for the church is another mode of expression entirely.

This construction of the martyr in the forty-ninth chapter must be brought to bear on the climactic final chapter, where Tertullian's apologetic is at its peak. As in past works, he parades a litany of examples of pagan martyrs, but this time his reasoning is more explicit (50.5–9). These men and women, Tertullian claims, died for friendship or country, but it is not permissible to die for God, as do the Christians (50.10)? Then follows a frank assessment of monumentalization:

> And yet for all of these you cast statues, you paint likenesses, you inscribe titles to give them immortality. As far as you are able by monuments, you yourselves perform, in a lesser way, a resurrection of the dead. He who hopes for a true one from God, if he suffers for God, is insane! (50.11)

While Romans valorize heroic historical deaths, they dismiss Christian ones. Tertullian's contention for the value of these deaths lies in a hierarchization: those for man, these for God. Earthly monumentalization is but a substitution; the community attempts to perform the actions of the divine. The implication, then, is that Christians, who recognize the vanity of such idols, would not structure their remembrance in that way. These accusations are ironic when considered against imperial Christianity a century later. The suffering and forgotten martyrs of a forlorn sect would have their turn at remembrance; any distinction between their will and the will of the community would be obliterated until it was obvious only that Christian martyrs died so that the community might live. Their stories became substitutionary atonement for the anxiety of death and the violence of the hegemonic power of the institution over the living and the dead.

The apologist's imagined community, however, was one of action and not remembrance. The words of Cicero and Seneca were outshone by the actions of Christians (50.14). What was the *telos* of those actions? Not remembrance or faith, but death. He seemed aware this singular focus rendered him vulnerable to critique. As the chapter opens, he puts the hypothetical question in the mouths of his opponents: why complain if when suffering, you are getting what you want? Just as the soldier in war, the Christian complains during the trial but rejoices in the victory (50.2). He "procure[s] a complete pardon by the payment of his own blood. Indeed, all offenses are forgiven by this work" (50.15–16). Tertullian's

Christianity is community only in an ephemeral sense, for its confirmation of membership is a death sentence.

Given his vision of Christianity, it is unsurprising that Tertullian grew gradually more disenchanted with the lenient position of the church in the first decade of the third century and began to align himself more strongly with the Montanist movement. His exhortations to martyrdom used a strict, if sometimes tendentious, reason. *On Flight in Persecution* is the most representative of these, written around 212 CE. Tertullian here argues that God wills persecution either as a judgment or a contest (1.5). If persecution comes from God, then one should not run from it, since all that God wills is good (4.1). To the arguments for flight from the gospels, Tertullian counters that those expired in the Apostolic age (6). Rather, he cites the Montanists: "Do not ask then to die on bridal beds, or in miscarriages, or from gentle fevers; rather, seek to die a martyr that he may be glorified who suffered for you" (9.4). He considers his exhortation superfluous, however, since those who have the Spirit already know neither to flee nor buy their safety from persecution (14.3).[42]

Clement's appeal to discernment as the true martyrdom may be seen to resonate with the direction that the Spirit gives for Tertullian. For Clement, though, this redirection is to remove the ultimate burden of proof from the death. While he contends against the Valentinians that the martyr who had lived a less than virtuous life would be redeemed through a virtuous death, the only external evidence he provides for determining the true martyrdom is that of a virtuous life. The only correlation is that Clement himself, in the stead of the church, is determining the true martyr. In contrast, for Tertullian, in no position to legislate for the church (nor seemingly desirous to), salvation is finally proven by the death, not the Spirit. Martyrdom, as he declared in *Scorpiace*, was the one guarantee of salvation (6.11).[43]

In any case, the Montanism to which Tertullian subscribed toward the end of his days was no less an appropriation of the violence of the willing suicide than the proto-orthodox position, although it certainly enjoyed much less favor. Montanism lacked essential qualifications for group sustainability. The recognition that exhortation to death was not beneficial for institutional growth spawned a mitigation and qualification of martyrdom, and this attempted control rubbed rigorists such as Tertullian the wrong way. It provided them an "other," a proof for the argument that the world is corrupting and corruptible. If the Spirit were to be the ultimate governing authority in the life of the Christian, the hierarchical church was attempting to play God with their lax requirements for witnessing, and for reentry after apostasy. Tertullian's conviction and intransigence has cast him in a fated role as revealing of the grim realities of Christian growth. His writing is more revealing of struggle within the Christian community than it is of the community's fight against Rome. There is thus some irony in Tertullian's position as the preeminent representative of Latin Christianity in the third century.

From the above discourses we can see how controlling the death was an implicit part of making the martyr from the willing suicide well before the Constantinian era. What Tertullian and Clement lacked, however, was the ability to spread their ideas on a broad enough scale. For Tertullian, it was not even practically conceivable that Christians could be emperors.[44] It was plain to the apologist that the Christian and the emperor each had their role to fill. The machine of state had a capability beyond all others to spread uniform ideas of control throughout the empire, and when this mechanism was allowed use by the church, ecclesiastical influence was given a substantial boost. Bowersock claims that without Rome, "martyr" would have simply remained "witness."[45] It might be more accurate to suggest that because of Rome, or at least with its help, the violent death of the willing suicide became the martyr of the Christians.

Cyprian and the Martyrs: Martyrdom's Challenge to Institutional Authority

A further example of the need to control martyrdom is shown in the letters of Cyprian. Like Tertullian, the Carthaginian bishop is given little attention by Eusebius, but his letters written around the middle of the third century illustrate the development of control by the Christian institution in the area where Tertullian had written only a half-century earlier.[46] Cyprian's letters were written while he was in self-exile during the brief reign of the Emperor Decius in 250 CE. The fact of his exile should not be forgotten, and not only because it gives us a written record of events and difficulties that might otherwise have been dealt with in person. His authority and actions were called into question by his choice to flee Carthage, which he defends in a letter to Roman church authorities. He argues that he has but followed the instructions of the Lord given in the gospel of Matthew, which prescribe flight upon persecution (10:23), the same passage that Tertullian had argued was meant for the disciples alone. However, his anxiety over a tenuous position manifests in a more exposed structure of rhetoric and authority than we might otherwise have.

Cyprian's limited ability to control his flock in his absence during a trying time results in his even stronger desire to enforce a strict hierarchy against rash judgments and consequential decisions from fear of persecution. Following the letters chronologically, we can trace Cyprian's growing concerns over the disintegration of the church in Carthage.[47] In initial letters, he sends general instructions to his presbyters to continue caring for the flock and taking supplies to those in prison (5.1.2). His letter to the first confessors of the Decian persecution—those in prison for their refusal to sacrifice—congratulates them on their fate and prays for them to be made martyrs (6.1.2, 6.4). When some of the confessors begin to perish in prison from torture or starvation, and the first of the martyrs is crowned, Cyprian takes an exultant tone, declaring that from the tortured "there flowed blood such as to quench the blaze of persecution" (10.2.2), and he prays that the rest are martyred as well (10.4.4).

It is, unsurprisingly, upon the deaths of some of the confessors that competition for authority begins. Many more have lapsed than have remained steadfast, either purchasing a certificate of sacrifice in concession to Rome or even themselves sacrificing under pressure. Some of these entreat the would-be martyrs for recommendations to allow their readmission to the church (15.3.1). All parties, the confessors, the lapsed Christians, and even the Carthaginian clergy are cooperating to allow this readmission to take place, an action that circumvents the authority of Cyprian as bishop. In writing to the remaining confessors, Cyprian places the blame on those lapsed and the clergy but gently chides the confessors not to write open certificates, which would allow entire households and extended families who had lapsed to be returned to the church (15.4). Cyprian wishes for the matter of the lapsed to be dealt with when the persecution has ended—when he is able to return to Carthage. Understandably, however, there were those who were anxious to receive readmittance to the church. To those, Cyprian dryly suggests that they redeem themselves through entering the contest for martyrdom again (19.2.3).

As the martyrs of Lyons and Vienne, the confessors of Carthage become more magnanimous as they feel they are coming closer to death. One Lucianus writes to a companion Celerinus in Rome, giving some indication of the suffering undergone by those in prison.[48] As Lucianus writes, he and the other confessors were crammed into two small cells and given no food and water in order to secure their cooperation with the imperial edict (22.2.1). On his writing, they had been subjected for eight days to another period of forced starvation (22.2.2). In the midst of this trial, Lucianus claims, he and the other confessors decided to issue a universal absolution: "Everyone of us whom the Lord has deigned to call away in this time of great tribulation, we have all together issued a joint letter granting peace to everyone together" (22.2.1). This peace was not immediate; rather, it was to allow readmission to the church after the time of persecution when confession had been made to the bishop (22.2.2). Nonetheless, Lucianus's letter represents an affront to the authority of the church and Cyprian himself.

This challenge is made more pointed in the following letter in Cyprian's collection. It is short and rich enough to be quoted in full:

> All the confessors send greeting to pope Cyprian. This is to inform you that all of us have together granted peace to those whose conduct since their fault you shall find, upon examination, to be satisfactory. It is our wish that you should make this resolution known to other bishops also, and it is our desire that you should be at peace with the holy martyrs. Written by Lucianus, in the presence of an exorcist and a lector from the clergy. (23)

In response to Cyprian's request for moderation, the martyrs confirm in no uncertain terms their intention for universal peace for lapsed Christians. As Clarke observes, they "adopt an even more supra-hierarchical stance."[49] This moment, still in the midst of the uncertainties of the Decian persecutions, allows unique examination of the potential power of the martyr's death. The extended period in prison has convinced the martyrs that their deaths are imminent, and this fact is critical to their resolution.[50]

In his previous letter to Celerinus, Lucianus prefaces the granting of peace to the lapsed upon the general peace of the church. This goes unmentioned in his terse letter to Cyprian, but had it been restated, it seems unlikely to have assuaged the bishop's indignation. At issue is the potential destabilization of authority against which the bishop has little recourse. In his next letter to the Carthaginian clergy, Cyprian mentions the letter and, without condemning it, calls the clergy to maintain the course of action he had previously recommended, which was to forestall all readmittance "until peace has been restored to use by the Lord and we are thus able to gather together and investigate each case separately" (26.1.2). While in his previous letters, he has admonished his presbyters for their lack of care, he now flatters them. In implied contrast to the sweeping gesture of the soon-to-be martyrs, he continues, "I would not dare to prejudge such an issue nor to take on myself alone a decision which is everyone's concern" (26.1.2). The bishop's rhetoric, certainly superior to that of the confessors or his fellow clergy, is at its finest here. Without negating the importance of the confessors' letter, he reiterates the necessity of having each case judged separately. The confessors seemed to envision the confession to the bishop as a formality, only based upon conduct after having lapsed. Cyprian agrees so far that the lapsed should confess but implies that the full details, including possibly the circumstances of having lapsed, should be considered by the clergy before readmittance. By delaying implementation, Cyprian is attempting both to mitigate desperate concern for obtaining certificates and delay important decisions until his return.

It is in a letter to Rome that Cyprian vents his fury over the actions of Lucianus and his companions. He credits the confessor with strong faith and courage but little grounding in the Scriptures. In his general exoneration of the lapsed, Cyprian vociferates that Lucianus "undermined well nigh every bond of faith, and fear of God, and command of the Lord, and the sanctity and stability of the gospel teachings" (27.2.1). The bishop's underlying fear, which he expresses more clearly to Roman clergymen than his own, is that if they actually weigh the evidence in the cases of individual lapsed Christians, they will be denying the absolution of the martyrs and will lose face. "This procedure fans even greater animosity against us" (27.2.2). He blames the flippant attitude of the would-be martyrs for widespread panic and rebellion against Carthaginian clergy who have no other choice but to readmit the lapsed into the church. The purpose of the letter, it seems, is to reiterate the separation of the confessors' actions from Cyprian's (and the clergy's) own.[51]

The case of Lucianus is a somewhat unique one. Cyprian contrasts him with other martyrs, Mappalicus and Saturninus, the former who issued certificates only to his mother and sister and the latter who issued none at all (27.1.1). Both of these men, of course, are dead, and that should not be underestimated. They obviously can produce no further certificates, so their authority is no longer a threat. It is impossible to discern whether their thoughts on certificates were substantively different from the living confessors or they were just the first to perish, having had less time to issue certificates. Lucianus, while as indicated in his letter to Celerinus resigned to death in prison, had not yet perished. However, he was not only speaking for himself but also for the entire group of confessors in prison. In addition, he claimed to have been originally inspired by a fellow martyr Paulus, who died in prison. Before Paulus was "called away," as Lucianus explains, he requested the confessor to grant peace in his name to any who should ask (22.2.1). Lucianus, then, as a confessor and soon-to-be martyr, claimed to have been granted power in the name of the martyr to confer peace to all who asked. In a magnanimous gesture, the remaining confessors proclaim universal forgiveness in one fell swoop.

The unruliness ensuing from the confessors' blanket certificate of reconciliation is evident in a group of lapsed Christians who wrote directly to

Cyprian demanding, as he interpreted it, their immediate reconciliation based on the peace granted by Lucianus in the name of Paulus. In response to anonymous letters, Cyprian contrasts two groups of lapsed: the first that audaciously styles themselves the church and demands reconciliation and the second that patiently awaits the end of persecution and Cyprian's approval to be reconciled to the church. Both groups apparently have in their possession certificates of absolution; the distinction, of course, is that the latter group recognizes the authority of the bishop while the former does not. Cyprian responds to the belligerent group that "they should not compose letters 'in the name of the church', for they are well aware that it is rather they who are writing *to* the church," that is, Cyprian himself (33.1.2).

The clergy in Rome respond to a letter from Cyprian by nuancing the position of the martyr in the time of persecution. Martyrs become martyrs in the name of, and for the sake of, the gospel. Consequently, it is not possible that they set themselves up as a rival to the gospel (in allowing for reconciliation outside of the proper hierarchical channels of the church), because in doing so they would be forfeiting their status as martyrs (36.2.1). With this logic, they shift the blame from the martyrs to the lapsed. They argue that the confessors acted correctly in attempting to refer requests for peace to the bishop and, in doing so, provide a precise formulation for bringing them under the church's control:

> It would appear that martyrs become martyrs with this precise purpose in view, that by refusing to sacrifice they may preserve their peace with the church even at the expense of shedding their own blood; what they are anxious to avoid is that they may be overcome by the pain of torture and thus may lose their salvation in losing their peace. Now if this is the case, how is it that they reckon that this salvation, which they thought they would not themselves possess if they had offered sacrifice, should be granted to those who are said to have offered sacrifice, whereas, in fact, they ought to uphold the same law in the case of others which in their own case they clearly imposed upon themselves previously? (36.2.2)

Having been convinced by their own logic, the clergy conclude that the martyrs could not have contradicted themselves; the lapsed have misinterpreted their commands and demanded immediate reconciliation. It is true that according to Lucianus's letter to Cyprian, the lapsed were to be subject to an interview from the bishop, albeit simply a formality. It is apparent, then, that groups of the lapsed were too impatient to await what seemed a foregone conclusion. What is more important here, however, is how the presbyters and deacons of Rome subtly reassert the control of the church over the martyrs. Notably, the clergy do not mention the imitation of Christ as part of the martyrs' motivation; the refusal to sacrifice is present, but it is to "preserve their peace with the church." The martyrs go to death in order to uphold the reputation of the church. The church was willing to acknowledge that martyrdom was an intimate relationship with God; indeed, it either ensured salvation or, upon failure, guaranteed its loss. Implicit in the church's acceptance of the importance of martyrdom was an exclusive right to dictate the terms of such a martyrdom. The transaction between confessors and the lapsed was a breakdown of that system.

In presuming that martyrs become so for the church and only through refusal to sacrifice, the Roman clergy point out the illogic of freeing others from the consequences of having failed such a test. This understanding of the martyrs should be set in contrast to that of Lucianus, who in light of his sufferings, with his fellow confessors, issued a blanket certificate of peace, implying that it was not desirous for others to undergo the same suffering they had experienced. In the first scenario, the power of the martyr's death is transferred to the church for redistribution under its control; in the second scenario, it is transferred to the lapsed themselves. The power and the politics of martyrdom are on clear display here. The clergy, the lapsed, and of course the martyrs themselves are all aware of the power of the willing suicide and are claiming it for themselves.

Cyprian denounces the blanket certificate of peace to the lapsed Christians for several stated reasons: it causes panic, it stirs up animosity against the clergy, and it is contrary to the gospel. These can be summed up by the problem that the would-be martyrs compete with the authority of the church. The ensuing panic (27.3.1) is a rhetorical distraction; Cyprian comments upon the disorientation caused by the Decian edict even before the first certificates were issued. G. W. Clarke's commentary takes Cyprian's remarks at face value, observing that Cyprian's primary goal was to maintain unity and implying that had such a response not occurred, the bishop would not have been so frustrated.[52] However, just as with the total number of martyrs in the pre-Constantinian era, one must be careful to interpret Cyprian's letters, written in a time of uncertainty, conservatively. If the relatively nearby bishop Caldonius could write a letter to Cyprian oblivious to the happenings in Carthage, one might reasonably assume that the throngs of people clamoring to the presbyters numbered in the tens rather than the hundreds. Cyprian writes that martyrs do not make but are made by the gospel (27.3.3). However, it was precisely the self-sufficiency that the potentiality of death provides that caused such a recognizable threat to Cyprian. The martyrs were destabilizing the church. Cyprian himself would supply the model of a controlled martyr, one in accordance with and for the church, only a few brief years later.

In retrospect, the bishop's own martyrdom under the emperor Valerian in 258 justified his flight under Decius years earlier.[53] Though he had only become a Christian a short time before, his death simplifies his history, rendering his life monocausal. There is a consistency to be seen in the manner of Cyprian's death and his discourse with the confessors of the Decian persecution: martyrdom was an action that needed to be circumscribed. In contrast to other martyrdoms such as that of Perpetua or Pionius, and certainly later martyrdoms, Cyprian's death is controlled throughout the entire process, seemingly with the complicity of both bishop and proconsul. According to the story of his martyrdom, Cyprian first willingly goes into exile in 257 CE before being recalled under the subsequent proconsul the following year (1.3, 2.1).[54] If not a spectacle, Cyprian's trial drew a crowd from the Christian populace, his entire congregation having slept in the street to await his sentencing (2.5). Upon the verdict, they beg to be martyred with him (5.1). Failing that, they spread cloth around him to catch his blood (5.4).[55] The death itself required a mere sentence (5.6). The account exhibits evidence of control throughout.

There is thus a tension displayed between the reserved certainty of Cyprian and the officials and the fervency of the crowd. From the ecclesiastical perspective, the bishop successfully walked a fine line that allowed him to fulfill insofar as possible both Roman law and that of the church. He was willing to accept the consequences of legislation against his person as long as it did not change his chosen identity. Notably, it is not only that of a Christian but also that of a bishop (1.2). It is his role as bishop, as well as his societal standing, that influenced his decision to go willingly into exile, as the law specified. He did not demand immediate fulfillment of the death, as the crowd would later do at his sentencing. Nor, however, would he divulge the names of his presbyters, citing both Roman law and Christian discipline in his defense (1.5).[56] When the laws were intensified the following year, Cyprian complied with his recall from the countryside by the new proconsul. On the sentencing, the proconsul states: "Discipline will be confirmed by your blood" (4.2). Cyprian and his community wholeheartedly agreed. Blood affirmed both Rome and the church. Though it is manifest subtly in Cyprian's story, control of the death is more carefully managed, and as the events unfolded rather than in their wake.

The type of Cyprian's martyrdom served as an alternative to that of Pionius or, in the case of North Africa, Perpetua and Felicitas. The account of one Bishop Fructosus closely followed the manner of Cyprian. Though sentenced to immolation, the bishop and his companions, deacons Augurius and Eulogius, accepted their fates without fanfare.[57] Two other North African martyrdoms said to have occurred during the Valerian persecution, the *acta* of Marian and James and that of Montanus and Lucius, displayed the elaborate and visceral tendencies of "spectacle" martyrdoms.[58] Neither of these latter pairs occupied significant positions in the church. The comparison reveals a correlation between levels of spectacle and levels of class. It also clearly shows the evolution of control over death that would soon be imperially legislated.

David Potter's examination of "Martyrdom as Spectacle" evaluates the distinguishable perspectives in the act of martyrdom. Potter values the martyr acts as unique because they provide a view of Roman justice from the perspective of the victim.[59] Working from a Foucauldian paradigm, he presents the process as a power struggle between competing authorities, using the third-century accounts of Perpetua and Pionius as evidence. Martyrdom obviously became a problem for a church interested in growth, Potter notes, and he exemplifies the efforts of Cyprian to moderate its usage.[60] He argues that because Cyprian was concerned about the "socially disruptive aspects of martyrdom," the bishop wanted to minimize its continued occurrence; this coincided with an increased reticence of imperial officials to publicly condemn Christians of high standing.

Regarding the public, torturous execution of the guilty for their crimes, Foucault himself notes, "The pains here below may also be counted as penitence and so alleviate the punishments of the beyond: God will not fail to take such a martyrdom into account, providing it is borne with resignation."[61] The "martyrdom" Foucault describes consists not of willing suicide but acquiescence to—and affirmation of—the power of the state. The power of the death is present, yet the institution appropriates its meaning. Tertullian writes of martyrdom differently. It was not passive acceptance of punishment in order to secure future reward; rather, the outright mockery of the torture inflicted was to secure the martyr's reward. Potter argues that "a person sentenced to die in the arena lost human identity, lost control of his or her body, became a slave."[62] For the willing suicide, it was precisely this scenario that became an alternative source of power.

The death of Cyprian and the martyr acts that were modeled after it display an accused who has ties both to a Christian identity and at least residual standing in a secular community. This manifested in a mutual reluctance by accused and accuser to foreground the ambiguities of justice inherent in the trial and a fear of jeopardizing the class identity shared by both. His comparatively sterile death by beheading contrasts to the virile affair of "voluntary" martyrdom, in which all attempts at negotiating on a common social milieu are refused by the accused.

Potter rightly sees this model in the foil of Pionius, who boldly refused pleas based on his standing and intelligence. The result, says Potter, was a disaster for all involved, except Pionius.[63] While this likely gives the source too much credit, it does model a significant difference between martyrdom when isolated from class privilege and the martyr mitigated by ecclesiastical authority. This latter, "true" martyrdom, became the church's model.

While giving sparse treatment to the Decian persecution in North Africa, Eusebius gives considerable space to the persecution in Alexandria, which serves as a helpful confirmation of the struggles of the Carthaginian bishop to the west. He yields the floor to Dionysius, who had become bishop of Alexandria in 247 CE and subsequently fled Alexandria during the Decian persecution. Eusebius records a letter of Dionysius to one Germanus in which Dionysius justifies his flight by citing, just as Eusebius did with Origen, a divine mandate. As he writes, Dionysius had waited for the arrival of troops to carry him away, but they apparently did not think to check his residence (6.40.1–3). When a short time later he was actually captured, his companions rescued him, against his will, from the guards who were transporting him to trial (6.40.6–9).

Following this tale Eusebius records a letter written from Dionysius to fellow bishop Fabius in Antioch describing in detail the nature of the persecutions in Alexandria, persecutions from which, presumably, Dionysius himself was absent. The bishop of Alexandria explains that actual persecution by Alexandrians themselves preceded the Decian imperial edict by about one year. He describes four martyrs who were horribly tortured and killed but suggests that virtually no Christians apostatized (6.41.6). When the edict arrived, though, apostatizing Christians came forward in great numbers, some reluctantly and others readily. Dionysius has little sympathy for these, calling the reluctant cowards and damning the willing apostates (6.41.11–12). These serve as a contrast to around twenty Christians whom the bishops named who stood firm in refusing to sacrifice (6.41.14–23). The majority of these were subsequently martyred, but some were tortured and subsequently released. Dionysius makes no distinction, calling the latter group martyrs as well. Herein may lie the reason for Dionysius's letter to Antioch. The "divine martyrs," those who had survived the Decian persecution, were issuing pardons to certain repentant Christians who had previously sacrificed. Unlike the letters of Cyprian, the bishop of Alexandria reveals uncertainty. "What do you counsel us, brothers, concerning these things? What should we do?" (6.42.5). If they agreed with the confessors, their authority was undermined, but if they countermanded the martyrs' judgment, they risked the ire of the martyrs, the lapsed, and the congregation (6.42.6).

If there was a response, Eusebius does not record it, perhaps because to him there could be little doubt as to the route Dionysius chose. The historian instead immediately frames the Dionysian question as a response to the rigid sect of the Novatians, who had set themselves up as the elect and refused the readmission of apostates. For Dionysius, however, the question had not been decided. He had been placed in a similar position to Cyprian. He was not present during much of the enactment of Decius's edict; consequently, he had no immediate access to the events as they unfolded. It was likely complicated in the aftermath to reassert control over the Alexandrians. Cyprian had done all he could to prevent readmission of lapsed Christians during his absence so that he did not have to counter a practice already in place. Dionysius was faced with the same difficulty. Though from a similar background, Dionysius seems to have been less assertive than his Carthaginian counterpart; an authoritarian approach was ultimately untenable. Agreeing with the martyrs was strategic; it provided a base, albeit temporarily subservient, from which to regain control of the church. The rigorist Novatians would provide a foil against which the church could ally with, and consequently control, the legitimization of martyrdom. Set over against the intransigent separatism of the Novatians, just as the Montanists, the church of Cyprian and Dionysius could begin to define itself, following the pattern set by the martyrs, in order to return to a paramount position of authority. Martyrs co-opted by the church became the church's martyrs.

Conclusion: Christian Martyrdom and Christian Persecution

The seventh book of his history is the last in which Eusebius relies primarily on the accounts of others. Still following Dionysius, Eusebius relates briefly the events from the latter half of the third century up to the "Great Persecution." The Dionysian account of persecution under the emperor Valerian details suffering and exile but mentions no martyrdoms specifically.[64] Eusebius himself traces the outline of two further incidents of martyrdom, both from his home region of Palestine, of which his is the only account. A first group of martyrs from Caesarea during Valerian's persecution he describes in general terms. Three men who first shirked martyrdom "in a cowardly manner" later decided to present themselves to the judge for punishment. The explanation for their actions is ambiguous, which may explain Eusebius's brief treatment. Though they "treated it lightly" when others presumably took the opportunity for martyrdom, the three reportedly acted so as not to "seize the crown of martyrdom prematurely" (7.12). Their deaths allowed for a reconfiguration of their account from cowardice to timeliness.

The other martyrdom Eusebius relates provides a more appropriate model on several levels. The martyr Marinus was both a member of the upper class and a high-ranking soldier in line for promotion. Upon his Christian identity being revealed, he was brought before the judge, whereupon the local bishop took him aside and encouraged him to "hold fast to God" (7.15). Marinus returns to the judge with his confession and "finished his course by death." The social background of Marinus, his calm demeanor and presentation before the judge, as well as his clear acting under the authority of the local bishop all recommend this martyrdom as a model to be recounted. Marinus's military status in particular provides an effective counterpoint to the Constantinian era, Eusebius's climax, in which Christianity and military service were no longer at odds.

Once we arrive at events contemporary to Eusebius, the narrative of martyrdom and triumph becomes even more dominant. It could not fail to be so when the success of Christianity had been contingent on military victory. The bishop is forthcoming as to the content of his narrative. He plans to include neither the accounts of clergy who "failed" during the Great persecution nor the infighting within the church. Whether it be because of his own questionable orthodoxy or an elevated sense of propriety, his interest does not align with modern historical ideals:

> We determined not even to mention those who have been tried by the persecution, or have made shipwreck of their salvation, and of their own free will were plunged into the depths of the billows; but we shall add to the general history only such things as may be profitable, first to ourselves, and then to those that come after us. (8.2.3)

True to his word, he mentions no persons by name who apostatized but details for the following ten chapters the gruesome sufferings of the martyrs in the regions in the East, paying special attention to those of social standing.[65] History was not on the side of the unfortunate apostates, who were too recent for comfort, reminding the church of the boundaries of its authority and the individual Christian of the finality of death. Though it could not be denied, the momentum of apostasy was contradictory and counterproductive to the use of martyrdom in Christian triumph. It was not just a matter of managing the death through classifications of "active" and "passive" martyrdoms, although this would remain important. Several of the martyrdoms Eusebius details were by all accounts unabashedly aggressive. The well-known incident that opened the Great Persecution, for example, involved one bold Christian who tore up the imperial decree in Nicomedia while the emperors Diocletian and Galerius were in residence (8.5.1). In Egypt, the bishop claimed to have seen Christians thrust themselves into the imperial judge's presence and declare their affiliation (8.9.5). The uniting factor became, in a time of persecution, success rather than the means by which it was achieved. With this focus, the uncertainty of death could be mitigated. The martyrs who succeeded did so, as far as Eusebius was concerned, for the unity of the church.

Though he mentions many martyrs, in comparison to his earlier books he dwells on few, because the bishop's focus has begun to shift to Christian triumph.[66] The bishop attributes the first abatement of persecution under Galerius not to the steadfastness of martyrs but the grotesque and debilitating disease inflicted upon the emperor by a divine hand (8.16). He details a similar fate for competing emperor Maximin, who garners the attention of his ninth book. Contrary to the suggestion of some scholars, Eusebius was not averse to violence, if for the sake of Christianity, as evidenced in his tacit approval of the wholesale slaughter of Maximin's entourage after his death, complete with a great many tortures (9.11.6).[67] These are precursors to the jubilant panegyric with which the bishop opens the final book of his history. In it, the martyrs of the previous nine books are pressed into the service of an earthly Christianity. He writes,

> Such things as of a truth many righteous men and martyrs of God before us desired to see upon the earth and saw them not, and to hear, and heard them not. But they indeed, hasting with all speed, obtained far better things in the heavens themselves and were caught up into a paradise of divine pleasure; while we, acknowledging that even these present things are beyond our deserts, have been utterly astounded at the munificence of the bounty of which He is the Author. (10.1.4–5)

In this triumphant paradigm, the martyrs who volunteered for death wished to see Christian freedom on earth; for such a desire, they went to their deaths. Beyond the control of any earthly party, God chose to end the persecution in the bishop's day. The rhetorical hierarchy of heavenly over earthly life is given lip service in the same sentence that revels in the generous peace of the present. The martyrs can thus be honored in such a way that domesticates their radical action and controls its future possibility. For the church, of what need is death once the institution is legitimized? The powerful subtlety of this shift should not be underestimated. Circumscribing the location and time of the achievements of the martyrs not only homogenizes their identities and aims, sublimating them to the aims of the Eusebian church triumphant, but also drastically limits their import. The church here takes full ownership of martyrdom, redirecting its anti-institutional violence for the perpetuation of another institution.

In an unpublished paper at the turn of the century, G. E. M. de Ste. Croix points to one possible reason why the death of the martyr was subsumed into Christianity—because it serves as a distinction between the "pagan" Roman Empire's violence against Christians and the "Christian" Roman Empire's violence against pagans and heretical Christians. The former was unjustifiable, the latter justified. Although Ste. Croix is at pains to reduce the believed number of actual martyrs, he is quick to note that the psychological effect upon the Christian community was significant. This helps to explain why, in his words, "the Christian Church—or rather churches—became during the fourth and following centuries, and remained for more than a millennium and a half, the greatest organized persecuting force in human history."[68] This question no doubt is one of the most popular dilemmas in Roman and early Christian scholarship; surprisingly, one rarely sees the question posed in full, for the first half is typically left assumed. The full question might be, "Why, given the fact that Christians were vehemently and brutally persecuted in the first three centuries of their existence, did they do the same thing in the centuries following?"[69] Implied is the idea that one who suffers would be reticent to impose that suffering on another, a plausible but historically counterfactual conclusion. Interestingly, Ste. Croix has been criticized for simplistic thinking on this problem; although his position can be improved, his description articulates greater nuance than many of his critics. His argument is that Christianity persecuted because of a collective trauma and because, with their alliance with the state, the church was intent on enforcing unity.[70] He readily suggests that Christianity ideally should not have accepted the state's power of coercion.[71]

In an appendix to the article, editor Joseph Streeter apologizes for Ste. Croix's argument. He contends that the dichotomy of an intolerant Christianity against a tolerant Rome is problematic, and that toleration is an inappropriate term to describe the situation in Late Antiquity. Ste. Croix is identified in the genealogy of the Enlightenment arguments of Gibbon and Hume. Streeter contends that toleration, defined as the positive valuation of diversity for its own sake, is a product of the Enlightenment.[72] While accurate, one should note how this steers the conversation away from the question that prompted the debate. Streeter contends that toleration was essentially an argument made by a minority group that could not maintain their existence by any other means; in other words, no group in power, no emperor, would maintain a position of tolerance when firmly in control.[73] Ste. Croix, however, is not mandating an ideal of toleration but claiming that Christianity—admittedly like many other institutions—failed to live up to its own ideals.

Ste. Croix provides a valuable perspective on the early Christian martyr because he recognizes the inherent power of the death and the original distinction of the individual martyr from the church with which he would posthumously be identified. In this, he highlights the distinction between the ambivalent ecclesiastical use of the "voluntary" martyr and the seeming inability to deny the common people the martyrs they had already venerated.[74] Most importantly, he argues that, as mentioned, the construction of martyrdom allowed Christianity to appropriate even these martyrs as well as mark a border between the "Christian" martyr and the deaths of heretics or pagans in post-Constantinian persecutions.

It should be clear that we have limited empirical or rational means to measure the extent to which the Christian ideology contributed to its historical growth. The triumph of Christianity was an ideological construction impressed upon the ancient past. That construction was supported by the martyr, taking a figure representative of autonomy, resistance, and division, and recasting it as the paragon of a collective, unified institution. This appropriation redirects the force of willing suicide for ideological perpetuation, and it has been successful. For martyrdom to become what it needed to be for the church, a malleable element of propaganda and community growth, the willing suicide had to be transformed à la Tertullian's bold claim that the blood of Christians is seed for the church.

Thus, martyrdom was absolutely crucial to Christian development but not in the way it is usually described. The *telos* of the willing suicide is death. The triumph of Christianity in the Eusebian narrative effectively eliminated the political forum in which Christian martyrdom operated, making it a homogenous subcategory within Christianity. What this means is that scholars and practitioners alike have accepted that Christian martyrdom somehow belonged to the state-sponsored Christianity that would emerge in the post-Constantinian era, that martyrdom was "for" Christianity. It is necessary instead to recognize the anti-institutional directionality of the willing suicide, actual death that cannot be quantified or aggregated, as opposed to venerated martyrdom, which can and has been placed in institutional service. It is originally impossible for physical death to be *for* physical life in its action, whether on an individual or institutional scale. That is why the success of Christian appropriation of martyrdom is so paradoxical. As long as the paradox that death brings life is propagated, the institution maintains sovereignty and we fundamentally misunderstand the martyr.

5

"Voluntary" Martyrdom: Avoiding the Stigma of Suicide

On the morning of June 23, 2014, Charles Moore, a 79-year-old retired United Methodist minister, drove to the parking lot of a strip mall in the small town of Grand Saline, Texas. He paced the parking lot for several hours before he knelt on a small cushion, doused himself with gasoline, and set himself on fire. Though the fire was put out by people who rushed to his aid, he succumbed to his injuries at a hospital later that day. In a note left on the windshield of his car, Moore claimed he was dying in solidarity with African Americans who had been lynched in Grand Saline and in the hopes that "others ... may be moved to change the situation here."[1] On Moore's desk at home was found a copy of a 2013 article from the *New Yorker* detailing the scores of Tibetan self-immolations in recent years as well as previously penned "suicide notes" expressing concerns, among other things, over the acceptance of the LGBT community in the United Methodist Church and Southern Methodist University's bid to house a library for George W. Bush.

Though Moore invoked no explicit religious justifications for his actions, many processed his death according to his—and their—lifelong Christianity. As with John Chau, this interpretation process did not yield uniform results. Though one blogger and minister claimed Moore as a "passionate follower of Jesus" whose actions made him a martyr, most reserved judgment.[2] However, one cleric on a United Methodist forum explicitly denied Moore the status of martyr because "martyrdom is never something that, according to Scripture and our earliest witnesses, is ever [sic] supposed to be sought out."[3] The divided opinion over Moore's status is indicative of the explanatory work that martyrdom does in the Christian tradition as well as the Western cultural imagination.

Scholarly understandings of martyrdom—whether Christian or not—have often been interpreted through the overarching narrative of Christian tradition discussed in the last chapter. This brings me to my two-part argument here.

First, I contend that unverifiable criteria remain operative in determining the legitimacy of martyrdom in popular discussion. As one Christian author writes, martyrdom is "an experience that God in His providence bestows on select individuals for purposes ultimately known only to Him."[4] This perspective prevails in some scholarly discourse as well. I will illustrate this through a brief examination of a debate over the validity of "voluntary" martyrdom. A dichotomy is assumed between voluntary and "true" martyrdom, and it is a false dichotomy both because such a rigid divide is impractical and disingenuous and because it is based on arbitrary criteria that provide a facade for the ongoing institutional control of violence.

Where something like divine compulsion is operative in "true" martyrdoms, suicide provides a means of dismissing "voluntary" martyrdom. As we have discussed in previous chapters, suicide is a primary transgression against sovereign authority; from Christian late antiquity it is a mortal sin. It requires logical gymnastics to distinguish suicide from martyrdom, but this process has been, historically, mostly successful. However, if there are not any easily verifiable distinctions between martyrdom and suicide, in theory or in practice, we should question what function this distinction serves. I argue that from a social perspective, suicide is the name for such violence as no institution is able to—or desires to—repurpose for its own perpetuation. Recognizing the institutional significance, as well as the moral significance, of this distinction allows us to examine the institutional machinery at work behind categories of martyrdom and "mere" suicide.

One significant challenge to the cohesive narrative of early Christian martyrdom has been provided by the "voluntary martyr." We have seen that this debate animated discussion about early Christian martyrdom from second-century Clement of Alexandria forward. The term was reintroduced to the modern scholarly discussion by G. E. M. de Ste. Croix, whose contrarian approach was briefly noted at the conclusion of the previous chapter. Ste. Croix's aim was to disambiguate the four separate edicts against Christianity promulgated by the Roman emperor Diocletian in rapid succession in 303–304 CE and the conflation of these in the hagiographical literature and subsequent history. His introduction of "voluntary martyrs" provides a contrast to "voluntary apostates," upper-class Christians who willingly denied their faith, likely to avoid loss of personal wealth and status. (These may have included some of the lapsed of Cyprian's concern.) Voluntary martyrs, rather than publicly abandoning Christianity, "deliberately and unnecessarily went out of their way to seek martyrdom."[5] As Ste. Croix explains, this was not as easy to do as history has made it seem. In general, officials seem to have been reluctant to carry out the harshest penalties for refusal to sacrifice. In the Western portion of the Roman Empire, the last of the Emperor Diocletian's four edicts, which required all citizens to sacrifice, was unlikely to have been enforced at all. Volunteer martyrs were an important addition for Ste. Croix because, if volunteers, such martyrdoms should not be used as evidence of the enforcement of a general persecution against Christians.

Ste. Croix uses Eusebius's fourth-century *Martyrs of Palestine* as a case study to examine the proportion of volunteer martyrs in more detail. He concludes that only sixteen out of forty-eight—forty-four others having been set aside for lack of information as to the circumstances of their mass execution—were not likely volunteers. Two-thirds of the Palestinian martyrs for whom we have sufficient information to judge "attracted the attention of the authorities."[6] The author makes no differentiation of quality between types of martyrs other than the above-noted distinction that upper-class Christians were more likely to voluntarily apostatize because they were more likely to be known by public officials and had more to lose. His point is not to judge the martyrs themselves but the general portrayal of the "Great Persecution." He concludes that "the ordinary Christian … was most unlikely to become a victim of the persecution at all" and thus that the Great Persecution has been greatly exaggerated.[7]

In a subsequent article almost a decade later, Ste. Croix contends that when Christians were persecuted from the second century onward, they were persecuted for being Christian, a membership that was understood as antisocial and atheist.[8] Here he argues that Christians had a history of "going far beyond what their churches officially required of them, often indeed offering themselves up to the authorities of their own accord, and occasionally acting in a provocative manner, smashing images and so forth."[9] He concludes that voluntary martyrdom, far from being a result of persecution already in place, "contributed to the outbreak of persecution and tended to intensify it when already in being."[10] Voluntary martyrs can be seen as Christians who reinforced the idea of Christians as intransigent and unassimilable to Roman authorities.

So what can we draw from Ste. Croix's conclusions? To the extent that voluntary martyrdom took place, it challenges the narrative of diabolical Roman persecution and the assumption that persecution was evenly and consistently applied, because we cannot assume that the presence of a Christian martyr requires a zealous persecutor as well. The point for my argument is not who was and wasn't a volunteer—all willing suicides are voluntary by definition. It is the fact that Ste. Croix's conclusions, which have more ultimately to do with the persecutor than the martyr, are taken as undermining Christian martyrdom. As a result, they have been the locus of subsequent scholarly challenge.

Defending "Voluntary" Martyrs by Making Them Involuntary

P. Lorraine Buck is one of the recent scholars to challenge the applicability of Ste. Croix's voluntary martyrdom.[11] Importantly, Buck does not disagree with voluntary martyrdom as a concept. In fact, she takes the idea even more seriously than Ste. Croix. Rather, Buck contends the scope of voluntary martyrdom. She protests that Ste. Croix discounts forty-four of the ninety-one martyrs of Palestine right off the bat, and she attempts to reclaim these Christians as "true martyrs." Buck presumes that the martyrs were apprehended for being Christian and sent to the mine as punishment. She surmises that because they were not immediately martyred rather than having been sent to the mines, they cannot have been volunteers.[12]

Buck also takes issue with Ste. Croix's subcategory of "quasi-volunteer" martyrs, which he delineated in an article published posthumously decades after being written.[13] Buck accurately suggests that Ste. Croix considers quasi-volunteers a subset of voluntary martyrs, different in that they indirectly rather than directly effect their recognition by the authorities. Buck protests that "a willingness to die, however, which clearly all the martyrs displayed, was not necessarily an intentional bid for martyrdom, even when an action put the individual perilously close to arrest."[14] This assertion illustrates the flawed reasoning of a "common scholarly ideological disposition" and requires further exploration.[15]

In order to validate the claim that willingness to die is not *necessarily* an intention to die, we need to ask in what cases *would* willingness to die be an intentional bid for martyrdom? It appears that the use of "necessarily" is rhetorical here, since the only time a willingness to die can manifest, and consequently be demonstrated to exist, is through "an intentional bid for martyrdom." More important is the question of what "intention" denotes for Buck. Her attempt to make a distinction here implies that an intentional bid for martyrdom is exclusive to the voluntary martyr. This suggests that she equates intentional martyrdom with martyrdom for its own sake, being "consciously or unconsciously in love with death."[16] The implication is that these cases are not martyrdoms but forms of suicide, following a Christian distinction from Augustine forward.[17] This distinction is not based on any clearly defined criteria but relies on a morally weighted interpretation of actions, or their absence.

In using "an intentional bid for martyrdom" as the primary point of differentiation between more and less legitimate martyrdoms, Buck overlooks the easily measurable factor that these martyrdoms share that clearly displays intention to die: refusal to deny Christianity when denial meant acquittal, and thus continued life. For Buck—as well as for Ste. Croix, although for a different reason—the circumstances of recognition by authorities are a more potent indicator of intention to die than refusal to deny Christianity on pain of death. Ste. Croix clearly also believed that quasi-volunteers were not exactly the same as volunteers—thus the distinct categorization—but concluded that quasi-volunteers are on a spectrum that places them closer to volunteer martyrs than those Christians who perhaps stayed silent in the crowd or wisely remained home. Volunteers of all degrees drew attention to themselves, surely aware of the risk of death, when most others did not.

A comparable case might be the modern concept of collateral damage. The United States can and does claim that certain civilian deaths are unintended consequences of specific intended targets. Following the implicit moral logic, collateral damage lessens culpability because of a lack of intention to kill. However, if there is reasonable certainty, based on history, context, and technology, that there *will* be collateral damage, then the significance of the distinction between intended and unintended loses meaning. This is not necessarily to say that no amount of collateral damage is acceptable but that the language of collateral damage enables dissemblance about intention. Similarly for Christians, presuming the presence of active persecution, the distinction between public self-identification with an intention to be martyred and public self-identification without an intention to be martyred lacks significant meaning.

The larger reason that Buck cannot have volunteers in the same camp as other martyrs is that "only the voluntary martyr actively sought out martyrdom and was thus answerable for his or her own death."[18] Presumedly Buck means that the deaths in these cases are the martyr's own fault, whereas in the case of quasi- and non-volunteers the death is the fault of the persecutor and the martyr is blameless. But why is the critical difference whether the martyr actively sought out martyrdom? We know that regardless of whether the martyr was "active" or not, it does not make the punishment more or less just so long as the punishment was for maintaining Christian affiliation. It is not a matter, then, of claiming the punishment of death was justified in one case and not another. And if one's primary goal was to stay alive, certainly one would not affirm an ideology that was punishable by death directly in the face of death.

We recognize a distinction between, for example, an American combatant in a foreign country who is captured and killed by the enemy and an American foreign aid worker who is captured and killed, but we would likely agree that they had more in common with each other than they did with the millions who never ventured outside their country's borders, and we would also agree that they were—or had the opportunity to be—aware of the potential danger and put themselves in harm's way anyway. In either of these cases, we might also guess that, provided the opportunity to deny national or organizational affiliation as the only condition of complete release, some would take it. There must be another premise that makes the crucial factor whether or not the martyr "actively sought out martyrdom." Buck seems to associate voluntary martyrdom with a potential moral failing. But this only begs the question: Why would it be a moral failing to actively seek martyrdom?

It is increasingly understood in the psychological literature of the last few decades that we are not fundamentally rational creatures but creatures with an extraordinary ability to rationalize our actions in retrospect.[19] Joshua Greene notes that there are often significant discrepancies between our ethical intuitions—our hard-wired aversion to or affinity for certain actions—and the rightness or wrongness of such actions upon rational reflection. He exemplifies this with "The Trolley Problem," a hypothetical dilemma in which an out-of-control train is hurtling down the track toward five individuals who are unable to get out of the way in time. Subjects may choose to pull a lever that will divert the train to another track, but another individual is on that track and will be killed as a result. In short, the subject must choose between saving five and saving one. Typically between 70 and 80 percent of subjects choose to pull the lever given this scenario. However, if the scenario is changed slightly, where the subject may choose to push one victim in front of the train to save the five others, only about 20 to 30 percent agree to do so, although the result would be the same.[20] Greene argues we are using different methods of moral calculation when judging these two cases without necessarily being able to explain why. In the first case we make a decision based on a rational utilitarian calculation, but in the second, an instinctual aversion intervenes in our thought process, causing us to react differently.[21]

This aversion is usually explained through a distinction between harm as a means to an end and harm as a side effect, a principle introduced by Thomas Aquinas in his *Summa Theologica* as the "double effect."[22] Greene argues that while this distinction is seen as a moral justification for our intuitive aversion, it's actually our intuitions that justify the principle.[23] We attempt, in other words, to construct a rational justification for our instinctual aversion to action in the second case. The contemporary trope of collateral damage functions similarly.

The seemingly distinct variable of intention proves upon inspection to lack the moral significance it is typically given. Greene displays this through additional scenarios that combine elements of the above two trolley cases. In a third case, subjects can pull a lever to divert a train, but to get to the lever they must run on a narrow footbridge past a single individual who will fall off the bridge as a result. Though the scenario still forces the workman to his death, 81 percent of people approve of taking the action, roughly the same as the original lever case.[24] This might seem to support the significance of the means/side effect distinction. However, in other cases where the respondent can pull a trapdoor lever from a distance or step on a switch nearby to cause a workman to drop in front of and stop a train, roughly 60 percent choose to do so in order to save others, despite the use of that individual as a "trolley stopper." The impact of intended and unintended consequences is mitigated when an intervening mechanism is inserted into the scenario. This suggests that the means/side effect distinction at least sometimes masks an amoral aversion to using direct personal force, an aversion serving as a helpful evolutionary tool in encouraging people to cooperate with one another.

It may be that a similar process of rationalization appears in the distinction between voluntary and "true" martyrs. The voluntary martyr's death is like pushing the man—or in this case, throwing oneself—off the bridge into the path of the train. It is an aggressive and direct action that, even in its contemplation, "sounds an emotional alarm bell."[25] The "true" martyr's action, like pulling the lever, is an indirect action that seems to neither create a new outcome—out of the possible outcomes available—nor interfere with the operation of other variables. In both cases, however, given the action taken, the result is the death of one. There are seemingly no morally salient variables apparent in one case and not the other. Thus, one must ask why the more aggressive case is a moral failing, while the first is laudable.

As described, one difference is that the volunteers leave less to chance. Their actions are apparently meant to ensure a particular outcome: their deaths. Other martyrs who are not so direct, however, open up a realm of possibilities. Perhaps they did intend to die, perhaps not. Perhaps they were simply ignorant of the consequences of their actions. Whether out of fear or a sense of propriety, they leave an element to chance, to fate, or to divine compulsion. This allows Buck to suggest that martyrs in this category were not making an "intentional bid for martyrdom," though they were willing to die. In other words, the space left by the apparent absence of the martyr's intention allows for a more favorable institutional interpretation. Most importantly, these quasi-volunteers can be categorized with "true" martyrs who didn't seek death for its own sake but for some higher purpose.

It feels wrong to seek death too directly, and the martyrs have been defended from these charges and their implied pathologies for some time. Along with Ste. Croix, many others have understood martyrdom through pathologizing the martyr, the underlying assumption being that desiring death and effecting that end directly is an aberration. I'll discuss this idea further in the next chapter. One benefit to their approach is that it offers a concrete explanation for what was different about the martyrs: they were not entirely in their right minds. However, this approach also minimizes the influence of the Christian institution in that martyrs made a decision—with ideological support—that death was in their best interest, and perhaps even in the best interest of others.

As noted, this fragile balance of intention between the pure martyr and the culpable one has a symbiotic relationship with the ancient premise of "divine compulsion." Arthur Droge and James Tabor describe divine compulsion—*anagke* in the Greek—as the defining characteristic of the justified voluntary death from Socrates forward.[26] Across the ancient Greek, Jewish, and Roman milieux (although to varying degrees), the acceptable and even laudable voluntary death was the one approved by, or commanded by, the gods. The writers of the New Testament gospels placed Jesus in this tradition as well, who became a model for the Christian martyr.[27] The explanatory function of divine compulsion is clear. If the distinguishing characteristic of martyrs is that they were compelled by God, this validates those who succeeded in becoming martyrs and explains those who did not. The complication here is that the methods for determining this criterion are inconsistent and ultimately unverifiable. The way it comes to be uniquely inferred in the history of the "true" Christian martyr is through an absence of the agency of the would-be martyr. The martyr's agency, suggested by particular "willing" actions, competes with the divine will. Consequently, the overt action of the volunteer martyr is understood as selfish in opposition to the selflessness of the "true" martyr. The absence of evidence of the martyr's will is taken as the evidence of absence of the martyr's will and thus the presence of the divine will.

This provides insight into what concerns Buck (and others) about voluntary martyrs: the volunteers are seen as primarily selfish, while "true" martyrs are selfless. Because of the space opened through an absence of markers of aggressively seeking death—and sometimes the presence of seemingly helpful acts prior to death, such as attempting to comfort other Christians heading to their deaths—the quasi-volunteer martyrs can appear to benefit others both before and in their deaths. Buck redirects the actions of the quasi-volunteers by suggesting that they were "doing nothing more than was expected of them as Christians."[28] She continues that "it was these very acts of charity, compassion, and cohesion that set Christianity apart from paganism, especially during times of adversity, and made it an attractive option." Buck here follows a traditional Christian narrative, espoused by early Christian scholars such as E. R. Dodds and W. H. C. Frend, that Christianity succeeded because it offered more than competing ideologies, such as the conglomerate "paganism."[29]

This approach raises an interesting dilemma. If the quasi-volunteer martyrs were only fulfilling the minimum expectations of Christian membership, this should imply that the vast majority of Christians did not fulfill those expectations. One could perhaps argue that other Christians were charitable and compassionate in other ways, but if the charity and compassion of the "normal" Christian was acceptable, then we are faced with noticing that martyrs did *more* than the norm—they made their Christianity overt in a time when it was punishable by death. This affirms Ste. Croix's claim that the martyrs could have avoided martyrdom without any compromise in Christian principle.[30] One could argue here, as Buck and others do, that it is not the death but the affirmation of Christianity preceding it that matters.[31] Yet Christians do not memorialize all who affirm Christianity but those who suicide doing so.

Another possibility within this paradigm is that there was a range of acceptable Christian activity in which both martyrs and non-martyrs could presumably operate. Yet Buck implies that the most appropriate action was taken by the martyrs here, so this cannot be right either. Non-martyrs have in this particular case failed to live up to their Christian obligations, but this does not seem to have made them non-Christian. The tension here is a fundamental one in Christianity—namely, that one is both expected to meet a particular set of obligations to maintain membership and allowed at times to avoid those obligations without substantial or permanent consequence. Concern over this tension, and under what conditions it could be resolved, animated early church hierarchy over the question of lapsed Christians, as we discussed in the previous chapter. Precisely because Buck believes in the category of voluntary martyrdom that Ste. Croix presents but is also faced with the negation of a number of early Christian martyrs, she attempts to adopt a narrower qualification for voluntary martyrdom. In order to create a more exclusive category, however, Buck adopts a normative understanding of Christianity that is consequentially unable to accommodate the vast majority of Christians who were not martyrs of any kind.

In the end, Buck defends even the unabashedly volunteer martyrs, claiming that "in a world that offered nothing of value except the opportunity to leave it for a better one, surely voluntary martyrdom for the early Christians would have been, not self-destructive, but self-preserving."[32] This passage provides a hermeneutic key for understanding the premises of Buck's approach. She asks us to excuse the volunteer martyrs, and martyrdom in general, because of the sincerity of belief that death was a necessary cost for a greater gain. This is certainly true from the martyr's perspective—no one dies willingly for a net loss. In fact, Buck's sentiment here resonates with the one I have outlined in previous chapters—that we understand martyrdom not first as an act of self-sacrifice but of self-formation. Though I suggest that self-destruction—or as I've described it, willing suicide—is an appropriate description for the action prior to its institutional captivation, the trajectory is the same. Buck seemingly fails to notice that this same justification can be made of all willing suicides.

Few would contend, for example, that the members of the Heaven's Gate cult killed themselves for reasons that were legitimate, even as we likely understand those individuals to have killed themselves for reasons they thought legitimate. Of course, there was no persecutor in the case of Heaven's Gate, but that this is not a salient distinction can be seen in the fact that we also do not consider the deaths of the Branch Davidians outside of Waco, Texas, as any more legitimate for having died while surrounded by FBI and ATF agents, even if we consider the actions of law enforcement unjustified. We still think that these movements were, at best, misguided. The difference between these examples and orthodox Christianity is that the latter has a long history and significant cultural capital. Nonetheless, the premises upon which Christian martyrs went to their deaths are not more verifiable than the aforementioned cults. We do not honor or commemorate the deaths of Heaven's Gate or Branch Davidian members—even though the latter thought of themselves as Christian—certainly because we do not want to encourage people to imitate them but also because we worry that our commemoration would give credence to their actions or the beliefs behind them.

This argument over the extent of voluntary martyrdom in early Christianity illustrates the shared ideological premises upon which many scholars study deaths for a cause, particularly religious ones. Distinguishing categories of martyrs is premised upon the assumption that martyrdom—willing suicide with Christian ideological support—is honorable, even when denying that cause ensures survival. Because the validity of the cause cannot be verified, however, we do not have a nonideological basis for asserting that there is such a thing as "true" martyrdom from which to distinguish other types. This problem is not avoided by simply "bracketing" the question of the legitimacy of martyrdom and describing the context. This also potentially brackets reason by treating all claims equally. In purely descriptive spheres this method might be welcome, but it is used in the contemporary sphere for political claims about the essence of religion and religious practice, as well as distinctions between martyrdom and suicide.

Ste. Croix's challenge to the extent of early Christian martyrdom is thus welcome, since the notion of voluntary martyrdom presents a false dichotomy that shows the extent to which religious institutional paradigms determine the legitimacy of the individual death. As we have seen though, many scholarly responses have debated over the scope or legitimacy of the category, or who should represent the Christian position on the subject, and at what point in time, rather than examine the contingency of the debate upon an unverifiable premise.[33] "Voluntary martyrdom" assumes that "true" martyrdom is arranged by God. While it is undoubtedly the case that many in the modern world and even some in the ancient world judged the validity of martyrdom on this basis, this dichotomy is a facade for institutional politics, covering institutional self-promotion with divine approval. Utility for the institution tells us nothing of the motivations of the individual martyr. It does not allow us to conclude that a particular Christian martyr, for example, brought her death upon herself, or that she had "a hand" in her own death while others did not. Yet in order to categorize voluntary martyrs, one must infer an egoism or selfishness that is absent in the "true" martyr. As I noted above, these feelings may be simply the result of our psychological architecture, which creates an emotional response in direct cases and remains dormant in indirect ones.

There is a second, overlapping implication of "voluntary" in relation to martyrdom, that it expresses a point on the spectrum of willingness to die that is too eager for the circumstances. In this sense, "voluntary" comes dangerously close to a death wish, seeking death for its own sake—in other words, suicide. The most exemplary martyrs appeared as the unwilling-willing, exerting no effort to promote their own persecution but offering no resistance if and when it arrived. In an oversimplification of this spectrum, these reticent Christians are misunderstood as "unwilling," not in the sense that they willed not to die but in the sense that they made their own wills actively subject to God. If the thoughts and feelings of the martyrs, likely conflicted and doubtful, are relegated to the interior, then we can safely ignore them. If, however, the martyrs express their zeal outwardly, this inconvenient fact must be mitigated if the death is to become a suitable candidate for Christian martyrdom.

Preserving "true" martyrdom as exemplary of normative Christianity has little explanatory value for early Christianity because the vast majority of Christians took steps as necessary to avoid martyrdom, wisely so. The side effect of this understanding, which extends to the present, is that deaths that can be associated with the Christian institution are made meaningful. More importantly, though, deaths not supporting Christianity, or those in opposition to it, are left meaningless or given a negative valuation. As I mentioned at the beginning of the chapter, Charles Moore did not explicitly identify his Christianity as the operative factor in his decision to self-immolate, and few if any Christians would agree that to be Christian requires martyrdom. An article written few months after his death described the uniqueness of Moore in the earnestness with which he sought to right societal wrongs and the degree of responsibility he took upon himself for his perceived inaction. It also attested, both through Moore's own words and the testimony of others, that he was not suicidal.[34] But there certainly was something different about him, as one could argue is the case with all who take their own lives—and sometimes the lives of others—for a principle, belief, or cause. The cause itself does not tell the whole story.

There is another way that we can understand the integral association of Christianity with willingness to die without establishing a double standard for martyrs and non-martyrs. Rather than understanding Christianity as the only operative institution in regard to Christian martyrdom, examination of the degree to which other identities augment or mitigate willing suicide provides a more nuanced picture of motivations for martyrdom. Some efforts have been made to understand aspects of early Christianity from the perspective of inconsistencies between real and perceived social identities, but these efforts have not been widespread.[35] Even from Buck's offhand defense of voluntary martyrdoms—that the world offered nothing of value for them anyway—we can see that martyrdoms are connected with the degree to which Christian identity is mitigated by other social institutions with tangible, achievable rewards. Comparatively unburdened with the ideological weight of the study of religion, scholars from other disciplines are more comfortable with examining the confluence of religious identities with other sociocultural and psychological influences on enacting extreme violence, as I'll discuss in the following chapter. Although more difficult, it is not impossible to engage in similar work on ancient martyrdoms, as these have had a significant influence on our perceptions of the martyrdom in the contemporary world. For example, David Bradford notes that "the martyr's exchange of biologically determined priorities for spiritual values challenges the normal, irreligious person's understanding. Yet the attitude of some modern religious patients is similar, however many centuries and scientific discoveries separate the martyr from the modern patient."[36] He concludes that it behooves modern psychologists and psychotherapists to understand the history of Christian martyrdom, and I suggest it similarly behooves scholars of martyrdom to understand the psychology (as well as other factors) that may contribute to willing suicide, though it may lead us into territory contested by religious ideology.

Is Martyrdom Different from Suicide?

I have suggested that the tendency to separate martyrdom from suicide, particularly in the Christian context, is justified by the institutionally imposed stigma of suicide and the corresponding need to purify martyrdom for institutional use. While this relatively successful cultural conditioning presents itself as self-evident, the tendency to react to suicide as aberrant is in part the result of a hardwired emotional response. When that response is muted in other cases, we assume those cases are somehow qualitatively different. We use our emotional response or lack thereof, in other words, to justify a categorical distinction where one is not necessarily present.[37] However, is martyrdom distinguishable from suicide in any other ways?

Some potential distinctions are easily dismissible. The first is the notion that martyrdom involves dying *for* something, while suicide is simply selfish. To put this in a more charitable way, martyrdom is dying for something *else*, while suicide is dying for one*self*. These options, upon closer inspection, are indistinguishable. What does it mean to die for something here? It does not mean to die in place of something. Christianity would live on as a sociocultural institution without the death of a given individual, so this is not a case of trading places. It neither can be demonstrated that the self lacks "thing"-ness in a way somehow present in all other things without making a priori assumptions about the nature of humanity or the presence of a soul. The self is as much a "thing" as other "things" in the world. Dying for something, then, is common both to the suicide and the martyr.

One might argue that martyrdom, then, is dying for some*one*. We would need to note that it is certainly not dying for someone in a straightforward sense; that is, it is not ending one's own life in order to directly prolong the temporal and physical existence of another. This can indeed happen, but it is seen as heroism rather than martyrdom.[38] Martyrdom as dying for someone relies on a longer chain of events, perhaps one in which someone would notice the death of the martyr and be swayed toward the institution for which the martyr was said to have died. This impacted person could, if all went well, have not their physical but their spiritual life preserved through their acceptance of Christianity. To accept this scenario, however, one must presume the existence of the very thing in question. It immediately regresses to the previous explanation: dying for something. If anything less than demonstrably real, however, there is no distinction between the martyr and the suicide. The martyr does not literally trade life for the life of another in this case but in the most charitable scenario trades one's physical life for the prospect of another's spiritual life. It is a hope or a gamble, and while it is not necessarily culpable on that point alone, it is indistinguishable from the possible conviction of the suicide that life will be better for others with them gone.

Further, the claim that the death was *for* something cannot be validated by the individual alone; without community support, such a claim is worthless. And if community support is given in one instance and not in another, *that* may constitute the distinction between martyrdom and suicide, rather than that one death was self-interested and the other was externally focused. The verification of "for" is the presumed social legitimacy of the institution rather than an absence of a "for" in one case. I'll discuss this idea further in Chapter 7.

The implication of dying *for* is that it lacks the self-interest that the suicide seems to wallow in. The suicide, if for anything, is for oneself, which is interestingly believed not to be a "for" at all. This is indefensible as well. How is the martyr, compared to the suicide, not self-interested? Certainly if one believes the tenets of Christianity, it is in one's self-interest to die rather than deny Christian belief. (This is not to say that it is easy as a result, despite what some martyr stories may imply. Neither is it the case that the suicide is easy, despite some rhetorical claims in attempts to discourage it.) In fact, the more demonstrable absence of self-interest, given that one identifies as Christian, would be to deny Christianity, for this would seem to go against one's interest.[39] From a Christian perspective, one might argue that in this case—denying Christianity—the question of interest moves from the realm of Christianity to some other form of identification; one is not going against one's Christian self-interest but being selfish with regard to some other identity, hanging on to life, wealth, fame, and so forth. But this is inconsistent. It cannot be that dying for Christianity involves a unique lack of self-interest while dying for most anything else is selfish. Again, this assumes to be true the very thing one proves through the dying "for."

On the other hand, even if one is generally agreed to have died for something, it is another thing entirely to establish that something needed dying for. It is a calculation that by leveraging the value of one's own life, something of greater value can be accessed. Charles Moore's self-immolation, as well as John Chau's death, raises this issue. The problem is not that motives are uniquely complicated in Moore's or Chau's case—it is that they are *always* complicated. This is why the institution must vouch for—and in return benefits from—the martyr's death. It is clear, though, that the mere fact of institutional surety on one side and cultural condemnation on the other does not necessarily suggest altruistic sacrifice and suicide, respectively. So, the "dying for" explanations are insufficient to distinguish martyrdom from suicide because they presume the acceptance that a certain institutional "for" is legitimate, while an individual "for" is not, failing to recognize that both instances are institutional *and* individual. Are there any other contenders for a distinction between martyrdom and suicide?

The sociologist Jean Baechler describes suicide as a solution to an existential problem, a similar sentiment to how I have framed martyrdom.[40] As might be expected for such a fundamental condition, the motivations and means of suicide vary widely.[41] Theories of suicide have also varied by disciplinary field, and their development has been comparatively slow. Durkheim's theory of suicide is preeminent,[42] and it largely frames suicide socioculturally, as the degree to which the individual relates to the values of society.[43] As I noted in the first chapter, his definition of suicide clearly includes what is commonly understood as martyrdom: "Suicide is applied to all cases of death resulting directly or indirectly from a positive or negative act of the victim himself, which he knows will produce this result."[44] Charles Moore employed a positive act that directly resulted in his death. The voluntary martyr might employ a positive act that indirectly results in death. The ideal orthodox martyrdom might occur indirectly as the result of a negative act. This variety of approaches is nonetheless fully contained in Durkheim's definition. Durkheim adds that "life is none the less abandoned because one desires it at the moment of renouncing it," addressing a common differentiation of the martyr from the suicide on the basis that the former, unlike the latter, wishes to live. Of his four primary classifications, the martyr fits best into the category of the altruistic suicide, who is over-integrated into a collective society.[45] Unless a mass suicide, however, this description fails to differentiate among those in the same subculture who suicide and those who do not.

Many subsequent typologies of suicide also contain types that can be identified with martyrdom. For Edwin Shneidman, "cessation-ignorers" suicide with the belief that death does not result in extinction, often based on supernatural beliefs.[46] For R. S. Mintz, one of eleven possible motivations for suicide is rebirth or reincarnation.[47] The aforementioned Baechler's typology includes oblative suicide, which includes the subtype of "transfigurational suicide," estimated to make up less than 5 percent of all suicides.[48] A recent literature review concludes that these typologies are helpful but limited because of their sample sizes and thus difficult to replicate; they also tend not to account for any role of genetic and neurobiological factors in suicide.[49]

Thomas Joiner suggests that there are three significant factors that, if present, constitute serious risk for suicidality. The first is a lack of belongingness. The second is perceived burdensomeness. These first two in combination are likely to lead to a desire for suicide. The third, and comparatively most critical, factor is acquired ability to enact self-harm.[50] Note that any one or two of these factors might be present in the individual without suggesting serious risk of suicide. Though suicide is undoubtedly difficult, many through their life circumstances, both chosen and imposed, have acquired the ability for self-injury but feel efficacious enough and/or connected enough that they have no desire for suicide. On the other hand, there are many who may have a desire for suicide without the ability to carry it out. (This is not simply the access to a means of suicide; it is the ability to follow through with it, regardless of the means.)

On the face of it, there would seem to be distinctions we can make between martyrdom and suicide on the basis of Joiner's theory. Perhaps the most obvious is "lack of belongingness." The martyr, one might argue, belonged to the group for which she was martyred, so she would not be suicidal on that account. Belongingness is not simply identification with a group but a feeling of being connected with that group. Nonetheless, it would seem that death for Christianity would presume a sense of belonging within that sociocultural milieu. There may be something unique to religious belongingness in this regard. What does it mean to have a sense of belonging to an institution in which a substantial thread predicts and praises the "sacrifice" of the individual for institutional aims? Is the martyr nonetheless, insofar as they "belong" to the group, not a suicide? Or does a group ideology promoting "sacrifice" direct that belongingness right back toward suicide? To put this another way, what does it mean when belongingness appears fulfilled *through* death?

Note here that belongingness is not verified externally but can only be felt internally. Indeed, in the wake of suicide, eulogies often reflect on the group membership—and the seeming benefits received from it—of the dead. On the other hand, group membership can neither be denied on the basis of suicide. "Clearly she was not *x*, because they don't commit suicide." This is particularly the case, as mentioned above, when there is a history of praise of violent death in certain forms.

So it remains questionable whether group membership in this case contributes to a sense of belongingness, particularly when this belongingness to the group is constructed vis-à-vis perceived lack of belonging to a broader social milieux, as is often emphasized in stories of martyrdom. Joiner's second factor, perceived burdensomeness, may also seem to be a reason for disqualification of the martyr from suicide. Again, though, the assumption that the perception of burdensomeness would not be present in the case of the Christian martyr is complicated by the fact that death for the institutional cause is praised. To the extent to which one adopts this aspect of institutional knowledge, one's continued existence may well be perceived as a burden. Clearly for most Christians this does not rise to the level of significance, so for the martyr the perception of burdensomeness, if present, is likely augmented from elsewhere.

As noted above, Joiner considered the ability to self-harm the comparatively larger hurdle to serious suicidality, in large part due to our hardwired aversion to self-harm or desire for survival.[51] The acquisition of the ability to enact self-harm has been explored—though not to support a connection to suicide—by some scholars of early Christian martyrdom. I suggest in the next chapter that widespread "martyrdom training" was unlikely in early Christianity, but that is not to say that the acquired ability to self-harm was not important to follow through with martyrdom. As Joiner explains, the ability to fatally self-injure may be able to be acquired through repeated, less significant attempts of increasing seriousness. It may also be acquired through less direct means of increasing pain tolerance, intentionally (tattooing, piercing, etc.) or unintentionally (childhood abuse, repeated exposure to violence).[52] Exposure only to violence as mediated through the narratives of a religious tradition may be insufficient to acquire ability to commit suicide, but it certainly could contribute to this acquisition.

There is an indirect element to ideal accounts of martyrdom that may complicate ability to self-harm. In many suicides, harm is directly self-inflicted, whereas in martyrdoms—again in the ideal sense—harm is inflicted by others on the agent; the agent's role, in a successful martyrdom, is not to resist that harm. Though the end result is the same, the means appear different. Support of a distinction is connected to the notion of selfishness discounted above—directly self-inflicted harm appears as an indicator of self-interest. Conversely, absence of directly self-inflicted harm, and thus self-will, leaves room for divine will. There is also the emotional response activated in the case of direct self-harm (or the observer's anticipation of another's direct self-harm) and remaining dormant in the case of allowing harm to oneself by another. But I can see no necessary—or really even any indirect—distinction here. Even if the distinction was rooted in the supposition that other-inflicted harm was somehow more courageous, one could make the opposite claim—relying on another to commit the act one is unable to do is selfish and cowardly. Such accusation is sometimes leveled in the phenomenon we label "suicide-by-cop."[53] Note, though, that here the act is still labeled as suicide. In these cases one might argue that the agent still had to take provoking action. In the ideal circumstance, law enforcement does not assume guilt; they use lethal force when their own lives are threatened. If the "suicide-by-cop" took no action, they would not be dead. And certainly there are analogues in early Christian martyrdom, such as those who offered no physical resistance may yet have assaulted their accusers verbally. They also did not resist violence against themselves.

So, how does lack of physical action relate to ability to self-harm? One might argue that martyrdom is not suicide because lack of physical action is at least an absence of evidence for ability to self-harm. Some recent studies have shown that individuals who are suicidal experience higher pain thresholds that non-suicidal individuals.[54] This would seem to indicate that ability to self-harm encompasses not only enactment of harm against oneself but also ability to experience self-harm. The perceived distinction may be based not on any real difference but in our inability to process on a psychological level a secondary chain of action. We thus "discount" an action that does not occur on the primary chain of action.[55] In both cases, there is an intent with knowledge that the result of such intent may be death. The action/inaction dichotomy is only such from a fixed perspective. With regard to intent, inaction is equally action. In other words, insofar as it is intentional—a requirement both of suicide and the martyr—inaction is merely a subset of, and not differentiable from, other types of action.

It may be difficult to conclusively identity lack of belongingness, perceived burdensomeness, and ability to self-harm among ancient martyrs. Neither is it obvious that these factors were not present among them, given the potential correlations in more recent cases such as Chau's or Moore's. The larger challenge appears to be disentangling the search for any salient distinctions from theologically or morally motivated (but unwarranted) arguments for martyrdom and against suicide.

There is a lay understanding within religious circles as well as in the general public that martyrdom represents a significant or perhaps the ultimate commitment to something. For followers of a specific tradition, that view is conditionally held. It may be true of Christian beliefs about Christian martyrdom, but Christians may be comparatively reticent to attribute Muslim martyrdom to sincere commitment to Islam, and even if so, they are certainly not convinced of the logic that it "proves" the faith that is ascribed to for their own tradition. As fifth-century Bishop Augustine of Hippo suggested regarding heretical Christian martyrs, it is not the death but the cause for which the martyr died which legitimizes it.[56] This was in the context of a polemical attack on Donatist Christianity and certainly not representative of all or most thinking within burgeoning Christianity. Nonetheless, clearly Augustine saw martyrdom as involving commitment to a cause. In contrast, suicide is seen within Christian circles as sinful and/or cowardly, representing at best a misplaced, and at worst a complete absence of, commitment.[57]

Joiner seeks to counter in his work the misconception that suicide is cowardly or a sign of weakness. His theory of suicide reinforces rather a sort of courage that is required for the suicide in order to overcome the will to survive and the potential pain of killing oneself, despite the "reward."[58] The notion of commitment certainly aligns with Joiner's model. So is the primary connection between the conventional suicide and the martyr, a commitment to death, a point of similarity, regardless of the possible difference of the "for?"

Interestingly, this approach to understanding martyrdom was fairly common among scholars in the early and mid-twentieth century. As noted above, E. R. Dodds suggested martyrs were simply "in love with death."[59] While it may be inappropriate to ascribe an emotion to the suicide's attitude toward death, can we say she is committed to death? It seems in the case of the current research on suicide, this may be hasty. There is anecdotal evidence in some cases of what Joiner calls the merging of life with death preceding suicide, which is indicated by positive or affirming indicators of symbols associated with death or looking on the potentiality of death with fondness.[60] Certainly this can be seen in traditional martyrdom stories as well. However, there is also evidence to suggest it is not always the case that suicide is ultimate commitment. Joiner reports of individuals, having survived "jumping" suicide attempts, for example, who experienced regret as soon as they jumped. Commitment may be unstable until the end.

Even if it were the case that we believed suicide represented ultimate commitment to something, insofar as that something is death itself, it is unhelpful in making any predictions about propensity for suicide or religious suicide. So, suicide as "ultimate commitment," true though it may be, cannot help us any more than suicide as arranged by the divine or suicide as identity-specific commitment.

In the abstract, the difference between suicide and martyrdom, as well as the difference of each from other forms of death, seems clear. It is much more difficult to substantiate by empirical means. Charles Moore clearly died by his own hand; he was not persecuted, except perhaps by his own despair over the insufficient response of his community, his denomination, and himself to societal injustices. He did not die for Christianity in the traditional sense, nor did he die for himself. The reason for this ambiguity is not that this is an exceptional case, but that there is no basis on which to make a definitive categorical distinction between martyrdom and suicide. Those who wish to make such a claim are stuck between a rock and a hard place. On one hand, there is no way to verify a distinction between suicide and martyrdom; on the other, there is significant stigma attached to suicide and praise attached to Christian martyrdom. Thus arises significant debate over whether Moore qualifies as a martyr and scholarly attempts to defend against implications that Christian martyrs exhibit secondary characteristics associated with suicide. This is not to say that the effects of this distinction, if successful, are not significant. The death of the "martyr"—having been determined by a theological distinction—serves to validate the institution for which it ostensibly took place, an institution whose sovereignty can be supported by no other means. The power of the suicide, as suicide, cannot be assimilated. So why not assimilate more willing suicides as martyrdoms? I've suggested this is in part because of our psychological architecture. Death achieved through direct physical force elicits in us a powerful emotional response; deaths, even willing ones, achieved by less direct means do not activate the same responses. They do not set off the alarm bells that we often use to determine right and wrong. There is more work that should be done to substantiate these connections between our psychology and our sense of morality vis-à-vis martyrdom, but it is clear that the distinction of suicide from martyrdom is maintained by the moral stigma placed on the former, and that the acknowledgment and removal of that stigma would not only benefit appropriate societal responses to suicide but also clear the way for an examination of the "why" of martyrs themselves. Do their alarm bells function differently? I turn to that question in the next chapter.

6

"In Love with Death": Pathology and Identity in Martyrdom

As we explored in the previous chapter, the history of the Christian martyr has been plagued by its association with suicide.[1] This is partly by design, as early Christian apologists were at pains to reinforce the legitimacy of the orthodox Christian martyr while delegitimizing the claimed martyrdoms of heterodox Christian sects, those that competed with the authority of the institution. Nonetheless, it remains a delicate dance for the institution that employs martyrdom, as the markers that attract us to the agent represent first willing suicide. The application of martyr requires institutional interpretation. Modern scholars have often assisted in this task of interpretation, reaffirming traditional boundaries between the "true" and "false" martyr established by early Christian bishops. While the boundary markers for legitimate martyrdom have been narrowed in scholarship over time, the consensus that there is indeed a boundary to be marked, a categorical distinction to be respected, remains. There are clear motivating factors for this as a defense of the religious institution, but reasons for its support in modern scholarship are less clear. Undoubtedly it is in part a function of the history itself. Certainly a distinction so prevalent throughout time is too obvious to be questioned. As one philosopher puts it, "While martyrdom involves giving up one's own life, it is not, of course, suicide."[2] She calls for other Christian philosophers to aid against martyrdom's "corruption in the service of vicious ends"—namely, an association with suicide. Another recent text has suggested that we "reclaim" the word martyr from its association with "suicide bombers, immolators, and victims" because "the miracle of martyrdom depends on us."[3]

More recently, another thread of scholarship has (perhaps wisely) exited the struggle over legitimate and illegitimate claims that has animated much of modern scholarship on early Christian martyrdom. Instead, an increasing number of scholars over the last forty years have understood martyrdom not in terms of its legitimacy, nor primarily in terms of death at all, but as an identity discourse. Martyrdom functions as "a narrative that creates or maintains group identity."[4] In this paradigm, more than a physical act, martyrdom becomes a symbolic means of communication, an important way to understand oneself as a Christian and to mark the boundaries of Christianity.

The use of "identity" as an analytical tool began in the mid-twentieth century and has become ubiquitous in the social sciences and humanities.[5] This approach has some potential advantages for studying martyrdom in comparison to prior approaches. One advantage is that it shifts the scholarly discourse about martyrdom from historical verification to analysis. It is certainly important on some level to know which martyrdoms are likely to have had some root in historical reality and which are likely to be fabrications, but we have limited examples to work with and remain uncertain even about the most likely candidates for historical veracity. Identity discourse largely sidesteps this issue because it reorients the discussion about martyrdom around the stories told and not the purported events behind those stories. Thus, it reclaims all martyrdom stories for study, historically accurate or not, because accuracy is secondary to the culture-building work that early Christians could put martyrdom to. Clearly, all stories of martyrdom were important to some early Christian groups, and this approach recognizes and values them.

There is also a certain collaboration of identity approaches to early Christian scholarship and a sense of atoning for past sins in regard to the Christian imperialism embedded in the study of religion. It is now commonly understood that the study of religion—indeed the very category of religion—was defined and maintained from the perspective of the hegemonic Christian tradition. Other religions were encountered on the basis of the extent to which they aligned or did not with an orthodox understanding of Catholic or Protestant Christianity.[6] In the social sciences, identity is a potential tool with which to counter hierarchical understandings of diverse cultures and perspectives and appreciate them on their own merits. Ironically, although "Christian" is an oppressor identity according to this decolonizing approach to the study of religion, the early Christian identity is different enough—as oppressed rather than oppressor—to be excepted from this categorization.

Note that there are at least two givens about early Christian identity at play here, and they sit in tension with one another. The first is that early Christian identity, when taken as an abstract whole, is distinct from Christian identity as it came to be associated with imperial power. This starting point allows scholars of early Christianity to retain the now standard critique of imperialist approaches to studying religion while excluding early Christian identity from that critique. The second given of early Christian identity is that part of its difference from later Christian identity is that it was developing, not yet fully formed. It seems particularly appropriate to identify rapid change in the first few centuries of the appearance of the Christian identity. The tension when these givens are taken together, however, is that early Christian identity is being understood here as both formed—in identifiable juxtaposition to a broader or modern Christian identity—and developing. Early Christian identity is a not-yet identity and an identity in its own right. Identity scholarship attempts to clear space for appreciation of early Christianity on its own terms without articulating a clear method for doing so.

A third perceived advantage of the trend toward identity in discussions of early Christian martyrdom is that it enables a critique of earlier generations of scholars who employed a "pathological approach," implying that martyrdom (often or always) is enabled by psychological abnormality. An identity approach instead roots the difference of martyrdom, as noted above, in the difference of early Christians as a group. However, a nearly exclusive focus on martyrdom's function as identity formation and maintenance leads to the martyr in martyrdom being effectively erased. This presents an incomplete picture of the past and renders early Christian martyrdom scholarship unable to contribute to a broader understanding of martyrdom.

The identity approach to early Christian martyrdom is insufficient for three reasons. First, as it has been deployed, the identity approach preserves an essentialist understanding of religion that roots the impetus for "Christian" martyrdom in Christianity, in line with a long-standing theological-historical discourse about martyrdom.[7] In the traditional Eusebian theological approach, martyrdom took place because of and for Christianity. The fundamental flaw in this approach is that martyrdom more often didn't happen. The identity discourse approach to martyrdom reproduces the essential connection between martyrdom and Christianity while relegating the "action" of martyrdom to discourse. It reduces the martyr to one identity—Christian—which precludes appreciating the context and motivations of the individual agent. As I have suggested, it creates a significant logical gap to ascribe the impetus for martyrdom to an affiliation with Christianity when most who adopted that identity past and present have not been martyrs. Obviously religious identity does not tell the whole tale. What was different about martyrs? This is the question that the pathological approach to martyrdom was better prepared to answer. Even if we were to argue that it is impossible to know whether *any* ancient martyrdoms actually took place, we can certainly verify the occurrence of potential martyrdoms in the present day such as John Chau or Charles Moore. Whether that be in a mimetic fashion or not, we need to recognize that occurrences do take place, and it is the occurrence, or at least the potential occurrence, that animates our interest in and excitement about martyrdom in the first place.

This leads to the second failure of the identity approach: it avoids the universal existential phenomenon represented by the martyr. In using martyrdom as an ideological trope, this approach cannot countenance the embodied essence—both existentially and historically—of martyrdom. Our fascination for martyrdom is primordially grounded in the paradoxically willing suicide of the agent. We covered this ground extensively in the second chapter.

Third, the very term "identity" has become ambiguous in its overuse and thus has limited explanatory capability.[8] It is deployed to signify both similarity (of early Christians with each other, of Christian martyrs with Christian non-martyrs, and of Christians across time and space and difference) and difference (of some early Christians from others, of some early Christians from some modern ones, of early Christians from Romans, and of early Christians from the modern readers of whatever text is being written) in ways that are contradictory. Because the martyr is first characterized by willing suicide, not by religious identity, understanding the "why" of the martyr—which includes, but is not exhausted by, the identity discourse around martyrdom—necessitates a revitalized focus on the existential and psychosocial difference of the martyr-agent. A nuanced understanding of Christian martyrdom that reunites the identity narrative with the death, drawing on recent insights of psychology and sociology in addition to history, is not only desirable for its comprehensiveness but can also contribute to an understanding of willing suicide with ideological support across ideological boundaries.

The Challenge of the Eusebian Narrative

Several components contributed to effective Christian institutional meaning-making with martyrs. The necessity of martyrdom had to be predicted, or at least seem to have been. This is evidenced in canonical early Christian writings as well as early Church apologists and clergy, and whether these texts reflect actual teachings or sayings of Jesus and his immediate followers is less important than their establishment in the textual tradition. Christian martyrdom appears as both a consequence of and vindication of the death of Jesus; the narrative of

Christianity could only develop if seen as a natural and intentional progression from the death of its progenitor. Thus follows a theoretical basis for understanding the *telos* of Christian identity as suffering unto death. The gospels are at their most similar in their understanding of Jesus through the lens of his death, and identification with Jesus, *imitatio Christi*, brought expectations of suffering and death, though lacking its lasting sting (1 Cor. 15:55).

Second, the "right" number actually had to commit willing suicide. While there was almost certainly a lower number than specific tales of martyrs—not to mention the institutional narrative of Christianity—represent, it's also nearly certain that some fulfilled this role. Too few and the narrative would not have had worth; too many and the institution would not exist. As I have suggested, the latter would have been unlikely beyond a small number since relatively few are suicidal and ideology is insufficient to induce suicide.

Finally, these willing suicides had to become Christian. This is not to suggest that the agent involved in a willing suicide did not believe themselves to be doing so in some way for their Christianness. Rather, it is to suggest that insofar as Christianity was to become a sustainable social institution, the charisma expressed in martyrdom needed to be routinized, subjected to Christian authority.[9] As the movement that would become Christianity had spread, it adapted to comparatively better circumstances than its original socioeconomic purview on the fringe of empire.[10] Without economic or social scarcity of resources, and especially in the absence of an active persecutor, martyrdom has comparatively less explanatory power. The willing suicide of the agent, which is both autonomous and anti-institutional, is minimally representable from a position of institutional sovereignty, as I discussed in Chapter 3. Thus the fundamental paradox with martyrdom from an institutional perspective. The death of its founder was the beginning of Christianity, but like the charismatic leader, martyrdom itself eventually had to be transformed in order for the institution to succeed.

It was only in the fourth century that martyrdom could retroactively become a central character in the story of Christianity. The patronage engendered by the emperor Constantine promoted the solidification of a Christian orthodoxy and enabled martyrdom to play a role in that orthodoxy.[11] Christianity for the first time had dogma and substantial—albeit certainly not total—power of enforcement. The existential and theological appeal of martyrdom needed to be reinterpreted in a new era where the possibility of practice was slim and, more importantly, where the persecuted minority had gained official status. The image of the "true" martyr as represented by writings of Clement and the martyrdoms of Polycarp and others prevailed in part because it was the easiest institutional form to manage. It enabled willing suicides for Christianity to preserve a temporal Christian kingdom in perpetuity.

As I discussed in Chapter 4, the first comprehensive history of Christianity written by Bishop Eusebius of Caesarea in the fourth century CE established a narrative of Christian expansion that has been generally accepted since, and this narrative featured martyrdom prominently. If Eusebius's *Ecclesiastical History* was a targeted media campaign, stories of martyrdoms made for catchy headlines.[12] Within the Eusebian paradigm, a written focus on suffering and martyrdom transparently reflects an increasingly persistent persecution of Christians throughout the first centuries of Christianity, culminating in the "Great Persecution" of the early fourth century under the Roman Emperor Diocletian and his successors. The deaths of Christians rose in direct proportion to the willingness of Rome to persecute.

As modern historical study failed to reveal evidence for widespread persecution, however, this narrative seemed to require interpretation.[13] If early Christians were not constantly under threat of death, why were these often gruesome stories passed down through history? Early modern explanations began to focus on difference—the difference of the martyr from other Christians and the difference of Christians from others in their social milieu. Early-twentieth-century scholars increasingly saw something pathological in the actions of martyrs and even in the behaviors of those who celebrated them. "Normal" people do not become martyrs; therefore, there must have been something aberrant about those Christians who welcomed martyrdom.

This paradigm challenges the traditional understanding of early Christian martyrdom, since viewing even select martyrdoms as aberrant taints the enterprise with the stigma of suicide. As Lacey Baldwin Smith remarks, "The possibility that martyrdom might be only faintly disguised suicide on the part of emotionally disturbed people who were determined, consciously or unconsciously, to end their own lives is a deeply worrisome proposition, because it strikes at the teleological roots of a performance that for many Christians is regarded as being providential."[14] Conscious of this "worrisome proposition," no scholars question the legitimacy of Christian martyrdom, preferring to critique particular martyrdoms or create lesser categorizations such as "voluntary martyrdom" to differentiate from "true" martyrdom, as discussed in the previous chapter. Nonetheless, even questioning the psychological state of some martyrs undermines the long-held assumption that the martyr was central to Christianity's success. Even further, it may imply that Christianity exploited vulnerable individuals for institutional gain.

The identity approach reconciles the infrequency of martyrdom with the consistent focus on suffering in Christian texts, reintegrating martyrdom as the quintessential expression of Christianness. Christian texts dedicated to suffering and death do not reflect pathology but a Christian identity discourse. As many scholars have explored, Late Antiquity martyr cults were a potent means to promote Christianity in a time when martyrdom at the hands of pagan imperial persecutors was nonexistent.[15] However, in normalizing martyrdom as identity formation before this period—when martyrdoms *were* occurring—this approach subordinates the question of what made martyrs different from non-martyrs: why did some Christians choose to die when most did not?

Training for Death

Judith Lieu suggests that within early Christian martyr texts "the label 'Christian' belongs pre-eminently to the martyrs, to the rest only in a shadowy and derivative sense."[16] Martyr texts and Late Antique bishops promote this reading of the martyr as a model for Christianness. In concluding a homily on the martyr Gordius, for example, the mid-fourth-century Cappadocian bishop Basil of Caesarea explains to his audience, "The account of men who have lived a good life produces, as it were, a light for those who are being kept safe with regard to the road of life." In a separate sermon on the Forty Martyrs of Sebaste, the bishop exhorts, "Bless the martyred sincerely, so that you ... end up being worthy of the same rewards as theirs, without persecution, without fire, without blows."[17] Embracing a similar approach in modern scholarship, though, does not address the event of martyrdom. Martyrdom, clearly, impacts the martyr differently than those who remain, and identity discourse flattens this consequential distinction.

If the martyr is the ideal Christian, however, then it might imply that many Christians would hope, prepare, and seek to become martyrs. A significant thread of scholarship has pursued this implication. The argument that Christians trained for martyrdom is a telling example of the conflation of the martyr and group perspectives on Christian identity. In the early twentieth century, Donald Riddle argued that early Christianity exerted a unique control over Christians that enabled them to undergo suffering.[18] One way, he suggests, was through training, preparation for impending suffering at the hands of the

Roman government.[19] This took place through practices such as the recitation of Scripture but more importantly through the veneration of previous martyrs. He credits church leaders and the writers of martyrologies for valorizing martyrs to such an extent that others were willing to imitate them in death. Riddle concludes from the presence of martyrologies exhorting Christians to martyrdom not only that these martyrologies indicate a large number of Christians-in-training but also that the training impelled many Christians to martyr themselves. While he does not employ identity as an analytical category, he does take for granted the existence of a homogeneous group called Christians. Riddle takes a normative Christianity as the starting point to show why individual Christians became martyrs but talks about these individual Christians only as groups, which reinforces the homogeneity of his starting construct. The homogeneity that serves as Riddle's starting point is no longer fashionable in scholarship, but it remains largely in place behind cursory disclaimers about the diversity of Christian identities.

Recent scholarship has redeemed martyrdom as a normative practice in early Christian self-understanding. Candida Moss explains that "suffering as Christological imitation was not just a passive interpretive move; it was an active practice to which Christians were constantly encouraged."[20] The modern martyrdom training argument is a version of this attempt to normalize the early Christian martyr. As with Riddle's argument, it begins with the assumption that Christian martyrdom was critical to Christian success and tries to posit just how. Maureen Tilley, for example, argues that regular ascetic practices prepared martyrs to remain silent in the face of torturous deaths. She examines an impressive number of martyr stories to suggest that martyrs prepared for martyrdom through such means as denying themselves food and water and practicing a "fugue state" to be able to flee the body in the face of unbearable pain.[21] With exculpatory caveats—"while it is true that exaggeration has a place in these stories" and "of course, Christians had little reason to preserve stories of failure"—she seems to take the stories at face value and with little reference to provenance or context. Without these specifics, the general success of martyrs is assumed, and that success is attributed to a consistent training program.

Presenting martyrdom as the enactment of a public liturgy, Robin Darling Young similarly concludes that martyr texts indicate that early Christian communities underwent an intentional program of training in anticipation of martyrdom. She continues, "Christians expected [martyrdom] and trained for it in the communities where it occurred, and its possibility was proven by the exceptions to the rule, namely those volunteers who buckled under persecution, or who found ways to avoid it."[22] Young makes a case for a chronology of martyrdom in particular places like Asia Minor from Bishops Ignatius and later Polycarp in the second century to Pionius in the third but implies that this developing public liturgy was spreading throughout Christian communities. Her conclusion is paradoxical: "The developing practice of training for martyrdom suggests by its very existence that not many could imitate the ones they admired."[23] This implies that both martyrdoms taking place and martyrdoms not taking place—as well as martyrdoms succeeding or failing—indicate a program of training for martyrdom. Thus, she concludes that the belief in the need for martyrdom training was a "consistent and widespread Christian teaching in the first three centuries of the church."[24]

Nicole Kelley more conservatively suggests that even if martyr texts don't show that Christians prepared for martyrdom, the texts tried to present training as part of a Christian ideal. She also considers—as had Ste. Croix nearly sixty years earlier—that few Christians in the early Christian era were actually threatened with persecution and thus posits "a small number of hearers who viewed themselves as training for martyrdom, as well as a larger number of readers and hearers whose perspective on suffering and Christian identity were shaped quite apart from any desire or opportunity to train for the event of persecution."[25] She acknowledges that martyr texts were used for a variety of different purposes beyond martyrdom training. However, the rest of her article focuses on this "small number" of Christians who, when they did hear or read martyr stories, ostensibly used them in active preparation for their own sufferings. While there is nothing wrong with examining a small group that created a particular type of Christian self-understanding, there is still little basis beyond inferences from the texts for believing that Christians actually did so. It seems prudent to explore the possibilities that these authors were indeed promoting a particular Christian self-understanding, but this says little about the subsequent actions of the text's audience. The continued emphasis on hypothesized groups that could have been the audience of these texts misrepresents their size and status as part of the whole of Christianity.

Kelley makes a broader point about how martyr stories served as "training mechanisms": "They also allowed a much larger group of Christians, who were never in any real danger of martyrdom, to internalize the religious principles exemplified by the martyrs ... the martyr acts may have helped to prepare some of their readers for an untimely death, but more often they changed their hearer's perception of the Christian life."[26] This construction is a distinct step away from direct institutional training for martyrdom. While Kelley's claim is accurate, it is important to reiterate that this is no small paradigm shift. The death of the Christian martyr is redefined as life for the institution and those who remain within it. This is what enables the connection of martyrdom and Christian identity, but we should not lose sight of the critical importance of institutional interpretation in this radical transformation.

Kelley bases much of her exploration on Judith Perkins's book-length work on suffering as critical to Christian identity.[27] Recently, in reaction to the assumption that self-narrated martyr stories such as that of Perpetua are an indication of greater historical accuracy, Perkins argues instead that "the martyr narratives … provide a shared discourse that offers a basis for a Christian group identity … martyrs modeled an ideal subjectivity based on an imitation of Christ, especially his suffering and death. The martyr texts are not individuals' stories, but Christian ones."[28] Rather than a historical account, in other words, Perpetua's story attempts to establish a hierarchically superior Christian group-ness over and against other competing social categories. She surmises that insofar as Christians had access to texts such as these, they would "already possess a script both for their own behavior and for interpretation of their sufferings."[29] However, the next step she takes reifies that "ideal subjectivity" as a group identity, implying that the authors of Perpetua's tale were recording the natural consequences of Christian identity rather than the creation of an ideal subjectivity through the narrative. She concludes that "the martyr narratives suggest that Christians were prepared and trained for martyrdom."[30] As before, this requires the assumption that because narratives like Perpetua's were produced, there must have been broad contemporary Christian audiences actively consuming them, an assumption that is not warranted by the fact of their production. Perkins presents the ideal construction of the martyr as normative Christian identity, first indicating that this was the rhetorical intent of the Perpetua narrative but then accepting it at face value. This step is revealing of the slippage between group constructions of identity and their individual manifestations, a dynamic relationship that is often represented as unidirectional.

She later expands: "Christians believe that their public suffering, their imitation of Christ's death, manifest for their contemporaries to see just how much they trust the power and reality of Christ's promise of an eternal community. Their deaths legitimate their beliefs and likely helped to convince others to follow them."[31] She repeats Tertullian's reference to the blood of martyrs and concludes that "their deaths were powerful testimonies to their commitment, training, and endurance." If "Christians" here refers to the small subset of Christians who would die as martyrs, this makes little practical sense, as the dead clearly no longer believe anything. Yet if this implies all Christians share in the suffering of the martyrs, it participates in erasing the existential difference of the willing suicide. What differentiated those who became martyrs from those who held up martyrdom as an ideal but did not suicide? The implication seems to be that the differentiating variable is found outside an identification with Christianity.

The assumption that martyrdom contributed greatly to Christian success or that martyrdom was widely held as an identity among the ancient Christian populace reaffirms an outdated assumption of a homogeneous early Christianity. It leads us to misunderstand the relationship between the death of martyrs and burgeoning Christianity as well as the institution that would be given the force of the state from the fourth century onward. There is insufficient justification to believe that even a significant minority, much less the majority of Christians, underwent training for martyrdom, particularly given the general consensus that persecution was generally sporadic and spontaneous before the middle of the third century. Outi Lehtipuu refers specifically to the validity of the martyrdom of Perpetua, but her comment is applicable to theories of martyrdom and Christian identity more broadly:

> Deep down, it is a question of how scholars weigh the often inconclusive and indirect historical evidence. Personally, I cannot help but wonder how much the readiness to accept Perpetua's diary as written by the martyr herself has to do with the fact that the majority of scholars working on the text, myself included, represent the western, Christian (or post-Christian) culture which makes Perpetua part of "our" heritage and "our" history. Would the conclusion be different if the Passion of Perpetua were, say, a story of an early Islamic martyr?[32]

Christian martyrdom has the weight of culture behind it, testifying to the success of an institutional Christian inculcation of a perceived "willingness to suffer" to all Christians, but it is reliant on an appropriation of the martyr's death for institutional life.

Some groups of early Christians actively cultivated ideas of persecution, but even for smaller groups the evidence for martyrdoms is similarly thin. In the absence of active persecution, the majority of Christians, marginalized in society though some may have been, were unlikely to pursue active training for death. This argument does more for buttressing the legitimacy of Christian ideology than understanding the phenomenon of martyrdom.

History of the "Pathology Approach"

Meanwhile, the choice to die remains an existential affront capturing our attention. In contemporary culture and scholarship a pathological approach remains a common means to grapple with violent deaths.[33] In the aftermath of mass murder, we question the mental state of the perpetrator; we measure the legitimacy of the lone suicidal death, such as Charles Moore's, against the agent's previous well-being.[34] Critics distinguish "true" Christian martyrdom from these deaths using theological criteria such as reluctance and passivity. These criteria mask concern that a pinnacle of Christian legitimacy be connected with psychological abnormality, and worse, that the religious institution be seen as encouraging the individual's avoidable demise.

Thus, neglecting the existential gap in studies of Christian martyrdom suggests lingering allegiance to the Eusebian theo-historical narrative, which assumes that the crucial factor in the martyr's death was Christianity, both justifying that death and reinforcing Christian legitimacy. Martyrdom as an identity discourse is valuable for understanding institutional Christianity but insufficient to understand the martyr. In the modern era of historical scholarship on early Christianity, numerous scholars challenged the normative Eusebian narrative. While their means of producing an "otherness" to martyrdom requires some correction, it also exposes critical questions that cannot be ignored.

As described above, Eusebius of Caesarea thoroughly integrated martyrs into early Christian history. Through the Middle Ages, early Christian martyrs were continually revered, but the religious tumult of the Reformation ushered in a new era of martyrs.[35] Coinciding with a new ability to distribute print material broadly, the stories of martyrs proliferated. Protestants, Anabaptists, and Catholics grounded martyrdom in the same Scriptures and stories of early Christian martyrs alongside their own "true" martyrs. In likening Queen Elizabeth I to Constantine, martyrologist John Foxe even styled himself as Eusebius in the first edition of his well-known book of martyrs, *Acts and Monuments*.[36] Parroting Eusebian style, Foxe posited an exclusive link between Protestant martyrs and early Christian ones, revealing Protestantism as the legitimate inheritor of Christian belief and the Catholic Church as diabolical persecutors. For Catholics, particularly in Foxe's England, contemporary martyrdom gave new life to traditions of revering early Christian martyrs, who were saints in the tradition.[37] The legacy of the early Christian martyr paradoxically served as guarantor for each side's Christianity. Analyzing this era of martyrdom of

Christians by Christians, Brad Gregory contends, "Martyrs were exceptional in their behavior, but not in their beliefs and values."[38] This claim provides a helpful way to recognize the pathological and identity approaches to Christian martyrdom: the identity approach tends to focus on common Christian beliefs and values while the pathological approach looks to abnormal markers of differentiation.

Edward Gibbon was one of the first modern historians to challenge the Eusebian martyr narrative; we see in his voluminous history the beginnings of a psychosocial approach to martyrdom. Building on his conviction of the "inflexible and intolerant zeal of the Christians," Gibbon suggests that some Christians "blindly sought to terminate a miserable existence by a glorious death," while others sought wealth from the charity of fellow Christians while in prison.[39] For Gibbon, martyrdom is an unfortunate action often taken when dogmatic certainty combines with poor material circumstances. He is skeptical of the ancient sources, particularly Eusebius, concluding that tales of martyrdom abounded as a result of assuming in the Roman Empire of previous centuries "the same degree of implacable and unrelenting zeal which filled their own breasts against the heretics and idolaters of their own times."[40] Critics point out that Gibbon critiques early Christianity according to contemporary standards,[41] yet he also recognizes that people responded differently to the Christian message—most avoiding but some seeking death.

The explicit identification of martyrdom with pathology begins in earnest in the twentieth century. As noted above, Riddle contends that the actions of the martyrs were socially constructed and describes martyrdom as an expression of "social control," blurring the line—as does more recent scholarship—between the agentive martyr and the martyr as a "social type."[42] However, Riddle also suggests that "the discussion of the attitudes which controlled the martyrs necessitates the recognition that in part, at any rate, they were of a psychopathic character."[43] The phenomenon of masochism, he says, was unquestionably present among martyrs and those who retold their gruesome tales. He adds that most martyrs were probably already psychically abnormal, and this abnormality formed a basis upon which a Christian doctrine of persecution was built. Christianity was successful, in other words, because it inculcated a mass psychosis among its followers, many of whom were already vulnerable. The doctrinal and ritual aspects of Christianity related to martyrdom—the celebration of suffering, the retelling of the martyr's tale, the promise of eternal reward—collaborated to produce martyrs. The extant writings from second-century theologian Clement of Alexandria and third-century Bishop Cyprian as well as the reflections of Emperor Marcus Aurelius or the satire of Lucian show that "the pathological desire for martyrdom had considerable currency."[44] Willingness to die was present as a social structure for maintaining loyalty, but as a result of that structure's success was also actualized by many Christians in death. His language appears sensational, yet though (like most) he overestimates the scope of early Christian martyrdom, he clearly identifies and differentiates social and psychological factors in his analysis.

G. E. M. de Ste. Croix's largely individual, psychological approach to martyrdom mounts an indirect critique of the Eusebian narrative as well. As I discussed in the previous chapter, the historian is building a case to suggest that martyrdom was more than a foregone conclusion for Christians, not only because it could be avoided without lasting social repercussions but also because Christians were not sought as relentlessly as the traditional Christian narrative would suggest. Within this argument, he surmises that first-century bishop and would-be martyr Ignatius had "an abnormal mentality" and suggests, like Riddle, that many other martyrs must have had the same.[45] Elsewhere he concludes many had a "pathological yearning for death" that should be further explored.[46] That many Christians avoided martyrdom without significant repercussion begs the question of why others courted death, and Ste. Croix seeks the answer in psychological difference.

Per Ste. Croix's request, other scholars continued to explore the influence of "political and emotional as well as doctrinal" motivations for martyrdom within well-known early Christian martyrdoms.[47] Representative of the controversial field of psychohistory, Seymour Byman, revisits Protestant martyrdoms in the Tudor period, characterizing the martyrdom of John Bradford as a function of internal guilt. Defending against critiques of the psychohistorical approach, Byman contends that twentieth-century psychological tools can be used to assess the past, since despite differences in context, the pressures of guilt and trauma were equally powerful. Further, he argues that "the martyrs themselves deserve our carefully considered attention" in order to counter their "flat, undeveloped characters, villains or saints according to the bent of the scholar."[48] Using Bradford's own writings, Byman recounts the tortured circumstances that led to his wish for death. Protestant doctrine is insufficient to explain Bradford's path, but "the roots of martyrdom can be found in the inner recesses of the martyrs' psyche."[49] Byman's critics argue that early modern martyrs "acted congruently with a culturally contemporary attitude toward death,"[50] though this conclusion, as Byman points out, fails to understand their unique demise. Gregory contends that although "modern psychological theories may be useful," approaches like

Byman's are "dubious," seemingly because they assume too much explanatory power.[51] Gregory agrees that certain early modern martyrs had a "death wish," yet because they wished to die as martyrs, "not simply end their lives," their deaths were not suicides but reflections of "deep religious commitment."[52] However, it is possible (and necessary) to consider the importance of both religious identity and psychosocial difference in an understanding of martyrdom. In other words, deep religious commitment and willing suicide are not mutually exclusive categories.

This scholarship I have categorized as the pathological approach is diverse, yet shares an understanding that martyrdom is not a normative phenomenon, even in Christian history. Thus, while not denying the contribution of religious doctrine or group interaction, this approach seeks the difference of the martyr through a psychosocial lens. In doing so, however, it may appear dismissive of early Christian martyrdoms vis-à-vis an orthodox Christian understanding of martyrdom, and it falls afoul of contemporary cultural standards. In an historical survey of select Western martyrs beginning with Socrates, Lacey Baldwin Smith suggests we need only "peel back the carefully contrived veneer of stereotyped piety and heroism imposed by hagiographers, and we sense the existence of the dark abyss of psychosis: the agony, the courage, and the distorted logic of personalities that have long since passed spiritual hypochondria by and are well on the road to madness."[53] Smith's provocative sentiment epitomizes the potential stigmatization of martyrdom opposed by subsequent scholars of early Christian martyrdom. In contrast, in his read of Bishop Ignatius, Bart Ehrman suggests "one person's pathology … is another person's common sense."[54] Ehrman's statement emblematizes a common retort to the pathological approach. Reacting to pathological "diagnoses" of martyrdom, subsequent scholarship has dismissed psychological approaches to martyrdom as subjective and largely abandoned exploration of the martyr-agent in favor of group identity as the explanation for martyrdom.

Evolution of the "Identity Approach"

"Identity" began to appear in social scientific literature in the mid-twentieth century and gradually seeped into adjacent disciplines.[55] An early example appears in a review of two prominent treatments of early Christian martyrdom. Peter Brown describes a dominant aspect of martyrdom as "a constant inward-going anxiety … to maintain one's identity, and that of one's group, as separate from one's past and one's environment."[56] The concept worked its way into the study of Christianity in the 1980s. Robert Markus contributed to a three-volume series that examines the process by which Christianity gained "consciousness of its own identity as a group visibly set apart from the common run of people."[57] He later describes Christian identity in the post-Constantinian era as grounded in the figure of the early Christian martyr, a link to the now-distant persecutory past.[58] Whereas many early uses of Christian identity were applied to Late Antiquity, however, identity as an analytical framework for early Christian studies has grown exponentially since then and remains a dominant interpretive framework for early Christian phenomena. The editor of the late Ste. Croix's work claims that "identity lies at the heart of the Christian persecutions."[59] Rather than the unusual expression of a minority of Christians, martyrdom here is the seal of Christianness.

The work of Judith Perkins presages this turn toward Christian identity and the integral link to martyrdom. Perkins recognizes that earlier scholarship saw martyrdom as pathology in response to the discrepancy between the relative lack of imperial persecution and the central focus in Christian literature on suffering and death. On the contrary, Perkins argues, the literature mirrors a widespread agreement among Christians that Christianity *was* suffering and death. "Christian emphasis on persecution, *rather than reflecting an actual situation*, reflects instead the place of suffering and death in the shared 'symbolic universe' of second-century Christian society."[60] Her shared symbolic universe resonates with the "Christian identity" of later scholarship. Nonetheless, this shared universe means that individual Christians "did not object to death," and that "contempt for death did, at times, verge on its pursuit."[61] The line between self-understanding as Christian and martyrdom begins to be blurred here; the former suggests a greater susceptibility for the latter.[62]

As the usage of identity has become more widespread, some voices have critiqued its overuse and consequent dilution. Brubaker and Cooper argue that "the social sciences and humanities have surrendered to the word 'identity'" and "that this has both intellectual and political costs."[63] They observe that identity is commonly used in multiple and contradictory ways, expressing sameness within a social group and difference of that group vis-à-vis society as well as flagging the multiple, unique configurations of characteristics within individuals or subgroups.[64] It is difficult to know to which sense of identity the scholar refers, and in order to gesture toward both, it may benefit the scholar not to make careful distinction.

Within the study of early Christianity, Lieu similarly cautions that "Christian identity" is much more tenuous than scholarship indicates; it minimizes the differences across early Christian communities.[65] As the implicit assumption of a universal identity among early Christians is increasingly criticized, one response is to acknowledge the diversity of Christian practice through discussion of "Christianities," not only over time but also contemporaneously.[66] Yet at this level the term functions in conflicting ways, paying lip service to diversity while still implying sameness. As Rebillard and Rüpke note, "Too often the result is a discourse that talks about the fluidity of identities while it simultaneously reifies identities by attributing them to groups (along with agency, interests, and will)."[67] "Identity" or "Christian identities" map phenomena onto the Christian ideological, institutional construct without significant explanation of the scope, location, and function of their influence. Rogers Brubaker and Frederick Coopecaution, "Stipulating that identities are constructed, fluid, and multiple ... leaves us without a rationale for talking about 'identities' at all."[68]

The relationship of martyrdom to identification with Christianity exemplifies the tension inherent in the use of identity. Subsuming martyrdom within Christian identity not only encourages blurring sameness and difference—Christianity and Christianities—but analysis and practice as well. Brubaker and Cooper distinguish categories of practice, which are used "on the ground," and categories of analysis, used by scholars to categorize aspects of culture. They argue that the contemporary use of identity as a category of practice does not necessitate its use as a category of analysis.[69] Use as a category of analysis carries even greater liabilities when there is no corresponding category of practice, as is the case with "identity" in the ancient world. When martyrdom is added as one aspect of Christian identity, it not only reifies "Christian identity"; it transforms martyrdom from a category of practice to a category of analysis, uprooting its essence.

As one illustration, after critiquing the notion of a consistent Christian understanding of martyrdom, Candida Moss instead "treats martyrdom as a set of discursive practices that shaped early Christian identities ... and provided meaning to the experience described by early Christians as persecution."[70] The category of analysis here—martyrdom—equals "a set of discursive practices." Though described as a set of practices, however, martyrdom itself is used as a category of analysis, which is part of a larger category of analysis—"early Christian identities." The similarly ambiguous set of Christian identities is, as noted above, often paradoxically built upon the assumption of a universal Christian identity, which is presumed commensurate with the totality of early Christian experiences.

Moss suggests that martyrdom and early Christian identities are tools for understanding persecution. This is appropriate so long as the goal is for scholars to examine "the experience described by early Christians as persecution," as she explains. The problem lies in forgetting that martyrdom was not understood by early Christians as a form of discourse. It was a social reality, an existential threat, or even a promise of salvation that was embraced by a few and avoided by most others. This discursive paradigm appropriately shifts from the presumption of a singular Christian identity to multifaceted and dynamic manifestations of Christianness, but the analytical value of identity becomes questionable as a result, and martyrdom is separated from the willing suicide with ideological support it is built on.

The strength of the identity paradigm is such that even critiques of its usage tend to reify it. In a review of Perkins's work, Richard Ascough ventures a mild critique of her seeming personification of Christianity. Individuals rose to power, not Christianity, he argues. The goal of examining Christian identity is "to understand the actors themselves, not the label." Yet, in the next breath, Ascough contends that "even the actors themselves had a collective identity ... we can bring back in the terminology of a 'Christian'—as a collective identity marker that houses many 'selves' who make particular claims together."[71] This passage shows the slipperiness of identity, signifying both the uniqueness of the individual actor and the particular characteristics of a collective understanding of self. The boundaries between individual and collective self-understanding are permeable, but without a careful delineation when deployed, identity is an imprecise tool. Ascough argues that "we need to resist reading [martyrdom accounts] through the individualistic lens ... and see how they function as communal stories."[72] This is an attempt to have it both ways, if indeed the goal is to "understand the actors themselves."

Christian identity is often treated as more totalizing than it operates on the ground. "Christian" is not an "either/or" but one among many dynamic aspects of self-understanding.[73] Moss points out that for many early Christian apologetic sources, the "true Christian" and the "true martyr" were inextricable concepts, and "what it means to be Christian ... is to die as a martyr."[74] There is a gap, however, between the sources and the daily lives of all who identified as Christian. For contemporary scholarship to similarly align Christian identity with "martyrdom" reduces the diversity of identity and ignores martyrdom's signification of an existential turning point, not only in Christianity but also in historical and contemporary cultural understanding. As I have explained, the power of martyrdom does not lie first in identification with Christianity but in its finalizing of all potentiality in suicide. How that finalization is achieved cannot be found in religious identity; it must be sought in the individuals—each with a multifaceted identity—who undertook the act.

Critiquing the Approaches

Moss rightly suggests that much scholarship on early Christian martyrdom is invested in the same distinctions between orthodox and heterodox martyrdoms that early Christian sources were. She contends that modern scholars, taking their cues from ancient writers, simply assumed the legitimacy of a distinction between what she calls normative martyrdom and voluntary martyrdom. However, modern scholarship developed this categorization further, stigmatizing voluntary martyrdom as "unnatural."

> It is the discourse of natural law that shaped suicide and, consequently, voluntary martyrdom as "unnatural" ... it betrays a commitment to a particular construction of normality, to an assumption that it is natural to want to live and that to desire otherwise is an aberration, a sign of mental dysfunction. This desire to diagnose and alienate the other is part of an assumption of self-normalcy.[75]

The implications of this argument are twofold: first, it suggests that seeing self-preservation as normative or "natural" is misguided; second, it implies that because cultural constructions of normalcy *can* be used for self-justification, it is "inappropriately pejorative" to describe martyrdom as an aberration.[76]

Criticizing the link between martyrdom and abnormality by scholars of the pathological approach requires equating a psychological discourse with a moral judgment. Moss implies that explaining martyrdom as aberrant behavior is making a moral claim. (She ironically—if making any moral claims is problematic—follows this with a moral claim of her own about this being "inappropriately pejorative.") While it is likely that some previous scholars were intending a moral distinction in labeling martyrs as unnatural or abnormal; that does not mean that any examination of martyrdom as nonnormative behavior constitutes a misguided moral critique. Just as scholars can wield pathology to dismiss aspects of Christian practice as aberrant, others can harness identity to uncritically normalize them.

Insofar as martyrdom is defined by death, it is impossible for it to be part of Christian identity. At the very point of martyrdom, the consummation of "martyr" as identity, the subject ceases to exist. As I have argued, it is simultaneously the assertion and finalization of the self. This is not a mere semantic point; rather, it cuts to the heart of martyrdom's relationship with the Christian tradition as well as the difficulty of the scholar to identify it. When we study the relationship between Christian martyrdom and Christianity, we should attend to the distinction between the individual Christian and institutional Christianity. To the extent that the individual Christian recognizes martyrdom as Christian, it is through the lens of a tradition. The individual's understanding of Christian martyrdom is mediated, and as the individual cannot identify with martyrdom itself, what she is actually identifying is something different, something that envisions the possibility of martyrdom, perhaps, but will not experience it. Thus, when we speak of martyrdom as a part of Christian identity, what we are expressing in the individual is a felt willingness to suffer for—or to prevent a transgression of—Christianness. Verifying willingness to suffer unto death can only be completed in death.

The difficulty of establishing an essential link between martyrdom and individual Christian identity can be illustrated practically in that the overwhelming majority of Christians who have ever lived have not been martyrs. Only a minuscule amount of the number of individuals who have identified as Christian have attempted willing suicide for Christianity, and an even fewer number have succeeded, both in the attempt and in being recognized by the Christian institution for such. If martyrdom were essentially bound with Christian identity, if to be the paradigmatic Christian was to be a martyr, one would expect high numbers of martyrs throughout history. In fact, the mischaracterization of martyrdom's role has long led to estimations of the number of Christian martyrs beyond the available evidence.[77] As mentioned, a low number of martyrs was actually necessary for Christianity to thrive as an institution, despite the implications of Tertullian's well-known rhetorical argument. If number of Christians did end their lives in martyrdom, Christianity would have minimal chance of success, both because of continuing institutional viability and individual disinterest in dying prematurely. As Ernest Becker and Terror Management theorists argue, the fear of death has driven the creation of much of what we label civilization, and any existing institution needs a thriving base with investment in the temporal circumstances of its existence.

This is not to deny that many Christians have seen martyrs as important for Christianity or have perceived martyrdom itself as a future possibility. As noted, this is based to a certain extent not only on narrative necessity but also on existential validity. In a historical sense the death of Jesus necessitated a reevaluation of his message and a justification of his death not as a thwarting but a fulfillment of his mission and message.[78] This embedded the death into the fabric of what would become Christianity. Existentially, death represents both the potentiality and the finality of life, the limit point at which the agent exhausts herself and the lens through which the rest of us assess her life. There are people throughout history who, by all accounts, have died in keeping with or in support of their convictions.[79] However, martyrdom and Christian identity converge in the individual only in passing. If we are to proceed with the normative idea that one can be a Christian without becoming a martyr, we must acknowledge the presence of some other element in the successful martyr that is not present, at least in sufficient quantity, in the vast majority of Christians.

One other possibility is that martyrdom is the whole of Christian identity; in other words, that to be Christian is to die, and to continue to exist is to have not become fully Christian. This for obvious reasons is an unpopular argument, but it may be more logically coherent. Robert Brimlow argues that the most Christian response to violence is to die, although he doubts his own ability to do so. In the end, however, he implies a spectrum of Christian practice with the martyr as the highest ideal, essentially returning to the default understanding of martyrdom and identity but with consciousness of his inability to measure up. He concludes that "the main difficulty in accepting the implications of our call [as Christians] to be peacemakers is our fear of death and dying."[80] A much more common approach is to affirm the martyr while denying the existential importance of the death. Johan Leemans writes, "It is not the event of the death per se but rather the martyr's disposition and testimony of faith that attracts and fascinates people."[81]

From a theological perspective, the seeming difference of the martyr is easily solvable. Martyrdom is only necessary as the circumstances require it. "The martyr acts almost unanimously declare that it is God who prepares the way for martyrdom."[82] If God willed the death of the individual Christian, that death was necessary; if not, it was not. Following this logic, the "martyrdom" that is embedded in Christian identity is a willingness of the agent to suffer that is, on occasion, chosen by the divine to be fulfilled in death. This criterion of divine compulsion, of course, is immeasurable, and the functional result for the individual Christian is an ability both to identify and not identify with martyrdom at the same time. By positing that one would be willing to die given the need to do so, one can continue to live as a martyr. The unlikelihood of a martyr's death for the vast majority of Christians allows for a charitable stance in self-assessing willingness to suffer.

Divine compulsion is immeasurable since there are no empirically verifiable signifiers to discern legitimate martyrdom. Even within Christianity, though, there is no readily apparent signifier of the presence of divine compulsion. Such a signifier had to be manufactured to demarcate the "true" Christian martyrdom and did not always match the body of evidence. In decrying voluntary martyrdom as suicide, for example, Augustine excepted past suicides by Christian women to preserve their chastity as have likely been the result of "divine wisdom" (*City of God*, 1.26). For lack of directly visible markers, a "preparedness" as displayed by outward disposition became the ideal for the "true" martyr and overeagerness a telling sign of alternative, selfish motives, shown as early as the martyrdom of Polycarp. Passivity and indifference toward suffering before and in death were taken as hallmarks of the "true" martyr. Since there is no necessary correlation between actions prior to death and the justification of that death, we should not accept those criteria, at least on theological grounds alone, even apart from the fact that a number of lauded ancient Christian martyrdoms do not meet the orthodox criteria.

A Different Way Forward

The identity approach to early Christian martyrdom highlights the importance of social meaning-making in interpreting early Christian texts. Thus it provides one justification for the perceived gap between early Christian textual rhetoric about martyrdom and its historical occurrence. Martyrdom represents a "discourse" or a "symbolic universe." With this move, however, early Christian martyrdom scholarship cannot answer the question that drove many scholars of the pathological approach, animates our universal fascination with martyrdom, and is of pressing concern today: What motivates a few to willingly give up their lives when so many who share the same identity do not?

Insofar as we understand evolutionary and sociocultural imperatives—including religious ones—to ordinarily drive us toward continued existence,[83] we should see any human activity in which one willingly gives up life as extraordinary. Foucault remarks that all the modern sciences of the mind are rooted in a process of individualization based on deviations from the normal.[84] The naming of these deviations is a means of power and can, as identity scholars have recognized, be wielded as an implicit (or explicit) tool of moral judgment. Moral judgment is also a means of power; it requires but is not commensurate with analysis. In response to the pathological approach, however, identity scholarship on early Christian martyrdom has avoided the agent almost entirely and, when unavoidable, made the individual a reflection of Christian identity.

The ostensible institutional purpose for which one dies has until recently been more accessible than the agent's psychological state. This fact should not preclude examining the difference of martyrs to the extent we have the tools to do so. While scholarship on ancient martyrdom faces obvious challenges to exploring the psychology of the early Christian martyr, contemporary research on motivations for martyrdom provides insights that warrant consideration. Post et al. contend that isolated psychological explanations are insufficient to understand suicide terrorism, yet remind that "we are left with the disquieting question of why among large numbers of people exposed to a common environment, only a few become suicide terrorists."[85] They suggest further research around low self-esteem, grief, and despair as contributing factors (while noting these need not be pathological) and conclude that continued research need to be multidisciplinary and collaborative to account for political, sociocultural, and psychological factors that contribute to willingness to kill and be killed.[86] Bélanger, Caouette, Sharvit, and Dugas do not find correlations between expressions of psychopathy, depression, suicide ideation, or fatalism and willingness to self-sacrifice; however, they do find positive correlations between willingness to self-sacrifice and neuroticism (one of the "Big Five" personality dimensions), antisocial tendencies, and willingness to engage in extreme means to achieve goals. Building on Viktor Frankl's notion of self-transcendence, they propose possible connections between a search for personal significance and willingness to self-sacrifice.[87] It is critical to note that there is an unbridgeable existential gap between willingness to die and the martyr. However, it is entirely different to decry any application of modern psychosocial means to illuminate martyrdom of the ancient past.

It should be clear that psychological or even genetic factors cannot constitute the full explanation for martyrdom, or even suicide more broadly. Thomas Joiner suggests that

> mental illness alone does not provide a satisfying explanation for suicide, because mental illness is much more common for suicide. How should we explain all those people with mental illness who do not die by suicide? ... Though it is rare for people without mental illness to die by suicide, it occasionally happens—a fact that an explanation centered around mental illness cannot account for.[88]

Limited research has suggested that genetic factors may play a role as well, independent of propensity for mental illness. Identical twin studies suggest a higher concordance for suicide than nonidentical twins. Other research has shown a correlation between lower serotonin levels and high-lethality suicide attempts, and potential correlation between particular genotypes related to the serotonin-regulating system and increased risk for suicide.[89] While it is impossible to conduct such research on past suicides, it would be irresponsible to dismiss the possible role of psychological, neurobiological, or genetic differences that would convey a higher likelihood of susceptibility for willing suicide with ideological support.

That some early Christians chose martyrdom is certain. The primordial question regarding martyrdom is not why it occurs within a particular institutional context, though, but why it occurs at all. Since the institution of Christianity has persisted to the present, and because of a past illuminated by the Eusebian narrative, recent scholarship has located martyrdom's meaning in a developing Christian identity discourse. To focus only on Christianity to understand martyrdom, even "Christian" martyrdom, is to put together a puzzle without all the pieces, and to insist on this line of inquiry is one indicator that it reinforces an ideological end.

The alternative is not stigmatization or moral judgment of the martyr. Recognizing the comparative uniqueness of the martyr's action opens the door to further research—in the Christian tradition as in other traditions—on the interplay of psychosocial factors that lead to the martyr's death. At the same time, moral questions cannot be avoided, and they are implicit in all contestations over the validity of martyrdom. This is why it is critical for martyrdom scholarship not simply to reaffirm notions of group identity, as if each tradition and time period has exclusive, incomparable means for producing martyrs.

The study of ancient Christian martyrdom is pertinent for the present. It can both benefit from and provide benefit to the contemporary study of martyrdom through a nuanced psychosocial approach that incorporates explorations of individual difference within the processes of group identity formation and maintenance. Such an approach begins with the understanding that martyrdom represents a complex, inextricable part of Christian history from the death of Jesus forward and yet signifies an individual act—willing suicide—that most Christians did not choose.

This is not important just for scholarship; there is a moral imperative here as well. The degree to which individuals or groups believe in persecution and death as part of or as a result of group identification impacts (albeit not exclusively) willingness to participate in acts of violence, martyrdom being one point along this continuum.[90] For example, as Jason Bruner notes, "Given how directly some calls for saving persecuted Christians seem to result in military interventions, one wonders whether the blood of today's martyrs may be the seed of American imperialism."[91] There exists a propensity within Christianity as with other religious traditions, founded as they are on universal claims, for acts of violence to act as self-fulfilling prophecy. This was the case in the first centuries of Christianity, and it is the case today. It is the responsibility of scholars of Christianity to represent the roles of violent acts like martyrdom accurately, and a small part of this is by disambiguating the connection between martyrdom and Christian identity.

7

The Immorality of Religious Martyrdom

If, as I have argued, there is no essential link between willing suicide and the Christian institution, but rather the power of the death is appropriated to authenticate the tradition, then the circumstances of that appropriation should be further scrutinized. Additionally, if following the previous chapter we see willing suicides with ideological support as reflective not of ideological validity but including a degree of psychological abnormality, we are confronted with the concerning nexus of institutional power enacted to leverage individual vulnerability for its own gain. This, then, is not only a neutral exploration but also a moral question: ought institutions use suicides—whose acceptance of institutional premises cannot be extricated from psychosocial factors—to indirectly substantiate their existence? Further, should scholars studying Christian martyrdom reproduce this cycle, affirming this exchange by examining willing suicide as a function of institutional identity?

In post-9/11 America, violence has increasingly been the topic of recent debates over religion. As discussed in Chapter 3, some have argued that violence is intrinsic to religion, or particular religions. Others have shifted the debate by arguing either that the bad actors are not truly religious or that the violence seemingly caused by religion is actually a product of economic, social, and political factors.[1] Still others have argued that religious justifications for violence are as acceptable as secular ones provided their premises are accepted.[2] There are few modern scholarly arguments that violence, as religious violence, is justified. So why are we in at least tacit agreement that religious violence is wrong?

To take 9/11 as a twenty-first-century example, one might say the violence was wrong because it took large numbers of innocent (i.e., noncombatant) lives. That response doesn't take into account the motivations of the attackers, but against how many and whom they were perpetrated. In other words, there is nothing particularly religious about that objection. It further seems indefensible to establish an arbitrary number of deaths above which an action becomes morally culpable. More importantly, the United States frequently takes innocent lives, and the distinction between intended targets and collateral damage has limited moral salience, particularly when it occurs repeatedly. Regardless, this gives no justification to single out violence whose source is at least partially religious.

How does religion specifically contribute to the immorality of the violence? One might argue it is because the religious motivations of the attackers are not shared by all; in other words, there is an imposition of belief—or an imposition of actions based upon that belief—on an unwilling group. The wrongness of this imposition seems obvious in any liberal system that prioritizes individual liberty and a fundamental right to life. However, the imposition of particular beliefs, whether imposed by a majority on a minority or vice versa, is not unique to religion; it is rather a common function of institutional life. Is there something uniquely wrong about violence insofar as it emanates from religion? I argue there is, and that we can make that claim without also claiming that religion is inherently bad or that religion is the source of all violence. Such an argument must begin before manifestations of religious violence, however. If we've agreed that our moral mechanisms for judging the morality of violence are not limited to religion, we must try to pinpoint what religion brings to the table.

Hector Avalos claims that unlike most other institutions, religion is based on unverifiable premises.[3] The conclusions of religious institutions may follow logically from the premises, but the premises cannot be tested. These premises may be explicit or implicit. Take the following example:

1. God commands adulterers to be stoned.
2. We must obey God.
3. Therefore we must stone adulterers.

In this logic are both the implicit, unverifiable premise that God exists and the explicit, unjustified premise that God must be obeyed. With those two premises granted, it does make logical sense to stone adulterers, but the premises must first be defensible. They can be defended only by begging the question. So, for example:

1. I was told that if I prayed to receive x, God would grant me x.
2. I prayed to receive x, and I did receive x.
3. God granted me x.

In this scenario, because the individual was instructed to expect divine intervention upon supplication, the receipt of something subsequent to requesting it is taken as evidence of the existence (and beneficence) of a divine entity. It should go without saying that the receipt of "x" does not substantiate the existence of such a being; "x" could have come from a number of other sources. However, concluding that receiving something after praying for it proves the existence of a divine entity can then be taken as evidence of (the unstated premise of) that entity's existence in actions commanded by it, as in the first example. Belief in unverifiable premises—valorized as faith—is not inherently wrong, but actions based upon these unverifiable premises are unjustifiable for those who do not share faith in them and cannot find alternative justification. Insofar as this prohibits cooperation or promotes partiality, these factors should not enter into any social moral calculus.

Joshua Greene describes morality as the set of psychological adaptations that promote group cooperation for mutual benefit.[4] Following this definition, religious violence can theoretically function within groups by placing the importance of the group over that of the individual. So long as all those within the group accept the same unverifiable premises, all within the group willingly subject themselves to the explicit and implicit consequences of those premises. (Of course, this is not how religions actually function. Far more people are born into religion rather than freely choosing it. As one recent text critical of religious indoctrination puts it, "Religion is a system of belief and a way of life dictated by that belief that a child is forced to adopt without understanding of the implications behind it."[5]) What can be done, though, when a group attempts to use unverifiable premises to govern interactions *between* groups? Insofar as these groups impose consequences for not accepting the implications of their unverifiable premises upon a group that does not accept those premises, they operate immorally.

Avalos concludes that because violence based upon religion must necessarily be based upon these unverifiable premises, it is always immoral.[6] There may be very few cases where we can successfully isolate a case of purely religious violence, and it would be artificial to do so. This is part of the problem, because it is also difficult to exculpate religion as a factor in violence where it is plausibly implicated without resorting to categorical separations of violence from religion. If to the extent that religion causes violence, that violence is necessarily unethical because it is based on unverifiable premises, it behooves us to remove religious justification from intergroup social interaction as much as possible. In other words, the answer is not to dismiss the connection between religion and violence through the unverifiable stipulation that religion cannot cause violence, nor is it to hold out hope that the elimination of religion is tantamount to the elimination of violence. It is to say that we are morally obligated to remove what Greene calls tribalism from (or reconfigure it for) intergroup interaction.

There is another notable conclusion here. The existence of religionists who do things we deem morally good or bad says nothing conclusive as to the inherent nature of the tradition. However, because the most fundamental tenets of religious belief are unverifiable, any intergroup violence taken based upon these beliefs is immoral, not simply because another group doesn't agree to the premises but because as a result violence cannot maximize the well-being of all involved. To the extent that religious institutions do promote good on an intergroup level, that good must necessarily be identified as such on the basis of publicly accepted criteria. As Barack Obama noted, "Democracy demands that the religiously motivated translate their concerns into universal, rather than religion-specific, values."[7] To put it another way, there is no common good found only in one social institution (such as Christianity) or subset (such as religion).

Thus, when we look at the 9/11 attacks, to return to our previous case, what should be morally relevant is not only that large numbers of "innocents" were killed but also that violent actions were justified at least partly on the basis of unverifiable evidence: that the attackers were carrying out attacks against "infidels" in accordance with the will of Allah and as a result had hope of martyrdom.[8] Clearly there are many points along the chain of reasoning where people might disagree with the sentiments expressed by the attackers, including with the existence/legitimacy of any supernatural entity, the existence/legitimacy only of a particular one such as Allah, or only specifically of the legitimacy of violence in the particular case. Yet there is no mutually accessible basis upon which to measure those disagreements. Compare this to the history of American intervention in the Middle East that contributed to the motivations for 9/11 or the subsequent "war on terror," the violence involved in which is also questionable. The difference between the 9/11 attacks and the subsequent actions, however, is that the evidence based on which the United States ostensibly invaded Afghanistan was *able* to be verified. It is now commonly understood that the evidence was often not verified, or it was lied about,[9] and the violence that occurred as a result was, in terms of sheer numbers, much greater than the original attacks.[10] It was possible to verify the information, though, and if for example we had verified that Iraq had weapons of mass destruction, or had the government made the lack of evidence for that conclusion public, there could have been an informed conversation about whether or not invasion with its consequent violence was a justified response. The violence in this case was not wrong because of its scope but because it was based on faulty premises. In the case of religion it is not even possible to verify the premises.

Hector Avalos argues that because religious violence is violence based on unverifiable premises, it is "even more tragic than nonreligious violence."[11] There are no criteria to indicate that the manifestations of religious violence are comparatively worse than other types. Insofar as one believes that violence is sometimes necessary to maximize well-being impartially, the question of violence turns on its justification. Religious violence is always wrong because it is inherently unjustifiable.

Criteria for Martyrdom

As I have repeatedly noted, sacrificing oneself for something greater is the commonest understanding of martyrdom. I have suggested instead that we understand martyrdom as willing suicide with ideological support. Willing suicide is not self-sacrifice from the perspective of the agent but self-formation. In order to suggest that the institutional promotion of martyrdom is immoral, it is helpful to delineate necessary criteria for promoting martyrdom. Delineating these criteria helps us make categorical—and consequently moral—distinctions between willing suicide, martyrdom, and the promotion of martyrdom. Even if one believes that suicide under some or all conditions is immoral, it would be naïve to think our efforts at preventing it would be best directed toward increasing stigmatization of the act itself,[12] particularly if this precludes applying a critical eye to institutions that benefit from claiming the willing suicide as their own. A primary reason for my work thus far has been to reframe the conversation around martyrdom in order to bring to light both how the willing suicide is institutionally promoted and how it is captured, so we can judge the morality of such a transaction.

The most fundamental criterion of martyrdom, of course, is the death. Without a death, there can be no martyr, though there certainly can be persecution and suffering. The death represents an important existential difference. The agent certainly may project his own martyrdom, but this projection is contingent upon the agent's being, which ends simultaneously with the beginning of martyr status. Death is a necessary criterion for martyrdom, but it is obviously not sufficient. Thousands of people die every day, and certainly very few of those are considered candidates for martyrdom.

One additional criterion for the martyr is willingness. As I have noted elsewhere, we do not consider the vast majority of deaths martyrdom in part because there is no indication of volition. The ideal martyrdom is one where the voluntariness of the death is made explicit in the death process. This is particularly apparent in early Christian martyr stories where the would-be martyr is given an explicit opportunity to renounce her belief. The would-be martyr's refusal symbolizes willingness to die. The active display of unwillingness, on the other hand, excludes one from martyrdom. In such cases where a willingness to die is not explicit, this volition must be inferred to create the martyr. It is impossible for the martyr to be named in the presence of unwillingness to die.

Before justifying the necessity of willingness to die for martyrdom, we need to establish what constitutes willingness to die. What are its necessary criteria? It is important to note that the institutional understanding of willingness to die is necessarily different from the individual perspective. Again, according to the commonest understanding of martyrdom, the martyr sacrifices him or herself for something else. For the institution naming and claiming the martyr, "something" must be either the institution or those entities and ideals it signifies. For the institution, willingness to die can consist of only one criterion: given circumstances in which the agent must choose between life and the institution (or its signifieds), the agent chooses to die. This criterion is not satisfied by an acceptance of death whenever it should arrive, because this does not express willingness to die in the particular. Acceptance of death as a possibility and inevitability and willingness to die are not the same. The martyr must have been willing to die under the circumstances of his or her death.

The necessity of willingness to die becomes most evident when its presence is not overt in a particular account, for it must be inferred. The inference of willingness to die can be seen in the well-known case of Cassie Bernall, who died at the hands of Eric Harris in the Columbine massacre in 1999. She quickly gained renown as a Christian martyr because she was believed to have explicitly affirmed her belief in God before being killed by Harris.[13] Subsequent evidence has shown that although Bernall may have been praying at the time of her death, Harris asked another girl a question about her faith and her response was misattributed to Bernall.[14] The evidence is taken seriously by her community, not because it calls Bernall's character into question but because her statement was thought to be clear evidence of willingness to die.[15] While not an explicit choice, the question of faith was thought, modeled after early Christian accounts, to have been posed as a life-or-death test. Adding to this uncertainty was the fact that the girl to whom the question was actually posed,

Valeen Schnurr, was not killed and had been shot earlier, not subsequent to the question asked her.

The key is that without Bernall's volition as evidenced by her statement, a necessary criterion for martyrdom is missing. As noted, it is possible in many cases for volition to be inferred when we have no record of the circumstances surrounding the death. This is true in the case of Alan Henning, a humanitarian aid worker delivering relief supplies to Syria and killed by ISIS. Henning was intentional not because he explicitly affirmed religious belief but because he was aware of the risks of his mission. Similarly, remarking on the deaths of journalists James Foley and Steven Sotloff at the hands of ISIS, the Committee to Protect Journalists noted, "Journalists know that covering war is inherently dangerous and that they could get killed in crossfire."[16] Both journalists were claimed as martyrs by their respective families.[17] While certainly neither wished to perish in horrific fashion, both needed to be aware of the situation they were in. While obviously not a sufficient justification for martyrdom, willingness to die is a necessary criterion.

The criterion of willingness to die might seem counterintuitive given the ideal of Christian martyrdom. Though it was contested, the emerging ideal of the Christian martyr from the second century forward was that one did not actively seek martyrdom or give the opposition cause for retaliation but did not shrink from the opportunity when presented. There were significant theological and practical reasons for this ideal, but they are not indicators of unwillingness to die. Moderating zeal is not the same as being unwilling, and had any candidate for martyrdom been unwilling, he or she usually could have taken opportunities for escaping when they presented themselves. The logic of Clement of Alexandria and subsequent apologists did not introduce unwillingness to die but attempted to specify those conditions that constituted a legitimate choice between life and the institution.

The cases of Bernall, Henning, Foley, and Sotloff point to the simplest types of evidence for willingness to die. The simplest evidence is the invocation of the institution or its signifieds by the agent. Both Thich Quang Duc, a well-known Buddhist immolator during the Vietnam War, and Charles Moore mentioned earlier wrote letters before death with specific invocations. Thich Quang Duc wrote a letter to his foreign-supported Catholic president calling for an ethic of love to prevail over the violence against Buddhists.[18] Acting alone, Moore left a letter for family and friends indicating that he was dismayed over not having done enough to change prevailing social oppression in the areas he lived. He hoped to inspire social justice through his death.[19] In both cases, others have further interpreted the meaning given by the agent. In the invocation of an ideal state, the agent indicates an alternate social environment. Thich Quang Duc implied a country in which Buddhists were not persecuted by the government, and Moore invoked a state where racism, biased incarceration, and homophobia had been mitigated or eradicated. In the case of affirming the supernatural, the agent's death is correlated with the existence and control of such a being. Ideally this is through the agent's communication prior to death. This provides credible corroborating evidence for the institution to name and claim the martyr.

In the absence of invocation by the would-be martyr, such information can be inferred. The simplest form of inference is group affiliation. Christianity is highly sensitive to the possibility of martyrdom and takes little confirmation to infer martyrdom. In the pre-information age, symbolic meaning given by the agent him or herself was more easily fabricated and group affiliation was rarely used as the sole justification of an institutional claim. An exception to this would be in martyrdom as a legal transaction when the meaning of the death was easily inferred from the actions of the persecuting party. Still in most of these cases, the would-be martyr expresses through bodily or verbal action the meaning of the impending death.

In more recent years, however, mere group affiliation can potentially serve as candidacy for meaning, if for no other reason than in the absence of affirmation by the agent it is increasingly difficult to fabricate. Alan Henning was claimed as a martyr by his religious and national community, though no one believes he invoked either his nation or his religion in his death. In this case, because he was admirably attempting to provide humanitarian aid, which is seen as a laudable action, both nation and religious tradition sought to recoup that action for their respective institutions.

Mere group affiliation is an initially fragile substitute for meaning-making completed by the agent and is thus easily contested. In the case of Cassie Bernall, the impetus for martyrdom was not simply her membership in the Christian community, although in the wake of her death, her family could certainly name her as a martyr. Her candidacy for martyrdom gained traction because of her purported affirmation of Jesus Christ immediately prior to death. There are many other factors that allowed this inference of course. An active persecution complex within Christianity plays a significant role, and one that had the ability to affect all parties involved. There were multiple emotional and psychological triggers involved as well: that children were targeted, that children were *doing* the targeting, that the killing seemed to be random, and so forth. All of these indicators flying in the face of norms for making meaning lead to desperation.

Christian affiliation facilitates an easy meaning-making opportunity. The tragedy can be recast as an echo of a much larger and ongoing cosmic battle over which larger forces ultimately have control.

In the case of Henning, we have no record of the moments preceding death, which increases the difficulty of claiming martyrdom. His death at the hands of ISIS might be seen as martyrdom both because of his affiliation with Christianity and his de facto opposition to ISIS as an extremist religious group. However, given that he wasn't engaging in explicit religious activity (evangelism, distribution of Bibles, etc.), other groups might contest his martyr status because the institution threatens to assume the totality of the death's meaning. The unspoken assumption in this case would be that Christianity provided the impetus for his charity. Those contesting this assumption would also contest the institutional affiliation through martyrdom.

Even invocation by the agent is open to question as well. The Columbine massacre again provides the most poignant example. Given that the tragedy was not a single death, but multiple, any attribution of martyrdom inevitably invites comparison with the other murdered students, who presumably were not martyred and thus were not institutionally meaningful in the way that Bernall was. This assumption was brought into the light when survivors, including the girl right next to Bernall, disagreed that she had indeed invoked God immediately before death.[20] As mentioned, this called Bernall's willingness to die into question, but it also exposed that her status of martyrdom—and difference from the other students who had died—was founded primarily on her fragile statement. It was also supported by the assumption that the killers, who had already been demonized in order to understand their actions, were specifically targeting Christians.[21] This was also questioned when it was understood that the student who actually affirmed her religious belief was not killed. The powerful meaning-making function of naming martyrs was displayed, then, in the vacuum created by loss of its meaning.

So far we have established two apparently necessary criteria for martyrdom: death and willingness to die. However, these are not themselves sufficient for martyrdom. Social interaction at the time of death is also a necessary component for martyrdom. This excludes a large majority of suicides that are not enacted publicly and points to the notion that the martyr's death was intended to have social meaning. There are two possible types of social interaction. In the first and most common the would-be martyr is acting directly with an opposing party, as in the case of persecutor and persecuted. This provides an "audience" for martyrdom, which could consist of only the persecutor or others as well. It also has the benefit of most easily verifying willingness to die, because it involves interaction between the parties, as in early Christian martyrdoms or the earliest story of Cassie Bernall.

In other cases, the would-be martyr is simply acting before an audience, one that is neutral or simply fulfilling the role of social interaction. John Chau would seem to fall into this category. Either way, a clear indicator of martyrdom is supposed to be whether the death was enacted by another or the self. If the latter, it was not martyrdom but suicide. This criterion attempts to prevent willingness to die in the absence of conditions deemed sufficient by the institution and indicates awareness of the distinction between the agent and the institution in terms of the death's meaning. I have argued that the presence or absence of an opposing agent, a persecutor, indicates at most a difference in subtype of suicide and not a categorical distinction between suicide and martyrdom. Despite this criterion, in any case, Christian and other institutional martyrdoms have been named without fulfilling the criterion of being directly enacted at the hands of a persecutor.

Unquestionably the process of naming and claiming the martyr is more complicated when the death is not directly enacted by an opposing party, not only because of the moral valuation of suicide but also because of the biological inclination toward preservation. In many cases, though, the death process is enacted either by the agent or assisted by his or her community. As noted, during the Vietnam War Buddhist monk Thich Quang Duc drove with a group of fellow monks to a busy intersection in Saigon and sat in the lotus position in the center of the street. His friends poured gasoline over him and lit him on fire. He was hailed by some as a martyr for protesting the Vietnam War and prompted others to imitate his death. Others, of course, decried the death as suicide. Charles Moore likewise drove himself to a strip mall parking lot in his hometown in Texas and lit himself ablaze.

These cases differ in important respects from most suicides. One way is they were played out—and were intended to be played out—before an audience. In addition, both would-be martyrs provided evidence of the circumstances that their deaths were enacted against. In order to become martyrs, however, the justifications have to be verified by and amenable to the institution. This is not a question of whether there is a prohibition against suicide, as noted above, but whether the circumstances for willingness to die are amenable to the continuance of the institution.

Even with willingness to die culminating in death in a social setting, the necessary requirements for martyrdom are not met. The most critical component is the institutional claim in response to a perceived threat. This is the most critical component because it is the only necessary and sufficient condition for martyrdom. The institutional claim is a sufficient condition because, given a desire to claim a martyr, all other necessary criteria could theoretically be fabricated. Classical myth as well as religious tradition likely abound with such partially or wholly fabricated tales, and most historical research on martyrdom has been dedicated to separating the factual from the fictional. These martyrdoms only work to the extent that they artfully simulate or document the other criteria mentioned. In an age of unprecedented availability and speed of information, modern martyrdoms may struggle to live up to the standard of early or medieval Christian ones, many of which emphasized extraordinary aspects of the death, which in turn seemingly provided evidence for supernatural involvement.

This is not to say that all other phenomena are necessarily wholly fabricated, that martyrdom could exist without any willing suicide in a social setting having ever taken place. I consider this to be possible but highly unlikely. It is in fact the danger of an exclusive focus on martyrdom as an identity discourse, which tends to forget the death itself and the existential fascination it demands in substantiating such a discourse. However, it is also clear that a single story of martyrdom, particularly that of a founding figure, can do a tremendous amount of work simply in its frequent and dynamic retelling.

The notion of perceived threat aligns well with resource scarcity, upon which Avalos founds most justifications of religious violence.[22] If there is a real or perceived scarcity of resources, this threatens survival. Fear of scarcity leverages our biological imperative to survive and thrive and indirectly a need to protect institutions that, for adherents, are also necessary for that survival. In such cases, violence is more readily justifiable because the alternative is extinction. As violence is often a comparatively efficient way, in the short term, of reaching institutional goals, it is unsurprising that in addition to real scarcity of resources, manufacturing scarcity is a common institutional tactic. In fact, it is inevitable when the viability of the institution is threatened. Avalos critiques religious institutions in particular here because their claims of resource scarcity, unlike many others, are unverifiable. While we can objectively investigate whether the water supply of a given community is poisoned, for example, we cannot verify through empirical means claims that it was cursed by supernatural agents from a rival community. In the absence of such means of verification, we cannot condone violence.

Thus the component of the institutional claim is flexible. Most explorations of martyrdom have attempted to explain the phenomenon around the institutional claim. Insofar as this sheds light on the nature of institutions in general or in the particular, this can be helpful. The problem is that martyrdom is taken to signify the would-be martyr as well. However, it is not the institution itself that is determinative of martyrdom but the institution's claim. If it were the cause alone that made the martyr, observances of martyrdom would be regular and predictable among martyr-making institutions. Clearly religious institutions that claim martyrs must describe an essential relationship between martyrs and the institution, but this relationship is a general one. The naming and claiming of martyrdom has nothing to do with the specific content of the institution or its signifieds but the type of content on which the institution is founded.

The irregularity of martyrdom within institutional ranks should be the clearest indicator that the institution itself has no necessary causal relationship with the martyr's death. It is clear then that the definition of martyrdom as a sacrifice is insufficient to describe the institutional relationship with the martyr and does not even approach an understanding of the agent before death. We can explore the distinction between the individual and institutional understandings of martyrdom. However, with the institutional claim we have sufficient criteria to describe martyrdom. I have suggested that martyrdom from the perspective of the individual actor is willing suicide with ideological support. From the institutional perspective, martyrdom is the social representation of an individual death that is institutionally meaningful, substantiated by the following components: a real or manufactured death, a real or manufactured willingness indicated by direct or indirect invocation of the institution and/or group affiliation, real or manufactured social enactment, and an institutional claim in response to a real or perceived threat. If these conditions are present, there are sufficient conditions for martyrdom, and this formula is applicable to religious institutions as well as political or social ones.

This demarcation of necessary and sufficient criteria for martyrdom may help to understand the negotiation process over recent martyrdoms, particularly those instances where there is contention over the institutional claim. The criteria for naming and claiming a martyr are also valuable for what they do not tell us. As mentioned, the criteria tell us nothing as to the inherent value of the institution that claims the martyr, much less any of the institutional signifieds. There is no quantity of martyrs that can substantiate the validity of the institutions to which they refer. This appears overly obvious, and yet in the traditional understanding of martyrdom there is a powerful transfer of meaning from the individual death to the institution, and the existential threat of death gives legitimacy to its claims. This culturally accepted institutional move co-opts the tremendously powerful signifier of willing suicide and leverages the desperate individual and social desire for meaning-making into institutional validity, although such a connection defies reason.

Neither can martyrdom show us the comparative value of institutions, as if the individual martyr weighed and balanced the value of multiple institutions before making a decision which one to die for. This already presumes the validity of the connection between the agent and the institution, which begs the question of how individual death translates to institutional validity. If it cannot uncover the validity of the institution or its signifieds in an absolute or comparative sense, we might argue martyrdom says something about the individual's beliefs about the institution or its signifieds, but to the extent that it does, it is impossible that these beliefs can be fully reconciled with institutional ones. To see why, we need to examine the phenomena that precede the would-be martyr's death from that agent's perspective.

Martyrdom Criteria from the Agent's Perspective

Using our criteria for martyrdom, the martyr literally cannot have been such to the would-be martyr; the martyr cannot become so until death. Like death, martyrdom can only be seen by the agent as a potentiality; it can never be understood by the agent as a component of being. Perhaps the "confessor," presumably having undergone suffering, but not yet death, as a result of willingness to suffer for a cause comes closest to martyrdom while still living, and as a result these confessors garnered prestige from their peers. Even with the confessor, however, there remains an existential difference. But there is more than just an existential difference, however great that might be. From an institutional perspective, the martyr must be able to perpetuate the institution. The martyr is a political statement. The martyr must advance the way the institution is seen. Whether or not it is an accurate reflection, it must in any case be a desirable one. As the religious institution is premised upon the supernatural, its founding premises are unverifiable. The result of the political act of naming and claiming the martyr, however, is that he or she is received as a blanket affirmation of the institution and effaces the distinction between the martyr and the individual before death.

Although the agent cannot be a martyr in the sense of embodying the criteria of death, this void is partially filled by the agent's willingness. Willingness to suffer and die from the individual perspective consists of one criterion as well, but it is different than the institution's. The individual's willing suicide is the calculation that given the right circumstances, it is better for the agent—according to the agent—to suicide than to live. The circumstances for willingness can obviously vary. In their most limited sense, they concern primarily the self. In the case of deaths traditionally labeled as suicide, then, the agent may calculate that the cessation of suffering in death is more valuable than the continued pain of existence.[23] This calculation may not extend to any ideological or institutional circumstances but stems from personal sensory experience. The calculation may consider that others such as family and friends will suffer because of the agent's actions, but this collective suffering is considered to be less than that of the agent. In other words, the agent may or may not believe in the morality of the death, but he or she must believe that, rightly or wrongly, his or her well-being will be maximized, or suffering minimized, in death.

It is also possible that the individual considers his or her death within a broader moral calculus. The willingness to die in this case would be based on the maximization of well-being for a broader social group. The individual may believe, for example, that his or her death will highlight the importance of a particular institution and its referents and draw other people into the fold as well as providing the individual with immortality. In these cases, the institution is served by the agent's death to the extent that its aims are reflected in the agent him or herself. All martyrs are drawn (or created) from this category, despite the common misunderstanding that the martyr is self-sacrificial, only considering institutional well-being and seemingly not taking his or her own happiness into consideration.

In cases where there is an actual willing suicide with ideological support, the most this could show us is the extent to which the individual adopted an ideology approved by the institution. In other words, the individual cannot sacrifice him or herself for the institution; the individual can willingly suicide, demonstrating the extent to which he or she has taken on signifieds that the institution claims as its own. It is not possible for the agent to willingly suicide for a net increase in his or her own suffering. This is true existentially as noted above; it must also be true biologically. We are structured on a rudimentary level to preserve our own lives at all cost. In order to violate that biological imperative, there is likely a permanent or temporary abnormality, as I discussed in the previous chapter, and a conscious belief that overrides the fear of death by providing a cognitive workaround, such as a belief in real or symbolic immortality.

Insofar as it is believed that the agent's willingness to die was informed by specific institutional content through direct invocation or group affiliation, the now-martyr's death provides the only support possible for unverifiable premises: the weight of human assent. As noted, this is always fragile and contentious because it is impossible to determine without doubt that the primary factor in the would-be martyr's calculation was some unverifiable premise of the institution. Nonetheless, when accepted, the martyr provides a response to a perceived threat to the institution's power through a recapture of the death. A loss of one or a few becomes a gain for the entire group, from the institutional perspective.

From the individual's perspective, it is possible that the death may be seen to be in the interest of the institution as well as his or her own, but the former cannot substitute for the latter. This differentiation is important in explaining why there is not an inexhaustible supply of martyrdoms for any existing institutional cause. The number of those who express a willingness to die under a given set of circumstances is certainly greater than those who would willingly die if those circumstances were to appear. This is sufficient to show that one cannot simply prefer institutional interests over one's own; to follow through in such circumstances requires belief that those interests are self-interests and not just institutional ones. For these reasons the agent and the martyr cannot be assumed identical.

The Immorality of Martyrdom

Following Avalos, I claimed that religious violence is always wrong because such violence is based on supernatural, and thus unverifiable, premises. Religion did not create violence; this distinction belongs most likely to the nature of social organization itself. Early on, however, religion served the political function of reckoning with unequal social systems. Although religious traditions could serve as a challenge to unfairness, they also often justified inequality and the violence that proceeds from it.[24] As a result, religion became a permanent and persistent factor in the perpetuation and maintenance of inequality, group affiliation, and their corollary violence.[25]

This is a strong indictment of religion, because due to unverifiable premises, religion must often be violent to advance those premises, by definition lacking empirical-rational means for agreement and compromise.[26] While often admitting the possibility of violence within religious traditions, defenders of religion vociferously argue against violence being inherent to religion. The misunderstanding seems based on the idea that many people and groups claiming religious identities have advocated against violence and become models for moral behavior. But inherency is not precluded by the appearance of nonviolent behavior. Indeed, inherent is defined as "existing in something as a permanent, essential, or characteristic attribute." From an empirical-rational perspective, violence appears as inherent in religion. It has been a persistent feature in religious traditions.

Again, violence is not unique to religion, which has become a common hang-up of contemporary discussions about religious violence. It is enough to note that violence is inherent in religion. One might also be able to claim, for example, that violence is inherent to politics. Violence manifests in social relationships on small and large scales as an arbitrary means to enforce cooperation. Political institutions often function on unverifiable principles as well, and the more that these often symbolic principles become separated from material reality, the more violence appears as a viable means for enforcing cooperation. This is not to say that every act of violence is immoral, even when used as a form of coercion. The morality of violence is tied to its justification, which provides the possibility for weighing the impartial maximization of well-being or minimization of suffering. The failures of political regimes that rely on unverifiable principles are exposed particularly when they manifest in gross inequalities. Yet, at least in democratic political systems there exists the possibility for fundamental principles that are accessible to all. This possibility does not exist within religious traditions.

So where does martyrdom fit in the scheme of religious violence? As an example of damaging behavior as an expression of power,[27] it certainly qualifies as violence. Even when religion appears as the victim of violence, as it is constructed in ideal cases of martyrdom, the institution that claims the martyr shares responsibility for the violence in the transaction. An institution that claims that violation or denial of its unverifiable premises is worse than death must be responsible for the deaths of individuals who adhere to its precepts. This is not to say that persecuting parties bear no responsibility for the violence of martyrdom. Insofar as the reason for engaging in violence is the religious affiliation of the agent or agents, the persecuting party is as culpable for engaging in violence on behalf of unverifiable principles. In other words, whether in support of unverifiable principles or in opposition to them, violence is as morally culpable. However, insofar as violence is motivated by other moral considerations, it is entirely possible for the moral culpability to reside solely on one or another side.

But it is more than this. The reason martyrdom appears as a religious phenomenon is precisely because religion is unverifiable. To put this another way, to the extent institutions rely on unverifiable premises, the deaths of adherents are used as substitute evidence for these premises. Insofar as institutions are justified by empirical-rational means, they have no need of martyrs for verification. Exploitation of human life for verification is a hallmark of both religious and political institutions.

This establishes the primary difference between the meaning of martyrdom from an institutional perspective and the would-be martyr's perspective. For the would-be martyr, the death must represent the maximization of well-being, even though the calculation of this may be based all or in part on unverifiable principles. As discussed, ancient conceptions of martyrdom, including Christian ones, were justified by divine compulsion. Divine compulsion serves to legitimize martyrdom and appears as additional evidence for the uniqueness of martyrdom. On a practical level, it prevents the explicit exposure of the inherent self-interest of martyrdom. The question of voluntary martyrdom turns around this concern. If a would-be martyr appears too eager to gain martyrdom, this overshadows the supposed institutional interest of the martyr. This is no less the case with "orthodox" martyrdom, but it is easier in the latter case to equalize the martyr's interest with the institution's because the martyrdom appears to have taken place without the initiation of the agent.

Because it appears as a violent side effect of the unverifiability of institutions, martyrdom is always wrong. Are martyrs then victims of the institution, or do they share blame? Both are the case. In the absence of institutional cultures that inculcate the value of unverifiable premises as equal to or more important than reason and evidence, the individual would not consider these premises significant in a willing suicide. However, there are likely few if any "pure" cases in which the individual is not exposed to any information that contradicts the unverifiable premises of the institution, and despite the confirmation bias that attends tribal identity, the agent must bear responsibility for his or her willing suicide. For the successful martyr this is a moot point because the very ground for reinforcing morality, the life of the individual, is negated in death. The point is not to assign blame to martyrs, at least insofar as their own deaths are concerned. As I have discussed, willing suicide, though a necessary factor for naming and claiming the martyr, is an unstable quantity, verifiable only by remnants left behind. Even in such cases where it is fairly certain that the would-be martyr's willingness aligns with institutional goals, assigning guilt to the martyr gains little in and of itself. This understanding of the martyr's culpability conveys the immorality of the action in order to expose the violence of the institution for those still living, both its adherents and detractors.

There is an additional reason beyond the mere categorization of martyrdom as a form of religious violence that calls the promotion of martyrdom into moral question. We have established that the vast majority of Christians throughout history have not become martyrs. While the level of immediate threat is one corollary for the creation of martyrs, we have also established that the perception of threat does not necessarily require an actual threat; thus the relative infrequency of martyrdom cannot be explained by the presence or absence of real threat. What we are left with, instead, is that martyrdom requires more than simply adherence to a particular religious identity. I have suggested that this additional factor is a psychosocial one that is augmented by the dogmas of religious tradition. There are certain among religious adherents that, through a combination of nature and nurture, are more susceptible to a message about the viability of martyrdom. The institution can be likened here to a virus: it establishes itself within the host and redirects its resource-creating processes to replicate the virus until all host material is exploited. The more vulnerable the agent is, the more likely the outcome will be that the rate of depletion of resources exceeds its replenishing from other sources, resulting in the death of the host.

Is there no way that martyrdom can maximize the well-being of humanity or minimize its suffering? We can examine this possibility through the quintessential martyrdom of Jesus, which is taken for approximately one-third of the planet to be the most efficacious martyrdom. But in order to believe that to be the case, one would first have to accept the unverifiable proposition that the death of Jesus effected the possibility of immortality in a paradisiacal setting for all people. This conclusion is based on other premises that would need to be specified. One would need to accept the further unverifiable propositions that every individual has the opportunity to receive this immortality and that this opportunity provides a means for immortality individuals would not otherwise have. Certainly it would be immoral if salvation was offered only to some people. (There are, of course, Christians who do believe in selective salvation using what ethicists describe as divine command theory, redefining fairness, love, or other commonly invoked moral qualities as whatever God says them to be.) It would of course also make the martyrdom of Jesus less efficacious if there were believed to be other viable means of obtaining immortality. Most difficult, we would have to believe it moral that the supernatural entity who created humanity not only created it lacking the immortality it desired but also required a bloody, painful death in order set up a system that required individual submission to this entity in order to receive salvation from a world created by this entity.

If these were all true, it would be the case that martyrdom, at least in the case of Jesus, is not only moral but also a moral necessity. However, we have absolutely no evidence that links this death with any shift in mortal status. Thus, even if all of these premises sound appealing, they cannot enter into a public moral calculus because there is nothing to recommend them as viable possibilities. We cannot weigh in the moral calculus any intangibles such as salvation. There would have to be another advantage to maintain the possibility of willing death being a moral action.

What if it is the case that while we cannot measure any supernatural effect of martyrdom, the change in perception of those individuals under the sway of these premises translates into a greater well-being while alive? In other words, is it possible for martyrdom to increase overall well-being or minimize overall suffering because it makes people think they will live forever and thus makes them happier? After all, there is nothing inherently immoral in a cultural fiction. The problem is that beliefs based on unverifiable premises make it impossible for the adherents to accurately measure the morality of a given action for others who do not similarly believe the given premises. The increase in well-being of adherents to a particular institution potentially involves an increase in suffering for at least some of those outside the institution, particularly insofar as conflict with outside groups is socially functional.[28] If my belief that the death of Jesus grants me immortality increases my individual well-being, regardless of whether that claim is true, my well-being and the well-being of others in similar situations would have to be weighed against the suffering of still others caused by the propagation and enforcement of that unverifiable belief on a cultural level, because my individual belief is premised on a certain level of social traction. It is also clear that I, as the believer, cannot solely do the weighing insofar as, having been convinced that this death effects my immortality, I am also convinced that the death increases the possibility of well-being for all. Consequently, I cannot make an active reckoning of others' suffering in relation to this belief because I place an inestimable gain in well-being on the other side.

Theoretically, then, it would be possible that the willing death of an individual, believed by that individual to maximize well-being impartially and creating an impact limited only to those who believe the same unverifiable premises, could be moral. It would be very difficult to examine this case in the world. Even if we believed, for example, that everyone involved in Jim Jones's Jonestown believed their own deaths to be a moral action (which is not the case[29]), it would be far from certain that their deaths maximized well-being impartially. The tragedy that preceded the mass death involved the deaths of others unconnected with the cult and caused significant suffering. There are substantial factors working against the possibility of a moral death whose primary premises are unverifiable. This likely matters very little to those involved, but it should matter greatly to the rest of us when we discount the particular event but affirm the overall enterprise of martyrdom.

It may be possible that an individual can maximize well-being impartially through the loss of his or her own life. One can imagine a parent giving life for a child or someone intervening to save the life of a significant individual or group of individuals and dying in the process. Because of the cultural ubiquity of martyrdom, we often mislabel such figures as martyrs. Though I disagree with their definition of martyrdom, I agree with Sophia Moskalenko and Clark McCauley that heroes or victims may be inappropriately labeled martyrs, in part because of the cultural ubiquity and benefit of such a claim.[30] Costica Bradatan writes about philosophers who died for their dedication to a cause: "for the sake of something bigger than oneself."[31] This sacrificial construction of the death relies heavily on ancient conceptions of martyrdom, but invoking martyrdom is not necessary in these cases, nor does it minimize the importance of the death to withhold the title. When the individual commits suicide neither on the basis of nor without a subsequent institutional claim, he or she is not a martyr and is free from the moral culpability of the claim.[32]

The well-known case of Socrates provides a likely candidate for a moral death. Socrates, as an old man living in a city-state ravaged and defeated in decades of war, chose to submit to his legal punishment for atheism and corruption of the youth. Plato's recounting explains Socrates's followers offering him the opportunity to escape, but this is not what makes his actions noble. This is simply an overt example of Socrates's ability to choose otherwise and gives an effective demonstration of his willingness to suicide. But there was no known institutional affiliation associated with Socrates's death other than the Athenian citizenship that condemned him. He claimed to prefer to die rather than flaunt the laws the city-state provided and the judgment they gave. At the time, however, few beyond his inner circle saw anything noble in his actions, and even many of his friends sought his freedom rather than death. In subsequent centuries, however, as the works of Plato have been disseminated across the world, some have come to see Socrates as a martyr for freedom, for wisdom, and a bulwark against tyrannical rule. Socrates was also elderly at the time of his death, a fact that must weigh more in favor of the morality of his actions than if he were a young man, both in terms of experience and remaining future. Primarily though, because the story of his life and death has come to be known by so many, and insofar as it has inspired others to stand for reason and against injustice, Socrates's voluntary death was likely a moral one. In addition, as Bradatan suggests, "it is true that these philosophers often become founding figures, but what they founded are not well-defined institutional structures … martyr-philosophers set the basis of philosophical lifestyles or broad movements of ideas."[33] Without an established institutional structure with an unverifiable referent, there is neither the core against which to establish a sense of group affiliation nor the means to enforce adherence to it. As such, the suffering that might be measured from the death of the philosopher is limited to his immediate family, friends, and associates. In such cases, the suicide might be morally beneficial and is so without recourse to martyrdom.

The persistent association of martyrdom with social institutions allows us to make some conclusions about the nature of their linkage. The only institutions that employ martyrs are those whose founding premises are unverifiable. Again, the martyr provides substitutionary evidence for the lack of institutional verifiability. Thus the Christian martyr dies to paradoxically validate the existence of an all-loving deity, and a soldier dies to protect America's freedom. Note the difference between the two cases. There is no amount of deaths, as mentioned, that can substantiate the existence of a supernatural being. It is possible, however, that we can justify a level of human freedom that maximizes overall well-being in society and see that, given that freedom, individuals are actually better off compared to other arrangements. In almost all cases, however, this cannot justify the soldier's death. In most cases where it is often invoked in the West, the protection of freedom is a disingenuous way of claiming the superiority of our tribe over others. The meaning of freedom has been circumscribed to mean the freedom of a particular group over others. In worse cases, it is haphazardly applied to national or corporate interests that have nothing to do with freedom in any sort of individual sense. Thus we can refine our claim to say that insofar as institutions employ martyrs, they do so on the basis of unverifiable premises.

When the institutions in question have a degree of social acceptance and employ martyrdom, then, it is immoral. At best, it is a self-serving means to allay the anxiety of death, and at worst it is a facade covering unjustifiable violence. How can one say, though, that a persecuted minority be immoral for claiming martyrs over and against a hegemonic norm? Say for example that Socrates had belonged to a voluntary association called "The Society of Questioners," and that this society was made up of Athenian citizens just like Socrates, with the same aims and concerns. In the wake of Socrates's death, it is quite possible that the society would capitalize on his death to advance those aims and concerns, particularly insofar as they served as an alternative to the status quo, and one that offered the possibility of maximizing happiness impartially. How then would these actions be immoral? They would become immoral when the signifier took the place of the signified, when "The Society of Questioners" became indistinguishable from the ideals of reason, freedom, and happiness that the society attempts to advance. Many institutions point to moral principles, but the signifiers of the institution are open-ended; they can take on additional meanings, even meanings that inherently contradict moral ones. Most would agree with the society's advancement of the goal to maximize individual freedom in an environment where it was lacking. However, equating the society itself with the maximization of individual freedom would be mistaken because of the fluidity of institutions and their symbols. In fact, the shorthand association of moral principles with particular institutions provides access to power that always supersedes its original aims. The institution that signifies a viable moral alternative to the sovereign institutional structure holds a precarious position, one in which the minority group must maximize the visibility of its aims without resorting to self-promotion. To maintain this position is to constantly flirt with failure, yet to succeed in establishing institutional viability fails to achieve the original aims as well.

Willing suicide is a gamble—we are unable to know all the variables because we have no knowledge of what if anything lies on the other side. Thus, though it is impossible to know for certain, it seems at least possible to construct a moral justification for suicide based on assessment of the variables we are aware of. Given the transitory nature of the majority of physical and emotional hardships, and the established ability of humankind to persist and even thrive in the face of such hardships, there also seems little to justify recommendation, much less valorization, of suicide on a general level. What we do know, however, is that there is no necessary connection between the life and death of an individual and the viability of an institution. As such, the institution that posits such a connection relies on a fundamental act of deception. We intuitively understand the value of life, and we seek reasoning for death. We do this in mundane cases such as old age, accidents, or homicides, but we presume that the victim in such cases was, like us, unwilling to die. In the rare cases where the "victim" chose death, however, the choice is counterintuitive and more demanding of explanation, precisely when there is no one to give it. The institution that originally creates the martyr from the willing suicide steps into that gap, exploiting our vulnerability for its self-promotion. This itself would be immoral but in isolation might be justifiable, particularly because we all, while we seek meaning, also know that "a thing is not necessarily true because a man dies for it."[34]

The religious institution cannot stop there, however, because despite ideological claims, the individual death does not have eternally lasting effects. Its power fades over time and must be replenished. Upon the original martyr, out of the conviction of those who buy it, comes conflict and violence that is necessarily unjustifiable. Violence is not solely created by the institution; the institution harnesses it, but insofar as violence proceeds from it or is promoted by it, it is immoral. On top of the manifold forms of human violence that result from the inability to enforce universal human order from tribal principles, martyrdom appears unique. Martyrdom recreates, with no foreseeable end, institutional validity from human death. That there have been many in the course of human history who have internalized the link between human death and institutional truth, aiming at martyrdom and subsequently becoming martyrs, adds no further validity to the linkage, but it does add further shame to the institution to the extent that it capitalizes on and promotes martyrdom. This is particularly the case because, given our biological and evolutionary resistance to knowing self-harm, it appears that martyrdom must rely on exploitation of those with a nonnormative lack of resistance to suicide. In short, martyrdom is not death for something greater; it is the fabrication of institutional validity upon the lives of vulnerable individuals who killed themselves for reasons we cannot fully verify.

A final note: though I am employing a consequentialist approach in assessing the morality of martyrdom, a non-consequentialist ethical approach provides an alternate conclusion. Margaret Watkins Tate argues for the possibility that the "Christian tradition's praise of the martyr constitutes an insight that may be central to the survival of civilized society and the promotion of human flourishing."[35] She explores and then discounts a neo-Kantian approach on the basis that one must violate one sacred value—preservation of human life—to avoid denying another transcendent good. Instead, she suggests that a virtue-based ethical theory might explain why "the loss of the martyr's life may be a discountable consequence."[36] If, for example, piety is virtuous, she argues, martyrdom might be justified because since piety considers "certain kinds of actions beyond the pale," the only alternative in certain cases may be martyrdom.[37]

There is, I think, an ultimately unbridgeable gap between our approaches. If we accept Tate's starting point of the existence of a transcendent value that either imposes itself upon the individual or a value that the individual takes to be virtuous, her approach seems plausible. In the latter case, this is also the reason that, despite my own possible feelings about suicide, my moral conclusion is irrelevant to the successful willing suicide. What does not explicitly enter into Tate's exposition, and what I think here critical, is the institutional influence on the possibility of awareness of transcendent values or legitimate virtues. At the least, I contend that coexistence in a pluralistic society requires a public employment of consequential reasoning in order not to unnecessarily violate the values of any particular facet of that society. We can, however, refuse to promote or sustain public support for ideologies that require human suicide for their substantiation. We can also employ all possible liberal means to persuade individuals and groups that because those ideologies are ultimately unverifiable, and because they can never be fully separated from the complex psychosocial environment in which humanity exists, the gamble of putting one's eggs in one ideological basket is a risky one indeed.

Conclusion

When Tertullian penned the dictum that the blood of martyrs was seed for Christian growth, he likely did so on the basis of sincere conviction. Nearly two thousand years later, John Allen Chau came to a similar conclusion and exchanged his own life for the institution's divine referent, with a long legacy of others behind him. Tertullian's words and Chau's actions express an important truth, just not the one they believed, so far as I can assess. What I can see is that we establish institutional truth upon human violence and death. Relying as they do on supernatural premises and rewards, religious institutions appear particularly prone to do so. While the proportion of the institution established on the blood of martyrs is debatable, then, it is the case that martyrdom has contributed to the continued existence of Christianity. While Tertullian and Chau might see this as secondary evidence of divine truth, though, I see it as a lamentable trick we play on ourselves. Martyrdom is used by Christians to validate Christianity, and this usage has been successful enough to be broadly accepted in scholarship and by the general public. As I've shown, religious belief or affiliation does not explain the martyr, and the martyr does not validate the religious institution. This fact sits in uneasy tension with the many forms of violence that modern liberal democratic societies roundly condemn.

I argued from the opening chapter that while martyrdom is commonly understood to be a sacrifice for something bigger or greater, this definition is simply an institutional one with the particular institutional referent stripped away. Insisting upon a different definition of the phenomenon known as martyrdom is an attempt to wrest control back from a socio-institutional operation that masks the root of the martyr in the willing suicide. Willing suicide is an indicator that the phenomenon of martyrdom is not categorically different from suicide but a subset of it: willing suicide with ideological support. This provides the first fundamental shift in our understanding of martyrdom.

Though it may be a contributing factor, Christian martyrdom cannot be fully (or even mostly) understood as because of or for Christianity.

There is a fundamental difference between the martyr and the non-martyr, and the exploration of that difference should begin not with the institution but with the obvious but overlooked existential difference of the martyr's death. The death is the hermeneutic key for understanding the draw of martyrdom both for the would-be martyr and those who are drawn to her memory and celebration. For the martyr, the death is a process of self-formation rather than self-sacrifice. Following a Heideggerian framework, it provides the exhaustion of potentiality in finality and, as such, a chance for wholeness, inauthentic though it may be. For those of us who remain, the martyr represents the possibility of avoiding our own fear of death, on an individual level and, through the institutional narrative, on a social one as well.

The process by which the willing suicide gains ideological support, becoming the martyr, is a socio-institutional function. The sovereign institution must control and exercise violence, and it does so not because of the inherent immorality of violence but in order to maintain sovereignty. The willing suicide is perhaps the most fundamental form of autonomous, and thereby anti-institutional, violence. The willing suicide that is salvageable by the institution becomes the martyr, a process that not only controls the violence of the willing suicide but also transforms it to validate the institution itself. When this process itself is institutionalized, the institution not only creates the martyr post hoc but also supports and promotes martyrdom, providing a potential vehicle for the willing suicide. As such, the institution is not just a passive beneficiary of the violence of the persecutor and the willing suicide; it actively employs violence for its perpetuation. In this form, religion and violence are inextricably intertwined.

The first three hundred years of Christianity, as narrativized by Eusebius of Caesarea, was a period in which Christians were regularly and in large numbers persecuted and martyred for their identification with Christianity. The phenomenon of martyrdom existed before Christianity, albeit by other names, but early Christianity provides an extended period to examine the institutional use to which willing suicide with ideological support can be applied, effectively and largely retroactively. Extensive historical research has attempted to disabuse widespread acceptance of the Eusebian narrative, but it still forms the wellspring from which the common cultural idea of martyrdom is sustained in the present day. Because human death is a powerful but arbitrary signifier, Christian bishops and apologists from Clement to Augustine worked with difficulty to validate the martyr, the willing suicide with ideological support, and separate that figure from the mere suicide. They largely succeeded, as today we accept without question not only the distinction between the two but also the valorization of the martyr and the demonization of the suicide. While the institution could not have created this distinction ex nihilo, it provides the individual a welcome script for meaning-making out of death. It validates our rudimentary hardwired fascination with willing suicide and redirects it toward Christianity.

Scholarship on Christian martyrdom has rarely questioned or challenged this fundamental dichotomy. That which has is met with resistance, not only by contemporary apologists but also by other scholars of the early Christian tradition who in the name of objectivity reinforce institutional norms. The scholarly discussion around voluntary martyrdom provides an interesting insight here, as it both echoes concerns in early Christian literature and, in the guise of conceding the overeagerness for death of certain martyrs, shores up the traditional boundary between "true" martyrdom and "false." It attempts to perform an end run around the obvious fact that "if martyrdom is not voluntary, it is not martyrdom."[1] Of course, what is overlooked in this oft-cited statement by Daniel Boyarin is that he is not critiquing categories of martyrdom that will be given moral value; he just prefers the term "provoked" rather than voluntary. The fundamental assumption that martyrdom is good, suicide bad, remains in place. I have argued instead that there is no apparent basis outside of theology by which martyrdom can be seen as categorically different from suicide; in the contemporary literature on suicide, martyrdom is a clear subcategory of it.

An adjacent thread of scholarship on Christian martyrdom has focused on its function as an identity discourse, following the trend of identity analysis in the humanities and social sciences since the mid-twentieth century. There is value to this approach; it is certainly true that conversations about and around Christianness, particularly in its formative first centuries, contributed to what it mean to identify with Christianity. However, as identity is used as both difference and similarity, this claim by itself is of minimal value. Insofar as analysis of martyrdom as identity formation minimizes the ultimate ground of the phenomenon in death, it reinforces institutional interests. It obscures the "why" of martyrdom, grounding it in unique religious identity and thus limiting comparison and understanding of what makes the martyr. We can recognize the much reduced historical number of actual martyrdoms in Christianity without dismissing the notion that willing suicides with Christian ideological support took place. This claim, in turn, can be recognized without validating the institution for promoting this phenomenon.

On the contrary, we should examine the morality of martyrdom, and upon examination we can see that the institutional promotion of martyrdom is immoral: it co-opts the voluntary, violent death of the individual for institutional promotion. If violence based on religion is immoral, grounded as it is in unverifiable premises, then martyrdom falls into that category of an immoral claim. Although willingness to die before a public audience constitutes most of the criteria for martyrdom, it also needs an institutional claim of support. It turns out that the institutional claim is not only a necessary condition, but building on the credibility of past martyrdom, in some cases it is a sufficient condition. This is where scholars of Christian martyrdom as identity discourse provide an insight. Stories of Christian martyrdom did work for Christianity whether the actual death of the martyr took place or not. This fact does not detract from the immorality of martyrdom, nor should it overlook the fact that Christians are still encouraged prior to martyrdom, and venerated after it, in further support of Christianity.

Martyrdom is indeed rare, and for good biological and psychological reason. What this may indicate is that the ideological message of martyrdom appeals particularly to those who are abnormal, who are more susceptible to the paradoxical message that ultimate meaning can be found by ending the possibility of any meaning whatsoever. While institutions are of course free to poorly treat any of their adherents who willingly agree to such treatment, martyrdom operates at the edges of the capacity for such willingness. In any case, this does not preclude outsiders from arguing against the perpetuation of this exchange of human death for institutional life without justifiable premises.

There is a risk in a work that roots martyrdom in willing suicide of appearing callous about the tragedies suffered by Christians throughout history. There are at least two potential points of resistance. The first doubles down on the ability to distinguish the "true" martyr from others who perhaps *were* suicides, who used Christianity as a means to fulfill an abnormal wish for death. This argument grants the latter group—dismissed as overeager and self-absorbed unfortunates—absolving Christianity from any responsibility for these exceptions and preserving a pure corps of legitimate martyrs. These pure martyrs might include those who were seemingly targeted and killed simply for being Christian. One might include in this category, with varying levels of justification, Martin Luther King Jr. and Oscar Romero, as well as more recent figures such as Cassie Bernall or Rachel Scott in the Columbine tragedy. And it is true that these individuals were not willing suicides. They were not given an explicit choice between renouncing their beliefs or their lives. They were thus not martyrs in the way I have been describing. They were simply victims.[2] Their description as martyrs is understandable for the reasons I've described throughout the last few chapters. Explaining their deaths as martyrdoms inserts them into a meaning-making framework. Their deaths seem tragic, but they were meant for some "larger" purpose, or at least they were reconfigured as such. They die so that I may live. More importantly, though, the institutionalization of violence, the recapture of bloody death to reaffirm the Christian institution, operates the same whether these individuals meet the ideal type or not. As I noted, though the ideal type includes willingness, public death, and an institutional claim, the latter is the most important. The remaining details can be manufactured. Thus, there are salient distinctions we can and should make among individuals who die and are given the label martyr. For example, it is worth noting that there is a significant difference between sanctioned executions, as many early Christian martyrdoms are described, and assassinations, which all the figures listed above were victim to. In describing the latter as martyrs, they are forcibly inserted into the mold of the former. They are not alike in many respects save one: their death becomes life for us who believe in them and for the institution that encourages, supports, and promotes them.

A second critique against my approach to martyrdom might be that this attention on martyrs as willing suicides, and the institution for making meaning from their deaths, is a form of victim-blaming. In the conclusion of his compilation of modern-day martyrs who graduated from the Moody Bible Institute, Marvin J. Newell rejects the idea that martyrdom and suicide are on the same spectrum rather than categorically different. He contends that this mistake "seem[s] to make the martyr responsible for the murderer's action, when in fact the one doing the killing needs to be held responsible for his own aggressive behavior."[3] Newell is not alone in perceiving that any attention on the role the martyr plays in their death as tantamount to giving sanction to the aggressor. It may indeed seem to be the case, but martyrdom is not a zero-sum game, and our belief otherwise has more to do with our genetic and psychological predispositions than any external facts. It should go without saying that any individual or group that kills someone, directly or indirectly, on the basis of their identification with a religious tradition, should be held to account. That is in fact the reason I wrote this book. While it seems obvious to me that most people clearly see the aggressors in cases of martyrdom as culpable, and rightly so, most also fail to consider the culpability of the institution that establishes the martyr's death as a viable transaction. Holding responsible those who kill unjustly is a societal imperative, and history has shown that we often fail to do so. Refusing to countenance the role of the individual and religious institution in the complex situation simply exchanges one form of injustice for another.

In addition to scrutinizing the moment of the willing suicide, we ought to be able to consider the social and institutional context that contributes to the event as it takes place. A common trope in the ancient world was that Christians were obstinate in their refusal to participate in many common aspects of Roman civic life.[4] The legitimacy gained officially by Christianity in the fourth century led over time to fundamental changes in the Western world and, in time, the globe.[5] Christianity is an institution with aims at sovereignty, and as such one that—albeit not uniquely so—rests uncomfortably among other institutions when it is not sovereign. It takes active vigilance for meta-religious institutions such as American democracy to balance the free exercise of religion and prevent the establishment of Christianity as a state religion, since this is fundamentally opposed to liberal principles and those upon which the country was founded.[6] This challenge is no less acute now than at any time in the common era, at a time when insiders and outsiders alike attribute the 2016 presidential election in the United States in no small part to Christian evangelicals who saw in their champion a chance for greater preference for their religious belief.[7]

To this competition for institutional sovereignty is added a well-established ideology of persecution, reinforced by scriptural texts and the centrality of martyrdom within Christian history.[8] No party, particularly in the United States, participates in or analyzes acts of religious persecution or martyrdom in a vacuum. This includes institutions responsible for unlawful persecution, those who commit willing suicide with ideological support, those who are victims as a result of their association with a religious tradition, and all the rest of us who are left to make sense of it all.

I have examined the phenomenon of martyrdom in Christianity while paying lip service to the existence of martyrdom in other religious traditions as well as outside the religious sphere. I focused on the Christian tradition in order to circumscribe the scope of my work, because that is where my personal and professional experience primarily lies and because the legacy of Christian martyrdom looms large in the Western world. To the extent that martyrdom as a phenomenon in other institutions relies on the exchange of human life for institutional validity based on unverifiable premises, however, I argue that the same analysis applies. It is my hope that we cast a more critical eye on martyrdom and that we remove the stigma of suicide to the extent we do actually want to help people in this life, and not just give them hope for the next.

Notes

Preface

1 Jason Bruner expresses a similar sentiment: Jason Bruner, *Imagining Persuasion: Why American Christians Believe There Is a Global War against Their Faith* (New Brunswick, NJ: Rutgers University Press, 2021), 88.
2 Ibid., 87.
3 My attempt to find the source of this story some thirty years later was unsuccessful. There are several stories with similar elements in a modern compendium of martyr stories: DC Talk and Voice of the Martyrs, *Jesus Freaks: Stories of Those Who Stood for Jesus, the Ultimate Jesus Freaks* (Tulsa, OK: Albury, 1999), 221–2, 268.
4 See, for example, "In U.S., Decline of Christianity Continues at Rapid Pace," *Pew Research Center* (October 17, 2019): https://www.pewforum.org/2019/10/17/in-u-s-decline-of-christianity-continues-at-rapid-pace/.
5 This remark resonates with the comment of the Bishop Eusebius about those Christians who he omits from his history, those who "have made shipwreck of their salvation" (Eusebius, *Historia Ecclesiastica*, 8.2.3). See also page 87.

1 Why Martyrdom at All?

1 Alex Perry, "The Last Days of John Allen Chau," *Outside* (July 26, 2019): https://www.outsideonline.com/2400030/john-allen-chau-life-death-north-sentinel.
2 Oral Roberts University, where Chau once attended, compiled an archive of news sources around his death. Thad R. Horner et al., "The John Allen Chau Archive: Citations to Primary Sources, Major News Reports & Commentary," *Digital Showcase* (2018): accessed June 18, 2021, https://digitalshowcase.oru.edu/chau/14/.
3 Paul Middleton, "What Is Martyrdom?," *Mortality* 19, no. 2 (2014), 118.
4 Moskalenko and McCauley suggest that "martyrs are people who have made a decision to accept suffering and possibly death for a larger cause." Sophia Moskalenko and Clark R. McCauley, *The Marvel of Martyrdom: The Power of Self-Sacrifice in a Selfish World* (New York: Oxford University Press, 2019), 6.

5 Jolyon Mitchell identifies the community-based way of viewing martyrdom as *creative* martyrdom, one of four scholarly approaches that also includes *evolutionary*, *evaluative*, and *inclusive* approaches. Jolyon Mitchell, *Martyrdom: A Very Short Introduction* (Oxford: Oxford University Press, 2012), 3. These might be translated as social, historical, theological, and descriptive, respectively. None encapsulates the existential/phenomenological approach I will attempt to foreground.
6 Émile Durkheim, *Suicide: A Study in Sociology*, trans. John A. Spaulding and George Simpson (New York: Free Press, 1979), 44.
7 J. Oliver Conroy, "The Life and Death of John Chau, the Man Who Tried to Convert His Killers," *The Guardian* (February 3, 2019): https://www.theguardian.com/world/2019/feb/03/john-chau-christian-missionary-death-sentinelese.
8 Eliza Griswold, "John Chau's Death on North Sentinel Island Roils the Missionary World," *New Yorker* (December 8, 2018): https://www.newyorker.com/news/on-religion/john-chaus-death-roils-the-missionary-world.
9 Durkheim, *Suicide*, 44.
10 Jeffrey Gettleman et al., "John Chau Aced Missionary Boot Camp: Reality Proved a Harsher Test," *New York Times* (November 30, 2018): https://www.nytimes.com/2018/11/30/world/asia/john-chau-andaman-missionary.html.
11 Griswold, "John Chau's Death."
12 Ibid.
13 Caleb Parke, "US Missionary Killed by Remote Island Tribe Inspires Others to Join Mission Field," *Fox News* (November 15, 2019): accessed February 10, 2021, https://www.foxnews.com/faith-values/missionary-john-chau-christian-inspiration.
14 Gregory Zilboorg, "Fear of Death," *Psychoanalytic Quarterly* 12, no. 4 (1943), 465–75; Larry C. Bernard et al., "An Evolutionary Theory of Human Motivation," *Genetic, Social, and General Psychology Monographs* 131, no. 2 (May 1, 2005), 129–84; Thomas Joiner, *Why People Die by Suicide* (Cambridge, MA: Harvard University Press, 2007), 22, 92. Robert Sapolsky notes that evolutionarily we are not about survival but reproduction of genes, and the latter doesn't always necessitate survival on an individual level. Robert M. Sapolsky, *Behave: The Biology of Humans at Our Best and Worst* (New York: Penguin Press, 2017), 329.
15 See, for example, Jay Newman, "The Motivation of Martyrs: A Philosophical Perspective," *Thomist* 35, no. 4 (October 1971), 594. I discuss this further in the next chapter.
16 W. R. Scott, *Institutions and Organizations: Ideas and Interests* (Los Angeles, CA: Sage, 2008), 48.
17 Perry, "Last Days."
18 Roger Friedland, "Institution, Practice, and Ontology: Toward a Religious Sociology," in *Institutions and Ideology*, ed. Renate E. Meyer, Kerstin Sahlin, Marc J. Ventresca, and Peter Walgenbach (Bingley: Emerald Group, 2009), 74.

19 Conroy, "Life and Death of John Chau."
20 Gettleman et al., "Chau Aced Boot Camp."
21 This draws on Jean-Paul Sartre's famous phrase: "Existence precedes essence." Jean-Paul Sartre, John Kulka, and Arlette Elkaïm-Sartre, *Existentialism Is a Humanism = (L'Existentialisme Est Un Humanisme); Including, a Commentary on the Stranger (Explication De L'Étranger)*, trans. Carol Macomber (New Haven, CT: Yale University Press, 2007), 20.
22 Conroy, "Life and Death of John Chau."
23 Joiner, *Why People Die by Suicide*, ch. 5.
24 Gettleman et al., "Chau Aced Boot Camp."
25 Albert Schweitzer argued that not only each era but each individual created Jesus in his own image. Albert Schweitzer, *The Quest of the Historical Jesus: A Critical Study of Its Progress from Reimarus to Wrede*, trans. W. Montgomery (New York: Macmillan, 1956), 4.
26 Hector Avalos, *Fighting Words: The Origins of Religious Violence* (Amherst, NY: Prometheus Books, 2005), 18.
27 Edward Gibbon, *The History of the Decline and Fall of the Roman Empire: Constantine and the Christian Empire* (London: Folio Society, 1995).
28 Herbert Musurillo, *The Acts of the Christian Martyrs* (Oxford: Clarendon Press, 1972).
29 Candida R. Moss, *The Myth of Persecution: How Early Christians Invented a Story of Martyrdom* (New York: HarperOne, 2013), 15.
30 Historian James Laine identifies this as meta-religion: "The precondition for the multicultural acceptance of multiple religions (tolerance) is the shared acceptance of something above religion, something with the power to set the political conditions of shared community." James W. Laine, *Meta-Religion: Religion and Power in World History* (Berkeley: University of California Press, 2014), 5.

2 "Willing Suicide": Martyrdom as Self-Formation

1 A portion of this chapter was previously published: Matthew Recla, "Autothanatos: The Martyr's Self-Formation," *Journal of the American Academy of Religion* 82, no. 2 (2014).
2 Divine influence is obviously untestable in any way, only arguable after the death of the subject, and cannot account for martyrdoms outside of a religious milieu. The ancient category of *anagke*, divine compulsion, fulfilled a similar role. This concept will be discussed further in Chapter 5.
3 Jay Newman, "The Motivation of Martyrs: A Philosophical Perspective," *Thomist* 35, no. 4 (October 1971), 581.

4 Ibid., 585.
5 Ibid., 592.
6 Ibid., 594.
7 Ibid., 596.
8 Ibid., 598.
9 The Maccabean martyrs are the prototype here. Scalped, dismembered, and fried alive, the martyrs retained enough composure to pronounce judgment on their persecuting king as they died (2 Macc. 7). The second-century Christian martyrs of Lyons and Vienne endure similarly terrible tortures with unyielding resolution. See Eusebius's *Historia Ecclesiastica*, 5.1. I will discuss the martyrs of Lyons and Vienne in Chapter 4.
10 Mel Gibson's 2004 film *The Passion of the Christ* is one popular and controversial example. *The Passion of the Christ*, directed by Mel Gibson (2004; 20th Century Fox Home Entertainment, 2004), 127 min., DVD.
11 There are numerous studies attempting to understand those few early Christian martyrdoms where we have purported access to the authors' own words. The third-century Perpetua probably tops the list, as she is a relatively well-born woman apparently new to Christianity. Mary R. Lefkowitz, "The Motivations for St. Perpetua's Martyrdom," *Journal of the American Academy of Religion* 44, no. 3 (September 1, 1976), 418. Lefkowitz directs Perpetua's account away from doctrinal interpretation and toward attempts to wrest agency from a patriarchal society; Marie Luise-Franz performs a Jungian psychoanalytic reading: Marie-Luise von Franz and Daryl Sharp, *The Passion of Perpetua: A Psychological Interpretation of Her Visions* (Toronto: Inner City Books, 2004). Second-century Bishop Ignatius is another frequent subject; both the aforementioned are novel in their seeming obsession with death in conjunction with an apparent lack of necessity. Unlike Perpetua, however, few if any scholars have been able to read Ignatius apart from his obvious Christian *milieu*. Allen Brent sees the bishop as the Christian representative in a Christian/pagan struggle: Allen Brent, "Ignatius of Antioch and the Imperial Cult," *Vigiliae Christianae* 52, no. 1 (February 1, 1998), 31–2. Robert Stoops indicates the fallacy of reading Ignatius as a martyr in the Late Antique developed sense of the term, but his reading simply turns instead to a modern interpretation of a first-century Christian reading, "living a life of faith … in unity with Christ." Robert F. Stoops, Jr., "If I Suffer … Epistolary Authority in Ignatius of Antioch," *Harvard Theological Review* 80, no. 2 (April 1, 1987), 166. He discounts the death as secondary to analysis of the martyr.
12 For a caution against a "romanticizing" approach to self-sacrifice from a different angle, see Saul Smilansky, "A Puzzle about Self-Sacrificing Altruism," *Journal of Controversial Ideas* 1, no. 1 (April 25, 2021), 7–8. On rational calculations about

suicide, see Avital Pilpel and Lawrence Amsel, "What Is Wrong with Rational Suicide," *Philosophia* 39, no. 1 (2011), 116.

13 Pilpel and Amsel, "What Is Wrong with Rational Suicide," 111.

14 David Daube, "The Linguistics of Suicide," *Philosophy and Public Affairs* 1, no. 4 (Summer 1972), 391, 394.

15 In a previous article on the subject, I used the term *autothanatos*, in part to avoid the negative associations with suicide, in part because the term had the benefit of minimal historical usage and in part because as a single term it is more aesthetically pleasing. However, *autothanatos* or its English equivalent "self-death" are, as Daube explains, "almost excessively passive." Ibid., 421. These considerations aside, with the expanded opportunity to treat multiple aspects of the phenomenon of martyrdom, I now consider the use of suicide a worthwhile endeavor. The change in term does not alter the direction but sharpens the thrust of my analysis. Recla, "Autothanatos."

16 This was true both inside and outside of the church. Hagiographic scholar Hippolyte Delehaye remarks that the Bollandists, a Jesuit society of scholars founded in the seventeenth century, had its beginnings when a Belgian monk told a visiting superior that "when reading the Lives of the Saints he had been surprised to find in them so many apocryphal stories, the orthodoxy of which might often well be questioned." Hippolyte Delehaye, *The Work of the Bollandists through Three Centuries, 1615-1915* (Princeton, NJ: Princeton University Press, 1922), 7-8. Orthodoxy and history are certainly not synonymous, but the proliferation of saints venerated in local churches leads to a wide variety in material that "suggested naturally" the need to be organized. Ibid., 59. In the twentieth century, historical work has also been completed by many others. A few follow: Timothy David Barnes, "Pre-Decian *Acta Martyrum*," *Journal of Theological Studies* 19 (October 1968), 509-31; Herbert Musurillo, *The Acts of Christian Martyrs* (Oxford: Clarendon Press, 1972); Gary A. Bisbee, *Pre-Decian Acts of Martyrs and Commentarii* (Philadelphia, PA: Fortress Press, 1988). The martyrdoms discussed in the following chapters are taken by nearly all scholars to have a firm historical basis.

17 Brad Gregory contends that "traditional confessional history" has been corrected by "atheistic history of religion," but that this latter perspective is equally biased. Gregory argues that the appropriate question to ask is, "What did it mean to them?"—"them" being a Reformation Christian other juxtaposed to a modern atheist "us." He approaches the martyrdom question by positing the need for what he claims is the sui generis methodology of religion. This approach perhaps builds a defense against "atheistic history" but dissolves the individual martyr into his Christian sect. Brad S. Gregory, *Salvation at Stake: Christian Martyrdom in Early Modern Europe* (Cambridge, MA: Harvard University Press, 1999), 8-15.

18 See note 11 for examples.

19 On the contrary, Gregory claims,

> There was nothing esoteric about the martyrs—their beliefs and worldview are stated in the period's most elementary catechisms. Accordingly, the extremism of martyrdom should not be understood as a fanaticism of the fringe, but as exemplary action. Martyrs were exceptional in their behavior, but not in their beliefs and values. Were this not the case, friends and family members would not have urged them to persevere. (Gregory, *Salvation at Stake*, 8)

This response downplays the action by implying that the "beliefs and values" were what was more important and what was shared by most. Thus while affirming the martyr, others can refuse to imitate the martyr.

20 For an excellent, concise summary of *Being and Time*, see Hubert L. Dreyfus and Mark A. Wrathall, *A Companion to Heidegger* (Malden, MA: Blackwell, 2008), 3–9. Heidegger uses "being" in two different senses. One is what he claims is the traditional understanding of being as the properties of a thing and the second sense is the modes of being, one of which is Dasein.
21 Martin Heidegger, *Being and Time*, trans. John Macquarrie and Edward Robinson (New York: Harper, 1962), 32.
22 Ibid., 37.
23 Ibid., 43.
24 Ibid., 72–5.
25 Ibid., 68.
26 Ibid., 119.
27 Ibid., 65, 227.
28 Ibid., 167.
29 Ibid., 231.
30 Ibid., 234.
31 Ibid., 235.
32 Ibid., 276–7.
33 Ibid., 280.
34 It is notable that the English word "authentic" comes from the Greek *autoentes*, which came into usage in the ancient period as a way of describing suicide. Daube, "Linguistics of Suicide," 401–2.
35 Examples abound. Mel Gibson's William Wallace roars,

> Fight, and you may die. Run, and you'll live. At least a while. And dying in your beds, many years from now, would you be willing to trade all the days, from this day to that, for one chance, just one chance, to come back here, and tell our enemies that they may take our lives, but they'll never

take our freedom! (*Braveheart*, directed by Mel Gibson (1995; Hollywood, CA: Paramount Pictures, 2000), 178 min., DVD)

Notably, Gibson's audience is a rag-tag embattled minority of Scots set to fight for their land against an invading English force. In contrast, the speech of Russell Crowe's fictional General Maximus Decimus Meridius is given to presumably battle-hardened Roman soldiers, themselves the invading party against Germanic peoples north of the empire:

Fratres! Three weeks from now, I will be harvesting my crops. Imagine where you will be, and it will be so. Hold the line! Stay with me! If you find yourself alone, riding in the green fields with the sun on your face, do not be troubled. For you are in Elysium, and you're already dead! [Laughing] Brothers, what we do in life … echoes in eternity. (*Gladiator*, directed by Ridley Scott (Universal City, CA: Dreamworks Home Entertainment, 2000), 155 min., DVD)

The former approach distracts from death by redirecting the audience toward a higher ideal; the latter minimizes death's importance as an unavoidable necessity; both contextualize the battle about something else than death, allaying understandable fear but obscuring the *telos* of conflict. Elaine Scarry examines the nature of war and the denial of its intent; injury, she posits, is the product, cost and goal of war. Elaine Scarry, *The Body in Pain: The Making and Unmaking of the World* (New York: Oxford University Press, 1987), 80.

36 See Heidegger, *Being and Time*, 297. Freud notes, "At bottom no one believes in his own death, or, to put the same thing in another way, that in the unconscious every one of us is convinced of his own immortality." Sigmund Freud, *On the History of the Psycho-Analytic Movement: Papers on Metapsychology, and Other Works* (London: Hogarth Press, 1957), 289. See also Ernest Becker, *The Denial of Death* (New York: Free Press, 1973), 2.

37 In *What about Hitler*, Robert Brimlow provides a beautiful example of the implications of this approach. His work will be discussed in detail in Chapter 6. Robert W. Brimlow, *What about Hitler?: Wrestling with Jesus's Call to Nonviolence in an Evil World* (Grand Rapids, MI: Brazos Press, 2006).

38 Heidegger, *Being and Time*, 284.

39 Ibid., 288.

40 Ibid., 305.

41 Many Christian martyrdoms in the post-antique period have been subject to greater scrutiny and some were officially declared martyrs only much later. Gregory notes that writers of Protestant Reformation-period martyrologies couched their stories in broader terms than their own denominational backgrounds and freely edited those that did not adhere to a particular outline. Gregory, *Salvation at Stake*, 185.

Some, though, had to simply bide their time. Thomas More, for example, did not gain official martyr status until 1935, four hundred years after his death. Lacey Baldwin Smith, *Fools, Martyrs, Traitors: The Story of Martyrdom in the Western World* (Evanston, IL: Northwestern University Press, 1999), 182.

42 See note 40.
43 Heidegger, *Being and Time*, 307.
44 Ibid., 308.
45 Talal Asad, *On Suicide Bombing* (New York: Columbia University Press, 2007), 64. Jonathan Haidt and Joshua Greene, both together and separately, are among those who have flipped the order of judgment and action on its head. At least on mundane levels, we more often make judgments first and subsequently ationalize our actions. See, for example, J. Haidt, "The Emotional Dog and Its Rational Tail: A Social Intuitionist Approach to Moral Judgment," *Psychological Review* 108, no. 4 (2001), 814–34; J. Greene and J. Haidt, "How (and Where) Does Moral Judgment Work?," *Trends in Cognitive Sciences* 6, no. 12 (2002), 517–23; Joshua David Greene, *Moral Tribes: Emotion, Reason, and the Gap between Us and Them* (New York: Penguin Books, 2013).
46 Talal Asad notes, "Ironically, it is only at the trial of someone who has failed to complete the operation that the motive of suicide bombers can be adduced." Asad, *On Suicide Bombing*, 45.
47 Heidegger, *Being and Time*, 313.
48 Ibid., 314.
49 Ibid., 349.
50 Ibid., 349–50.
51 Ibid., 434.
52 As Nietzsche suggests in his *Twilight of the Idols*, "Even the most courageous among us only rarely has the courage for what he really knows." Friedrich Wilhelm Nietzsche, "Twilight of the Idols or, How One Philosophizes with a Hammer," in *The Portable Nietzsche*, ed. Walter Arnold Kaufmann (New York: Penguin Books, 1982), 466.
53 Becker, *The Denial of Death*, xvii.
54 Ibid., 16. See also note 14 in the previous chapter.
55 Ibid., 11.
56 Ibid., 48.
57 Ibid., 180.
58 Ibid., 173–4.
59 Ibid., 207.
60 Sheldon Solomon, Jeff Greenberg, and Thomas A. Pyszczynski, *The Worm at the Core: On the Role of Death in Life* (New York: Random House, 2015).
61 Ibid., 13.

62 On this point, see also Leonard L. Martin and Kees Van den Bos, "Beyond Terror: Towards a Paradigm Shift in the Study of Threat and Culture," *European Review of Social Psychology* 25, no. 1 (2014), 58–9.
63 See Lee A. Kirkpatrick and Carlos David Navarrete, "Reports of My Death Anxiety Have Been Greatly Exaggerated: A Critique of Terror Management Theory from an Evolutionary Perspective," *Psychological Inquiry* 17, no. 4 (2006), 288–98; Marc Parry, "Death Denial: Does Our Terror of Dying Drive Almost Everything We Do?," *Chronicle Review* (May 22, 2015): https://www.chronicle.com/article/death-denial/.
64 Solomon, Greenberg, and Pyszczynski, *Worm at the Core*, 65.
65 Jonathan Jong, *Death, Anxiety, and Religious Belief: An Existential Psychology of Religion* (New York: Bloomsbury, 2016), 172–3.
66 See Andreas Lieberoth, "The Evolution of Martyrdom? Considerations in the Study of Religious Self-Sacrifice," in *Human Characteristics: Evolutionary Perspectives on Human Mind and Kind*, ed. Henrik Høgh-Olesen, Jan Tønnesvang, and Preben Bertelsen (Cambridge: Cambridge Scholars, January 23, 2009). This perspective, notably, would likely argue that martyrdom benefits both the individual *and* the group, but while death sustaining group identity requires no additional theological architecture, death in the individual's best interest has a higher bar to demonstrate validity.
67 Jonathan Jong and Jamin Halberstadt, "Death Anxiety and Religious Belief: Responses to Commentaries," *Religion, Brain & Behavior* 9, no. 2 (2019), 14.
68 Jocelyn J. Bélanger et al., "The Psychology of Martyrdom: Making the Ultimate Sacrifice in the Name of a Cause," *Journal of Personality and Social Psychology* 107, no. 3 (2014), 511.
69 Jong and Halberstadt, "Death Anxiety and Religious Belief," 23.
70 Becker, *Denial of Death*, 180; Solomon, Greenberg, and Pyszczynski, *Worm at the Core*, 57.
71 See, for example, Ian McGregor, "Offensive Defensiveness: Toward an Integrative Neuroscience of Compensatory Zeal after Mortality Salience, Personal Uncertainty, and Other Poignant Self-Threats," *Psychological Inquiry* 17, no. 4 (2006), 299–308; James K. Wellman, Jr. and Kyoko Tokuno, "Is Religious Violence Inevitable?," *Journal for the Scientific Study of Religion* 43, no. 3 (2004), 291–6.

3 "True Because a Man Dies for It": Martyrdom as Institutional Violence

1 O. Wilde, *The Portrait of Mr. W. H.* (New York: M. Kennerley, 1921), 29.
2 Curtin and Litke suggest that "we generally recognize a distinction between force, which may be morally justified, and violence." Deane W. Curtin and Robert Litke, *Institutional Violence* (Atlanta, GA: Rodopi, 1999), xi. Presumably, they believe

violence is morally unjustifiable, but I suggest the grounds for making such a distinction, however warranted, are given by the institution itself. In other words, there is no moral value of violence prior to social organization.

3 Curtin and Litke suggest that institutional violence, which they see as morally unjustifiable, is distinguished from systemic violence, which is also immoral but extends across particular institution into the broader social fabric. Ibid., xiv.
4 Georges Bataille, *Death and Sensuality: A Study of Eroticism and the Taboo* (New York: Walker, 1962), 41.
5 Ibid., 12. Italics in the original.
6 Ibid., 15.
7 Ibid., 13.
8 Ibid., 18.
9 Ibid., 72.
10 Dimitris Vardoulakis, *Sovereignty and Its Other: Toward the Dejustification of Violence* (New York: Fordham University Press, 2013), ch. 3.
11 Roger Friedland, "Institution, Practice, and Ontology: Toward a Religious Sociology," in *Institutions and Ideology*, ed. Renate E. Meyer et al. (Bingley: Emerald Group, 2009), 58–9.
12 Vardoulakis, *Sovereignty and Its Other*, 1.
13 Ibid., 4.
14 Ibid., 7.
15 Ibid., 11.
16 Ibid., 19.
17 Ibid., 11.
18 Foucault provides an extended description of this modern transition: Michel Foucault, *Discipline and Punish: The Birth of the Prison* (New York: Vintage Books, 1995).
19 In a previous article, I compared Giorgio Agamben's figure of *homo sacer* with the martyr as another way to understand the transformation of martyrdom from individual violence and death to institutional support. Matthew Recla, "*Homo Profanus*: The Christian Martyr and the Violence of Meaning-Making," *Critical Research on Religion* 2, no. 2 (2014), 147–64. I had a similar aim, which is to highlight the ways in which a reading of martyrdom as self-sacrifice is not only misleading but is also part of our acquiescence to Christian institutional norms of discourse about violence. There are a couple of distinctions that I signify differently in that article than I have here, though the signified objects remain the same. The first distinction is around violence. In that article I used Slavoj Žižek's "triumvirate of violence" made up of subjective, symbolic, and systemic violence. Slavoj Žižek, *Violence: Six Sideways Reflections* (London: Profile, 2008), 1. I am more concerned with the "concept creep" of the term violence than I once was,

and I have here distinguished instead between violence as physical force and "lawful violence," which is given other names in common parlance. (On concept creep, see Nick Haslam, "Concept Creep: Psychology's Expanding Concepts of Harm and Pathology," *Psychological Inquiry* 27, no. 1 [2016], 1–17.) I think it is important to note—perhaps in a way it was not even a decade ago—both that the means of enacting harm are subtle and not always easily observed, *and* that adjectival forms of violence such as systemic violence rely ultimately on physical force for their meaning. My intent is not to reinforce institutional norms of discourse around violence. It is instead to mitigate the opposite tendency to assume that any institutional use of violence is immoral. A second distinction I made in that article between "martyr" and "Christian martyr" is the distinction I am now making between "willing suicide" and "martyr." This is partly because where I tended to see the operation of the Christian institution as somewhat unique in this transformational process from one to the other, I now would classify this operation, part of the control of violence, as a necessary process for any institution. In connection with seeing these processes as common among institutions—though largely unappreciated in studies of Christianity and other religious traditions—I have come to see the comparison with *homo sacer* as provocative but more complicated than necessary for my purposes. Finally, I am no longer as enchanted as I once was about the redemptive possibilities of the figure of the martyr. However, I have not been completely disenchanted either, and perhaps in the future I will return to what I identified as *homo profanus*.

20 With "Afro-American," I intentionally follow the suggestion made by Fields and Fields. Karen E. Fields and Barbara Jeanne Fields, *Racecraft: The Soul of Inequality in American Life* (New York: Verso, 2012).

21 Among others describing this transition, see Howard Kaplan, "The Rule of Law and Civil Disobedience: The Case behind King's Letter from a Birmingham Jail," *Social Education* 77, no. 3 (2013), 119; H. A. Drake, *Constantine and the Bishops: The Politics of Intolerance* (Baltimore, MD: Johns Hopkins University Press, 2000), 150.

22 As Roger Friedland remarks, "Institutional transformations require power, the deployment of resources, self-conscious collective organization, and even— especially—the exercise of force. Shifts in institutional architecture are occasions in which hegemony fails, and power, denuded of legitimacy, is on display." Friedland, "Institution, Practice, and Ontology," 72.

23 Ernest Becker, *Escape from Evil* (New York: Free Press, 1975), 5. Italics mine.

24 Modern democratic institutions might be seen as exceptional in this regard as meta-institutions whose purpose is to preserve the plurality of institutions with limited power. See note 30 in Chapter 1.

25 Becker, *Escape from Evil*, 65.

26 Ibid., 43. This is a primary function of martyrdom in the absence of perceived existential threat: an object for, or a tool by which to, worship.
27 Ibid., 125.
28 Vardoulakis, *Sovereignty and Its Other*, 19.
29 Becker, *Escape from Evil*, 167.
30 Steve Clarke, *The Justification of Religious Violence* (Chichester: Wiley-Blackwell, 2014), 7. Friedland argues that "every institution is a religious institution: a linked set of practices, subjects, and an unobservable substance that joins the two." Friedland, "Institution, Practice, and Ontology," 64. I lean toward Clarke in thinking that while perhaps not qualitatively different, religious institutions, unbounded by rational-empirical approaches to knowledge, have a greater number of options for justification.
31 Evangelical leader Pat Robertson is exceptional in this regard, having interpreted 9/11, Hurricane Katrina, and the Haitian earthquake as just responses of the divine. Dan Fletcher, "Why Is Pat Robertson Blaming Haiti?," *Time* (accessed October 30, 2021): http://content.time.com/time/specials/packages/article/0,28804,1953379_1953494_1953674,00.html. More recently, in regard to Hurricane Florence, which killed fifty-three, Bruce Ashford intoned, "It was not God who broke this perfect paradise, but humans." Bruce Riley Ashford, "Daddy, Where Is God during the Hurricane?," *Fox News* (September 15, 2018): https://www.foxnews.com/opinion/daddy-where-is-god-during-the-hurricane. On the tendency both to assume agency for natural occurrences and create narratives of meaning out of suffering in the form of deities, see Brett Mercier, Stephanie R. Kramer, and Azim F. Shariff, "Belief in God: Why People Believe, and Why They Don't," *Current Directions in Psychological Science* 27, no. 4 (2018), 263–8.
32 For example, four days after 9/11, practicing Sikh Balbir Singh Sodhi was gunned down by a man who mistakenly profiled him as a Muslim. Moni Basu, "15 Years after 9/11, Sikhs Still Victims of Anti-Muslim Hate Crimes," *CNN* (September 15, 2016): https://www.cnn.com/2016/09/15/us/sikh-hate-crime-victims/index.html.
33 Karen Armstrong, "Charter for Compassion," accessed November 20, 2021, http://charterforcompassion.org/.
34 Karen Armstrong, *Fields of Blood: Religion and the History of Violence* (New York: Alfred A. Knopf, 2014), 4.
35 Ibid., 6. This is the approach of William Cavanaugh, who Armstrong relies on for this argument. William T. Cavanaugh, *The Myth of Religious Violence: Secular Ideology and the Roots of Modern Conflict* (Oxford: Oxford University Press, 2009).
36 Armstrong, *Fields of Blood*, 9.
37 Ibid., 43.
38 Ibid., 124.

39 James K. Wellman Jr. and Kyoko Tokuno, "Is Religious Violence Inevitable?," *Journal for the Scientific Study of Religion* 43, no. 3 (2004), 295.
40 A few examples follow: D. C. Talk and Voice of the Martyrs, *Jesus Freaks: Stories of Those Who Stood for Jesus, the Ultimate Jesus Freaks* (Tulsa, OK: Albury, 1999); Teresa Okure, Jon Sobrino, and Felix Wilfreld, *Rethinking Martyrdom* (London: SCM Press, 2003); Marvin J. Newell, *A Martyr's Grace: Stories of Those Who Gave All for Christ and His Cause* (Chicago: Moody, 2006); Brian Wicker, *Witnesses to Faith?: Martyrdom in Christianity and Islam* (Aldershot: Ashgate, 2006).
41 Herbert Musurillo's assembly of likely "authentic" martyr texts is the starting point for most works on martyrdom over the last four decades, though it has been amended by many in the intervening years. Herbert Musurillo, *The Acts of Christian Martyrs* (Oxford: Clarendon Press, 1972). Historian Lacey Baldwin Smith has put together an interesting diachronic compilation of remarkable martyr stories from within and outside the Christian tradition, though he has difficulty refraining from hierarchization of his tales. Lacey Baldwin Smith, *Fools, Martyrs, Traitors: The Story of Martyrdom in the Western World* (Evanston, IL: Northwestern University Press, 1999).
42 Elizabeth Castelli's work is a notable exception to this: Elizabeth A. Castelli, *Martyrdom and Memory: Early Christian Culture Making* (New York: Columbia University Press, 2004). Candida Moss makes the critical point that the misplaced belief of many contemporary Christians that they are persecuted—based on a narrative that relies heavily on early Christian martyrdom—"legitimates and condones retributive violence." Candida R. Moss, *The Myth of Persecution: How Early Christians Invented a Story of Martyrdom* (New York: HarperOne, 2013), 3.

4 Blood Is Seed: Martyrdom and the Triumph of Christianity

1 Tertullian, *Apology, De Spectaculis*, trans. T. R. Glover, Loeb Classical Library 250 (Cambridge, MA: Harvard University Press, 1931), 50.45.
2 W. H. C. Frend, *Martyrdom and Persecution in the Early Church: A Study of a Conflict from the Maccabees to Donatus* (Garden City, NY: Anchor Books, 1967), 12.
3 Timothy David Barnes, *Tertullian: A Historical and Literary Study* (Oxford: Clarendon Press, 1971), 156.
4 Ibid., 163.
5 Frend, *Martyrdom and Persecution*, 349.
6 Ibid., 392.
7 Glen Chesnut argues that Eusebius was attempting to move from the histories weighted with fate and fortune and give more emphasis to the individual will,

but the bishop was "tempted to put these accidents in a causal chain." Glenn F. Chesnut, *The First Christian Histories: Eusebius, Socrates, Sozomen, Theodoret, and Evagrius* (Macon, GA: Mercer University Press, 1986), 50. This tendency is especially manifest in the relationship of martyrdom and Christian growth, despite the strict incompatibility of the two notions being held with equal importance.

8 Eusebius, *Ecclesiastical History, Volume I: Books 1–5*, trans. Kirsopp Lake, Loeb Classical Library 153 (Cambridge, MA: Harvard University Press, 1926); *Ecclesiastical History, Volume II: Books 6–10*, trans. J. E. L. Oulton, Loeb Classical Library 265 (Cambridge, MA: Harvard University Press, 1932). Translations are from the Loeb volume unless otherwise noted and will be abbreviated as *HE* in subsequent reference.

9 Shelly Matthews notes that Eusebius also quotes the martyrs of Lyons and Vienne, referring to Stephen as "the perfect martyr." Shelly Matthews, "The Need for the Stoning of Stephen," in *Violence in the New Testament*, ed. E. Leigh Gibson and Shelly Matthews (New York: T&T Clark, 2005), 124–5. See also the introduction and first chapter of Shelly Matthews, *Perfect Martyr: The Stoning of Stephen and the Construction of Christian Identity* (New York: Oxford University Press, 2010).

10 Many other suggestions can of course be made; the obsequiousness of Pliny's letter to Hadrian gives a start as well as practical concerns over the sheer number of cases, not simply those of Christians, with which the governor had to reckon.

11 Pliny, *Letters, and Panegyricus*, trans. Betty Radice (Cambridge, MA: Harvard University Press, 1972).

12 It has been noted that Trajan doesn't directly answer Pliny's question as to the extent of punishments. However, it is clear he responds to the question by negating its value, stating it is impossible to establish a static formula for judging Christians. "It is not possible to establish anything universal, as if it had a definite form" (10.97.1). Neither does he sanction the execution of Christians. "If they are indicted and convicted, they are to be punished" (10.97.2).

13 In this case, the opposition comes from the lower class. Ste. Croix and others have noted that pre-Decian persecutions were sporadic and bottom-up, initiated by common people or local officials, in contrast to the coordinated imperial persecutions of the latter third century. G. E. M. de Ste. Croix, "Why Were the Early Christians Persecuted?," *Past and Present* 26 (November 1963), 26; G. E. M. de Ste. Croix, *Christian Persecution, Martyrdom, and Orthodoxy* (Oxford: Oxford University Press, 2006), 137. Eusebius seems to be suggesting at this point an imperial resistance to legitimizing persecution, if for no other reason than to prevent increased accusations and a backlog of cases.

14 On a death wish, see note 30 below.

15 Philip Schaff and Henry Wace, eds., *Eusebius: Church History, Constantine the Great, and Oration in the Praise of Constantine* (Edinburgh: T&T Clark, 1997), 166–7, note 4. For examples of modern scholarship on Ignatius, see note 11 in Chapter 2.
16 The mention of these martyrs comes immediately after Pionius; while for the latter, Eusebius refers the reader to his other work, for the former he notes only that an extant memoir exists (4.15.48). Doron Mendels suggests that Eusebius included those martyrdoms that could be considered public and therefore media-worthy. "Private" martyrdoms, those without a sufficient crowd, did not have the necessary draw. He contends, for example, that this is the reason Polycarp's martyrdom was recorded in detail and Justin Martyr's mentioned only in passing. Mendels's situates Eusebius's work as geared toward attracting more followers, and martyrdom was a good draw. "Eusebius believed that the society outside the Christian inner sphere was potentially ready to accept the Christian mission since the Logos is present everywhere in the world." Doron Mendels, *The Media Revolution of Early Christianity: An Essay on Eusebius's Ecclesiastical History* (Grand Rapids, MI: William B. Eerdmans, 1999), 68. It was also a time in Christian history in which the freedom to proselytize had no attached cost.
17 Herbert Musurillo, *The Acts of Christian Martyrs* (Oxford: Clarendon Press, 1972), 28–9. A Latin version of the same martyrdom has Aganothice burning at the stake for her refusal to sacrifice. When seen combined with the assignment of titles bishop and deacon to Carpus and Papylus, the account appears as an attempt to mitigate potential embarrassment at their aggressive behavior. Ibid., xv–xvi.
18 *Martyrdom of Polycarp*, in J.-P. Migne, *Patrologiae Cursus Completus: Series Graeca* (Paris: J.P. Migne, 1857), vol. 5, 1030–46; Ruslan Khazarzar, "Son of Man," accessed October 2021: http://khazarzar.skeptik.net/pgm/PG_Migne/. References are according to the *Patrologia Graeca*. See also *HE* 4.15.3.
19 Translation mine. Eusebius records only the first of these sentences. *HE* 4.15.3.
20 The dates for Polycarp's martyrdom traditionally range between 155 CE and 175 CE during the reigns of either Antoninus Pius or Marcus Aurelius. Musurillo, *Acts of Christian Martyrs*, 13. More precise dating is not particularly significant for the purposes here, since the cessation of persecution referred to was most certainly a local one regardless.
21 It is possible for the sentence to be read with the emphasis not on the fact that Polycarp waited but that he was "delivered up," martyred, both like Jesus and unlike voluntary martyrs. Do the Smyrneans intend to emphasize, in other words, "that we might become his imitators" in the waiting or the death? The end result is not significantly different. It still expresses that "waiting" produces successful results but volunteering does not. While the death still is the organizational motif for the story, it is the waiting that justifies it. The uncertainty that this intentionally or

unintentionally introduces into the forum of justifications for death both acts as a preventative measure and promotes the repetition of known cases of success, as we will discuss further below.

22. This became especially pronounced in the post-Constantinian era of pagan/Christian struggle, when the bold actions of the individual were feared to bring possible retribution from the opposition on the community as a whole. Ste. Croix, *Christian Persecution*, 163, 204.

23. Interestingly, this idea follows shortly after the selection of Paul's letter to the Philippians quoted by the Smyrneans: "And being found in appearance as a man, he humbled himself by becoming obedient to death—even death on a cross!" (Phil. 4:8).

24. Oskar Leopold von Gebhart, *Acta Martyrum Selecta* (Berlin: A. Duncker, 1902). References are numbered according to *HE*.

25. A gradual transition can also be observed in recensions of the martyrdom of one Justin, believed to be Justin Martyr, in which the account becomes more descriptive and the participants more recalcitrant; in other words, the account gradually loses its unique context and becomes a typecast representation of martyrdom ideals. Musurillo, *Acts of Christian Martyrs*, xviii–xix.

26. The Christian apologist Tertullian similarly accuses Rome of attempting to resurrect the dead with monuments in the final chapter of his *Apology*. See p. 68.

27. This would be a difficult point to defend, as even the stories of most orthodox martyrdoms hinge upon the refusal of the martyr to participate in a secular mandate, preferring instead to pledge allegiance to the higher law of the divine. Even in the cases of imperial officials who are diabolized, martyrdoms certainly took place according to God's law. Tertullian would argue for the universal requirement of martyrdom based upon God's omnipotence and goodness in his *On Flight in Persecution*. See pp. 69–70. Apollinarius's mention of unlawfulness is explained in his following comments.

28. Daniel Boyarin discusses this passage as well, illustrating the contested space of legitimate martyrdom. Daniel Boyarin, *Dying for God: Martyrdom and the Making of Christianity and Judaism* (Stanford, CA: Stanford University Press, 1999), 101–2.

29. There is an interesting dynamic established here in which Origen inspires his pupils so much that many are led to martyrdom, yet the teacher himself remains unharmed. The break from the expected storyline of inspiration through death may be responsible for Eusebius's earnest effort to ascribe Origen's survival to divine will. However, his death under Decius years later also goes a long way to rewrite his early history, and he was certainly not without zeal, as Eusebius's apologetic account of Origen's self-castration shows. *HE* 6.8.

30. G. W. Bowersock, *Martyrdom and Rome* (New York: Cambridge University Press, 1995), 61. This sentiment is also related by E. R. Dodds and attributed to a comment

of Clement. Dodds states matter-of-factly, "There is evidence for thinking that in these centuries a good many persons were consciously or unconsciously in love with death. For such men the chance of martyrdom, carrying with it fame in this world and bliss in the next, could only add to the attractions of Christianity." E. R. Dodds, *Pagan and Christian in an Age of Anxiety: Some Aspects of Religious Experience from Marcus Aurelius to Constantine* (Cambridge: Cambridge University Press, 1990), 135–6. "A good many" is the depth of quantitative analysis that has perpetuated the traditional valuation of the martyr, even for "outsiders" like Dodds.

31 Bowersock, *Martyrdom and Rome*, 64.
32 Ibid., 65–6.
33 Eusebius devotes two chapters to recording the works of Clement but goes little beyond summary notes. He uses the bishop earlier as a source for various events, such as the martyrdom of James the Just (2.1.3).
34 Note the resonance with the philosopher Newman in Chapter 2 (p. 20).
35 Bowersock, *Martyrdom and Rome*, 96. Notably, Barnes argues that Clement is redefining the term to be confession before God rather than man, which accomplishes the same end of limiting the autonomy of the act. Barnes, *Tertullian*, 168.
36 Philip Tite similarly emphasizes the innovative work Clement is doing in his tripartite division of martyrdom, with volunteerism on one side, wholesale rejection on the other, and Clement's own position resting appropriately between the two. Philip L. Tite, "Voluntary Martyrdom and Gnosticism," *Journal of Early Christian Studies* 23, no. 1 (Spring 2015), 33–4.
37 Barnes, *Tertullian*, 83–4.
38 As with Clement, Eusebius's greatest use of Tertullian, "a man well-versed in the laws of the Romans," is as a source for previous historical events. *HE* 2.2. For this, he seems only to know the *Apology* through a Greek translation not his own. Schaff and Wace, *Church History*, 105.
39 *Address to the Martyrs* was once thought to be contemporary with the martyrdom of Perpetua, but Barnes has suggested it was written in 197 CE, before the *Apology*. Barnes, *Tertullian*, ch. 5. For online access to Tertullian, see this excellent collection: Roger Pearse, "The Tertullian Project," accessed November 5, 2021: https://www.tertullian.org.
40 Barton discusses several cases of "the Roman paradigm of the redemption of honor through ferocious self-destruction." Carlin A. Barton, "Savage Miracles: The Redemption of Lost Honor in Roman Society and the Sacrament of the Gladiator and the Martyr," *Representations* 45 (Winter 1994), 46.
41 Geoffrey D. Dunn, *Tertullian* (New York: Routledge, 2004), 114.

42 His only concession to Christians who fear arousing suspicion by continuing to gather together is to meet in smaller groups or at night; again, what is God's will is both good and unavoidable and consequently not worth worry (3.4).
43 Barnes, *Tertullian*, 174. Barnes imagines Tertullian as a forgotten martyr, forgotten because considered Montanist, but the heavy usage of Tertullian's writings by later church fathers, particularly Cyprian, suggests a less dramatic passing. Had Tertullian wished to have been a martyr, he could likely have become one. It is not unimaginable that he, for whatever reason, was unable to allow himself to be placed in a position to be martyred; vehement rhetorical opposition often belies an inner turmoil and tension between word and deed.
44 After describing Jesus's death and resurrection and its witnessing by many, he notes that Pilate reported the happenings to Tiberius and remarks that even the emperor would have believed "if either emperors had not been necessary to the world or if it had been possible for Christians too to be emperors." *Apology*, 21.24.
45 Bowersock, *Martyrdom and Rome*, 54–5.
46 Eusebius first mentions Cyprian in connection with Novatus, who treated the refused the readmission of lapsed Christians to the church (6.43). He is subsequently mentioned as holding the opinion that the lapsed might be readmitted to the church upon rebaptism, a contentious position that Eusebius refrains from commenting on (7.3).
47 G. W. Clarke, *The Letters of St. Cyprian of Carthage* (New York: Newman Press, 1984). The chronology of the letters I follow is suggested by Clarke. See also Paul Middleton, "Enemies of the (Church and) State: Martyrdom as a Problem for Early Christianity," *Annali di storia dell'esegesi* 29, no. 2 (2012), 177–8.
48 One certainly wonders how Cyprian gained hold of these letters. Clarke asks whether Celerinus might have sent the letters to Cyprian out of deference, and Cyprian later speaks of the confessor highly, albeit in contrast to the seemingly naïve and grasping Lucianus. Clarke, *Letters of St. Cyprian*, 314. Cyprian himself explains, in forwarding the correspondence on to Roman clergy, that "nothing escapes our watchful zeal" (26.3.2).
49 Ibid., 340.
50 Ibid., 344.
51 While internally Cyprian chastises the presbyters and deacons severely, externally he presents them as victims in "malevolent" attack (27.3.1).
52 Ibid., 355.
53 Musurillo writes: "Cyprian's response ... dispels any suspicion that he had avoided a clash with the Roman authorities out of cowardice." Musurillo, *Acts of Christian Martyrs*, xxxi. In any case, it was less likely that he would follow the same course as he had under the Decian persecution, which had precipitated such a flurry of controversy and letter-writing; his actions needed to be clear this time. David Potter,

"Martyrdom as Spectacle," in *Theater and Society in the Classical World*, ed. Ruth Scodel (Ann Arbor: University of Michigan Press, 1993), 59.

54 *Acts of Cyprian, Holy Bishop and Martyr* in Gebhart, *Acta Martyrum Selecta*. Translation in Musurillo, *Acts of Christian Martyrs*, 168–75.

55 There is no mention of the community attempting to procure relics from his clothing or his person. Rather, "his body was placed nearby on account of pagan curiosity" until the day had expired (5.6).

56 There follows an amusing exchange between the proconsul and the bishop that reveals a sort of competition lying just below the surface of class niceties. After refusing to give Christian names, he retorts, "But if you seek them out, you will find them." Paternus responds: "I will seek them out from this community today." Cyprian repeats, "They will be found if sought by you." Paternus reaffirms: "I will find them" (1.6–1.7). The exchange, a jousting between social peers, suggests a more sophisticated but similar contention to that seen in the diatribes of other would-be martyrs against their opponents.

57 *The Martyrdom of Fructosus and Companions*. Translated in Musurillo, *Acts of Christian Martyrs*, 176–85.

58 Ibid., xxxiv.

59 Potter, "Martyrdom as Spectacle," 53.

60 Ibid., 55–6.

61 Michel Foucault, *Discipline and Punish: The Birth of the Prison* (New York: Vintage Books, 1995), 46.

62 Potter, "Martyrdom as Spectacle," 65.

63 Ibid., 70.

64 The Bishop of Alexandria claims that the names are superfluous, but many "of every race and age, some by scourging and fire, some by the sword, have conquered in the strife and received their crowns." The preceding serves primarily as a contrast to those such as himself who the Lord, for unknown reasons, preserved through persecution and exile (7.11.20–21).

65 He includes the prison account of one Phileas, Bishop of Thmuites, also a philosopher and civil servant, as well as a list of the clergy who suffered under the persecution (8.10, 8.13).

66 It should be noted that Eusebius is also considered to be the author of the *Martyrs of Palestine*, an account of many martyrdoms within Palestine from 303 to 310, commonly inserted between the eighth and ninth books of the *Ecclesiastical History*. Although it is complementary to the brief accounts of martyrdoms in other regions in Book Eight, it does not seem to have been originally intended to be within the history and fits somewhat awkwardly in its current position. With that consideration, the brief twelve chapter account adds little to our discussion, following the same general pattern as that of the history. Even after the fourth

imperial edict that compelled all Christians to sacrifice, Eusebius describes exclusively martyrs of high social standing and education, particularly those with positions in the church or whom Eusebius admired. He devotes only a sentence to those "benumbed in spirit by terror, [who] were easily weakened at the first outset." *Martyrs of Palestine*, 2.3. The remainder of the compilation is devoted to particular exemplars. G. E. M. de Ste. Croix discusses the text in his analysis of voluntary martyrdom. See Chapter 5.

67 Glen Chesnut suggests the initial pacifist approach of the bishop that only slowly accommodated the triumph of Constantine into a Christian worldview. Chesnut, *The First Christian Histories*, 131.

68 Ste. Croix, *Christian Persecution*, 201. Ste. Croix notes that in preparation for writing his article, he could find no works that dealt with persecution both before and after Constantine. He laments that scholarly treatment is weighted toward the persecution of Christians rather than by them. Scholarship in the last ten years has mitigated that trend slightly. Hal Drake suggests that continued persecution is best understood in primarily political and not religious terms. H. A. Drake, *Constantine and the Bishops: The Politics of Intolerance* (Baltimore, MD: Johns Hopkins University Press, 2000), 27. Michael Gaddis argues rather that continued post-Constantinian violence should be understood in religious terms but on a continuum between enacting and suffering violence. Michael Gaddis, *There Is No Crime for Those Who Have Christ: Religious Violence in the Christian Roman Empire* (Berkeley: University of California Press, 2005), 11, 175. Tom Sizgorich presents an even more nuanced view, recognizing the stand-in, sacrificial role that Christian purveyors of violence played in their communities. Martyrs and then ascetics were included in Christianity by their exclusion from it; they patrolled the boundaries of Christian corporate identity. Thomas Sizgorich, *Violence and Belief in Late Antiquity: Militant Devotion in Christianity and Islam* (Philadelphia: University of Pennsylvania Press, 2009), 24, 130.

69 See also Bart D. Ehrman, *The Triumph of Christianity: How a Forbidden Religion Swept the World* (New York: Simon & Schuster, 2017), 265; Drake, *Constantine and the Bishops*, 23.

70 Ste. Croix, *Christian Persecution*, 214–15.

71 "I suggest, then, that ideally the Catholics should have refused the use of force offered by the State to coerce their Donatist opponents." Ibid., 218. In Chapter 6, I discuss philosopher Robert Brimlow wrestling with this issue on an individual rather than institutional level.

72 Ibid., 231.

73 Ibid., 232.

74 Ste. Croix, "Why Were the Early Christians Persecuted?," 22; Ste. Croix, *Christian Persecution*, 130.

5 "Voluntary" Martyrdom: Avoiding the Stigma of Suicide

1 Kenneth Dean, "Madman or Martyr? Retired Minister Sets Self on Fire, Dies," *Tyler Morning Telegraph* (July 1, 2014): accessed March 12, 2022, http://www.tylerpaper.com/TP-News+Local/201968/madman-or-martyr-retired-minister-sets-self-on-fire-dies .
2 Jeff Hood, "Pushing into the Flames: Rev. Charles Moore and the Struggle against Racism," *Fellowship of Reconciliation* (June 23, 2015): accessed May 19, 2016, http://forusa.org/blogs/jeff-hood/pushing-into-flames-rev-charles-moore-struggle-against-racism/13205.
3 Drew B. McIntyre, "Heroism, Martyrdom and Suicide: Thoughts on Self-Immolation," *United Methodist Insight* (July 17, 2014): accessed May 19, 2016, http://um-insight.net/perspectives/heroism,-martyrdom-and-suicide%3A-thoughts-on-self-immolation/.
4 Marvin J. Newell, *A Martyr's Grace: Stories of Those Who Gave All for Christ and His Cause* (Chicago: Moody, 2006), 12.
5 G. E. M. de Ste. Croix, "Aspects of the 'Great' Persecution," *Harvard Theological Review* 47, no. 2 (April 1954), 83.
6 Ibid., 102.
7 Ibid., 104.
8 G. E. M. de Ste. Croix, "Why Were the Early Christians Persecuted?," *Past and Present* 26 (November 1963), 31.
9 Ibid., 21.
10 His claim that voluntary martyrdom may in some cases have encouraged Roman persecution is not given significant support. This may be because he intended to publish a longer work on the subject, as he claims in the opening footnote to the article.
11 Paul Middleton mentions others: Paul Middleton, "Early Christian Voluntary Martyrdom: A Statement for the Defence," *Journal of Theological Studies* 64, no. 2 (October 2013), 561.
12 P. Lorraine Buck, "Voluntary Martyrdom Revisited," *Journal of Theological Studies* 63, no. 1 (April 2012), 126–7.
13 Ibid., 127.
14 Ibid.
15 Middleton, "Early Christian Voluntary Martyrdom," 561.
16 E. R. Dodds, *Pagan and Christian in an Age of Anxiety: Some Aspects of Religious Experience from Marcus Aurelius to Constantine* (Cambridge: Cambridge University Press, 1990), 135.
17 Arthur J. Droge and James D. Tabor, *A Noble Death: Suicide and Martyrdom among Christians and Jews in Antiquity* (San Francisco, CA: HarperSanFrancisco, 1992), 5; Middleton, "Early Christian Voluntary Martyrdom," 556–7.

18 Buck, "Voluntary Martyrdom Revisited," 127.
19 See particularly Jonathan Haidt and the work built upon his scholarship. J. Haidt, "The Emotional Dog and Its Rational Tail: A Social Intuitionist Approach to Moral Judgment," *Psychological Review* 108, no. 4 (2001), 814–34.
20 Joshua David Greene, *Moral Tribes: Emotion, Reason, and the Gap between Us and Them* (New York: Penguin Books, 2013), 124–5.
21 Ibid., 213. Steve Clarke treats Greene's earlier work in relation to religious violence. Steve Clarke, *The Justification of Religious Violence* (Chichester: Wiley-Blackwell, 2014), 70–5.
22 Alison McIntyre, "Doctrine of Double Effect," *Stanford Encyclopedia of Philosophy* (Winter 2014): http://plato.stanford.edu/archives/win2014/entries/double-effect/.
23 Greene, *Moral Tribes*, 223.
24 Ibid., 219.
25 Ibid., 224.
26 Droge and Tabor, *A Noble Death*, 43.
27 Ibid., 126.
28 Buck, "Voluntary Martyrdom Revisited," 128.
29 Paradoxically, Bart Ehrman suggests that "paganism … die[d] a natural death, cut off from resources and abandoned by popular opinion." Bart D. Ehrman, *The Triumph of Christianity: How a Forbidden Religion Swept the World* (New York: Simon & Schuster, 2017), 277. This is a natural death, I suppose, in the same way that starvation from being locked away without access to food is a natural death.
30 See note 7.
31 See, for example, Johan Leemans, *More Than a Memory: The Discourse of Martyrdom and the Construction of Christian Identity in the History of Christianity* (Leuven: Peeters, 2005), xi.
32 Buck, "Voluntary Martyrdom Revisited," 132.
33 Candida R. Moss, "The Discourse of Voluntary Martyrdom: Ancient and Modern," *Church History* 81, no. 3 (September 2012), 531–51. Middleton similarly attempts to navigate the issue I've discussed, not only critiquing Buck's approach but also chastising Droge and Tabor, making the grand statement that "martyrdom, at least for those Christians who embraced it, was never an unfortunate necessity, and certainly not an act of self-destruction. For early Christians, embracing death was rushing toward life." Middleton, "Early Christian Voluntary Martyrdom," 560. This statement needs to be balanced against the reality that the vast majority of early Christians embraced death no less or more than non-Christians, as is the case throughout history. See also Paul Middleton, *Radical Martyrdom and Cosmic Conflict in Early Christianity* (London: T&T Clark, 2006).

34 Michael Hall, "Man on Fire," *Texas Monthly* (December 2014): accessed May 19, 2016, http://www.texasmonthly.com/articles/man-on-fire/.
35 See Wayne Meeks for one example: Wayne A. Meeks, *The First Urban Christians: The Social World of the Apostle Paul* (New Haven, CT: Yale University Press, 1983).
36 David T Bradford, "Early Christian Martyrdom and the Psychology of Depression, Suicide, and Bodily Mutilation," *Psychotherapy: Theory, Research, Practice, Training* 27, no. 1 (1990), 39.
37 In a response to Adam Lankford's *Myth of Martyrdom*, Rottman and Kelemen suggest a slightly different psychological response: suicide is stigmatized because it violates the moral foundation of purity, following Haidt's Moral Foundations Theory. Adam Lankford, "Précis of the Myth of Martyrdom: What Really Drives Suicide Bombers, Rampage Shooters, and Other Self-Destructive Killers," *Behavioral and Brain Sciences* 37, no. 4 (2014), 375–6.
38 Sophia Moskalenko and Clark R. McCauley, *The Marvel of Martyrdom: The Power of Self-Sacrifice in a Selfish World* (New York: Oxford University Press, 2019), 7.
39 This is a familiar theme in Christian existentialism. See, for example, Peter Rollins, *The Fidelity of Betrayal: Towards a Church beyond Belief* (Brewster, MA: Paraclete Press, 2008).
40 Cited in Talal Asad, *On Suicide Bombing* (New York: Columbia University Press, 2007), 40.
41 Jeffery Martin et al., "Typologies of Suicide: A Critical Literature Review," *Archives of Suicide Research* 24, no. 1 (2020), S25.
42 Thomas Joiner, *Why People Die by Suicide* (Cambridge, MA: Harvard University Press, 2007), 33. See also J. Maxwell Atkinson, *Discovering Suicide: Studies in the Social Organization of Sudden Death* (Pittsburgh, PA: University of Pittsburgh Press, 1978), ch. 2.
43 Martin et al., "Typologies of Suicide," S27.
44 Émile Durkheim, *Suicide: A Study in Sociology*, trans. John A. Spaulding and George Simpson (New York: Free Press, 1979), 44.
45 Martin et al., "Typologies of Suicide," S27.
46 Ibid., S28.
47 Ibid., S30.
48 Ibid., S31.
49 Ibid., S35, S36.
50 Joiner, *Why People Die by Suicide*, 39.
51 Ibid., 53.
52 Ibid., 68–9.
53 Ibid., 148.
54 Ibid., 76.
55 Greene, *Moral Tribes*, 234.

56 Droge and Tabor, *A Noble Death*, 170.
57 Ibid., 3.
58 Joiner, *Why People Die by Suicide*, 63.
59 See note 16.
60 Joiner, *Why People Die by Suicide*, 86.

6 "In Love with Death": Pathology and Identity in Martyrdom

1 Portions of this chapter previously appeared here: Matthew (Matt) J. Recla, "Pathology, Identity, or Both? Making Meaning from Early Christian Martyrdom," *Mortality* (2020), 1–15; Matthew Recla, "Martyrdom and the Creation of Christian Identity," in *The Wiley-Blackwell Concise Companion to Christian Martyrdom*, ed. Paul Middleton (Chichester: Wiley-Blackwell, 2018), 199–214.
2 Margaret Watkins Tate, "Martyrdom and Integrity," *Philosophia Christi* 9, no. 1 (2007), 101.
3 Sophia Moskalenko and Clark R. McCauley, *The Marvel of Martyrdom: The Power of Self-Sacrifice in a Selfish World* (New York: Oxford University Press, 2019), 151.
4 Paul Middleton, "What Is Martyrdom?," *Mortality* 19, no. 2 (2014), 130.
5 Rogers Brubaker and Frederick Cooper, "Beyond 'Identity,'" *Theory and Society* 29, no. 1 (February 2000), 2–3.
6 Jose Cabezon and Sheila Greeve Davaney, *Identity and the Politics of Scholarship in the Study of Religion* (New York: Routledge, 2004), 8. See also the classic essay on religion by J. Z. Smith: Jonathan Z. Smith, "Religion, Religions, Religious," in *Critical Terms for Religious Studies*, ed. Mark C. Taylor (Chicago: University of Chicago Press, 1998), 269–84.
7 Middleton, "What Is Martyrdom?," 120; Judith M. Lieu, "The Forging of Christian Identity," *Mediterranean Archaeology* 11 (1998), 74.
8 Brubaker, and Cooper, "Beyond 'Identity,'" 1.
9 Max Weber, *From Max Weber: Essays in Sociology* (New York: Oxford University Press, 1946), 262.
10 Wayne A. Meeks, *The First Urban Christians: The Social World of the Apostle Paul* (New Haven, CT: Yale University Press, 1983), ch. 1; Rodney Stark, *The Rise of Christianity: A Sociologist Reconsiders History* (Princeton, NJ: Princeton University Press, 1996), ch. 2.
11 H. A. Drake, *Constantine and the Bishops: The Politics of Intolerance* (Baltimore, MD: Johns Hopkins University Press, 2000), 28; Charles M. Odahl, *Constantine and the Christian Empire* (London: Routledge, 2004), 182–201; H. A. Drake,

"Intolerance, Religious Violence, and Political Legitimacy in Late Antiquity," *Journal of the American Academy of Religion* 79, no. 1 (March 2011), 217.

12 Doron Mendels, *The Media Revolution of Early Christianity: An Essay on Eusebius's Ecclesiastical History* (Grand Rapids, MI: William B. Eerdmans, 1999).

13 Hopkins connects minimal early Christian persecution to a low absolute number of Christians in the Roman Empire in the first centuries of the Common Era. Keith Hopkins, "Christian Number and Its Implications," *Journal of Early Christian Studies* 6, no. 2 (1998), 196. However, Barrett and Johnson inclusively calculate over seventy million Christians who have died in "situations of witness" throughout history—over half from the twentieth century forward. David B. Barrett et al., *World Christian Trends Ad 30–Ad 2200* (Pasadena, CA: William Carey Library, 2001), 32.

14 Lacey Baldwin Smith, *Fools, Martyrs, Traitors: The Story of Martyrdom in the Western World* (Evanston, IL: Northwestern University Press, 1999), 17.

15 See Daniel Boyarin, *Dying for God: Martyrdom and the Making of Christianity and Judaism* (Stanford, CA: Stanford University Press, 1999); Peter Robert Lamont Brown, *The Cult of the Saints: Its Rise and Function in Latin Christianity* (Chicago: University of Chicago Press, 1981); Lucy Grig, *Making Martyrs in Late Antiquity* (London: Duckworth, 2004); Michael Gaddis, *There Is No Crime for Those Who Have Christ: Religious Violence in the Christian Roman Empire* (Berkeley: University of California Press, 2005); Thomas Sizgorich, *Violence and Belief in Late Antiquity: Militant Devotion in Christianity and Islam* (Philadelphia: University of Pennsylvania Press, 2009). As orthodox Christianity developed throughout the fourth century, martyrs were certainly made from Donatists, Manichaeans, and other "heretical" Christian sects.

16 Judith Lieu, *Neither Jew nor Greek?: Constructing Christian Identity* (London: Bloomsbury T&T Clark, 2016), 233.

17 Johan Leemans, *"Let Us Die That We May Live": Greek Homilies on Christian Martyrs from Asia Minor, Palestine, and Syria (C. Ad 350–Ad 450)* (London: Routledge, 2003), 58, 68.

18 Donald W. Riddle, *The Martyrs: A Study in Social Control* (Chicago: University of Chicago Press, 1931), 2.

19 Ibid., 24–5, ch. 2.

20 Candida R. Moss, *The Other Christs: Imitating Jesus in Ancient Christian Ideologies of Martyrdom* (New York: Oxford University Press, 2010), 20. See also Paul Middleton, *Radical Martyrdom and Cosmic Conflict in Early Christianity* (London: T&T Clark, 2006), 6.

21 Maureen A. Tilley, "The Ascetic Body and the (Un)making of the World of the Martyr," *Journal of the American Academy of Religion* 59, no. 3 (Autumn 1991), 471–3.

22 Robin Darling Young, *In Procession before the World Martyrdom as Public Liturgy in Early Christianity* (Milwaukee, WI: Marquette University Press, 2001), 11.
23 Ibid., 60.
24 Ibid., 61.
25 Nicole Kelley, "Philosophy as Training for Death: Reading the Ancient Christian Martyr Acts as Spiritual Exercises," *Church History: Studies in Christianity and Culture* 75, no. 4 (2006), 727.
26 Ibid., 729.
27 Judith Perkins, *The Suffering Self: Pain and Narrative Representation in the Early Christian Era* (London: Routledge, 1995).
28 Judith Perkins, "Perpetua's *Vas*: Asserting Christian Identity," in *Group Identity and Religious Individuality in Late Antiquity*, ed. Éric Rebillard and Jörg Rüpke (Washington, DC: Catholic University of America Press, 2015), 144.
29 Ibid.
30 Ibid., 145.
31 Ibid., 146.
32 Outi Lehtipuu, "'What Harm Is There for You to Say Caesar Is Lord?' Emperors and the Imperial Cult in Early Christian Stories of Martyrdom," *Collegium* 20 (2016), 107.
33 See, for example, Adam Lankford, *The Myth of Martyrdom: What Really Drives Suicide Bombers, Rampage Shooters, and Other Self-Destructive Killers* (New York: Palgrave Macmillan, 2013); Ariel Merari et al., "Personality Characteristics of 'Self Martyrs'/'Suicide Bombers' and Organizers of Suicide Attacks," *Terrorism and Political Violence* 22, no. 1 (December 22, 2009), 87–101; Jonathan M. Metzl and Kenneth T. MacLeish, "Mental Illness, Mass Shootings, and the Politics of American Firearms," *American Journal of Public Health* 105, no. 2 (December 12, 2014), 240–9.
34 Michael Hall, "Man on Fire," *Texas Monthly* (December 2014): accessed May 19, 2016, http://www.texasmonthly.com/articles/man-on-fire/.
35 Brad S. Gregory, *Salvation at Stake: Christian Martyrdom in Early Modern Europe* (Cambridge, MA: Harvard University Press, 1999).
36 Gretchen E. Minton, "'The Same Cause and Like Quarell': Eusebius, John Foxe, and the Evolution of Ecclesiastical History," *Church History* 71, no. 4 (2002), 716.
37 Gregory, *Salvation at Stake*, 306.
38 Ibid., 8.
39 Edward Gibbon, *The History of the Decline and Fall of the Roman Empire: Constantine and the Christian Empire* (London: Folio Society, 1995), 94, 198.
40 Ibid., 167.

41 Candida R. Moss, "Discourse of Voluntary Martyrdom: Ancient and Modern," *Church History* 81, no. 3 (September 2012), 537.
42 Eugene Weiner and Anita Weiner, *The Martyr's Conviction: A Sociological Analysis* (Atlanta, GA: Scholars Press, 1990), 7.
43 Riddle, *The Martyrs*, 60.
44 Ibid., 63.
45 G. E. M. de Ste. Croix, "Why Were the Early Christians Persecuted?," *Past and Present* 26 (November 1963), 24.
46 G. E. M. de Ste. Croix, *Christian Persecution, Martyrdom, and Orthodoxy* (Oxford: Oxford University Press, 2006, 154).
47 Mary R. Lefkowitz, "The Motivations for St. Perpetua's Martyrdom," *Journal of the American Academy of Religion* 44, no. 3 (1976), 417.
48 Seymour Byman, "Guilt and Martyrdom: The Case of John Bradford," *Harvard Theological Review* 68, nos. 3/4 (1975), 307.
49 Ibid., 331.
50 Lamar M. Hill and E. Mansell Pattison, "Communications," *American Historical Review* 84, no. 4 (1979), 1230.
51 Gregory, *Salvation at Stake*, 100.
52 Ibid., 105.
53 Smith, *Fools, Martyrs, Traitors*, 16.
54 Bart D. Ehrman, *Lost Christianities: The Battles for Scripture and the Faiths We Never Knew* (New York: Oxford University Press, 2005), 137.
55 Brubaker and Cooper, "Beyond 'Identity,'" 2.
56 Peter Brown, "Review: Approaches to the Religious Crisis of the Third Century A.D.," *English Historical Review* 83, no. 328 (July 1968), 550.
57 R. A. Markus, "The Problem of Self-Definition: From Sect to Church," in *The Shaping of Christianity in the Second and Third Centuries*, ed. E. P. Sanders, Albert I. Baumgarten, and Alan Mendelson (London: SCM Press, 1980), 1.
58 R. A. Markus, *The End of Ancient Christianity* (Cambridge: Cambridge University Press, 1990), 92–5.
59 Ste. Croix, *Christian Persecution*, 34.
60 Judith Perkins, "The Apocryphal Acts of the Apostles and the Early Christian Martyrdom," *Arethusa* 18, no. 2 (1985), 221–2. Emphasis mine.
61 Ibid., 223.
62 The idea that textual focus on suffering—in Christian and non-Christian texts—is a reflection of a "widespread cultural concern" rather than individual obsession is echoed in her later work as well. Perkins, *The Suffering Self*. Perkins's partial step toward identity might also be characterized as a half-step away from pathology, as Candida Moss suggests—"from psychological to cultural pathology." Candida R.

Moss, *Ancient Christian Martyrdom: Diverse Practices, Theologies, and Traditions* (New Haven, CT: Yale University Press, 2012), 7.
63 Brubaker and Cooper, "Beyond 'Identity,'" 1.
64 See also Judith Lieu, *Christian Identity in the Jewish and Graeco-Roman World* (Oxford: Oxford University Press, 2004), 11–17, 23–4.
65 Lieu, "The Forging of Christian Identity," 74.
66 Jonathan Z. Smith, *Drudgery Divine: On the Comparison of Early Christianities and the Religions of Late Antiquity* (Chicago: University of Chicago Press, 1990), 110.
67 Éric Rebillard and Jörg Rüpke, eds., *Group Identity and Religious Individuality in Late Antiquity* (Washington, DC: Catholic University of America Press, 2015), 5.
68 Brubaker and Cooper, "Beyond 'Identity,'" 1.
69 Ibid., 4–5.
70 Moss, *Ancient Christian Martyrdom*, 17.
71 Richard Ascough, "Judith Perkins and Christian Identity Formation," *Westar National Meeting* (March 24, 2017), 15.
72 Ibid., 10.
73 Éric Rebillard, *Christians and Their Many Identities in Late Antiquity, North Africa, 200–450 CE* (Ithaca, NY: Cornell University Press, 2012), 2–5.
74 Candida R. Moss, "Notions of Orthodoxy in Early Christian Martyrdom Literature," in *The Other Side: Apocryphal Perspectives on Ancient Christian "Orthodoxies,"* ed. Tobias Nicklas et al. (Göttingen: Vandenhoeck & Ruprecht, July 17, 2017), 165.
75 Moss, "Discourse of Voluntary Martyrdom," 550.
76 Ibid. Gregory makes a similar critique: Gregory, *Salvation at Stake*, 8, 101.
77 Candida R. Moss, *The Myth of Persecution: How Early Christians Invented a Story of Martyrdom* (New York: HarperOne, 2013), 14.
78 David Friedrich Strauss, *The Life of Jesus*, trans. George Eliot (New York: C. Blanchard, 1860), 850–2.
79 See Smith, *Fools, Martyrs, Traitors*; Costica Bradatan, *Dying for Ideas: The Dangerous Lives of the Philosophers* (New York: Bloomsbury Academic, 2015).
80 Robert Brimlow, *What about Hitler?: Wrestling with Jesus's Call to Nonviolence in an Evil World* (Grand Rapids, MI: Brazos Press, 2006), 170. See also Moss, *The Myth of Persecution*, 5.
81 Johan Leemans, *More Than a Memory: The Discourse of Martyrdom and the Construction of Christian Identity in the History of Christianity* (Leuven: Peeters, 2005), xi; Erin Ronsse, "Rhetoric of Martyrs: Listening to Saints Perpetua and Felicitas," *Journal of Early Christian Studies* 14, no. 3 (Fall 2006), 284.
82 Kelley, "Philosophy as Training for Death," 735.
83 See note 14 in Chapter 1.
84 Michel Foucault, *Discipline and Punish: The Birth of the Prison* (New York: Vintage Books, 1995, 193).

85 Jerrold M. Post et al., "The Psychology of Suicide Terrorism," *Psychiatry: Interpersonal and Biological Processes* 72, no. 1 (March 1, 2009), 25.
86 Ibid., 26–9.
87 Jocelyn J. Bélanger et al., "The Psychology of Martyrdom: Making the Ultimate Sacrifice in the Name of a Cause," *Journal of Personality and Social Psychology* 107, no. 3 (2014), 499, 502–3, 511.
88 Thomas Joiner, *Why People Die By Suicide* (Cambridge, MA: Harvard University Press, 2007), 152.
89 Ibid., 177–83.
90 Moss, *The Myth of Persecution*, 9. See also note 68 in Chapter 4.
91 Jason Bruner, *Imagining Persecution: Why American Christians Believe There Is a Global War against Their Faith* (New Brunswick, NJ: Rutgers University Press, 2021), 143.

7 The Immorality of Religious Martyrdom

1 Karen Armstrong, *Fields of Blood: Religion and the History of Violence* (New York: Alfred A. Knopf, 2014).
2 Steve Clarke, *The Justification of Religious Violence* (Chichester: Wiley-Blackwell, 2014), ix.
3 Hector Avalos, *Fighting Words: The Origins of Religious Violence* (Amherst, NY: Prometheus Books, 2005), 18; Hector Avalos, "Religion and Scarcity: A New Theory for the Role of Religion in Violence," in *The Oxford Handbook of Religion and Violence*, ed. Mark Juergensmeyer, Margo Kitts, and Michael K. Jerryson (New York: Oxford University Press, 2013).
4 Joshua David Greene, *Moral Tribes: Emotion, Reason, and the Gap between Us and Them* (New York: Penguin Books, 2013), 23.
5 N. Innaiah, *Forced into Faith: How Religion Abuses Children's Rights* (Amherst, NY: Prometheus Books, 2009), 9.
6 Avalos, *Fighting Words*, 29.
7 Cited in Greene, *Moral Tribes*, 175.
8 "The Last Night," *Friends of Flight 93 National Memorial*: accessed October 15, 2021, https://www.flight93friends.org/learning-center/crime-scene-investigation/the-last-night-document.
9 The Center for Public Integrity, "False Premise for Going to War" (December 10, 2008): accessed October 15, 2021, https://publicintegrity.org/politics/false-premise-for-going-to-war/.
10 "Costs of War," *Watson Institute for International and Public Affairs at Brown University*: accessed October 15, 2021, https://watson.brown.edu/costsofwar/.

11 Avalos, *Fighting Words*, 18.
12 Thomas Joiner, *Why People Die by Suicide* (Cambridge, MA: Harvard University Press, 2007), 26.
13 Elizabeth A. Castelli, *Martyrdom and Memory: Early Christian Culture Making* (New York: Columbia University Press, 2004), ch. 6; Justin Watson, *The Martyrs of Columbine: Faith and the Politics of Tragedy* (New York: Palgrave Macmillan, 2002), 9–12.
14 Dave Cullen, "Inside the Columbine High Investigation," *Salon* (September 23, 1999): accessed January 25, 2014, http://www.salon.com/1999/09/23/columbine_4/.
15 Watson, *The Martyrs of Columbine*, ch. 1.
16 "CPJ Condemns Murder of US Journalist Steven Sotloff," *Committee to Protect Journalists* (September 2, 2014): accessed October 21, 2021, https://cpj.org/2014/09/cpj-condemns-murder-of-us-journalist-steven-sotlof/.
17 Alana Massey, "Must James Foley and Steven Sotloff Be Martyrs to Not Have Died in Vain?," *Religion Dispatches* (September 9, 2014): accessed June 17, 2019, http://religiondispatches.org/must-james-foley-and-steven-sotloff-be-martyrs-in-order-to-have-not-died-in-vain/.
18 "Thích Quảng Đức," *Wikipedia*: accessed October 22, 2021, https://en.wikipedia.org/wiki/Th%C3%ADch_Quảng_Đức.
19 Kenneth Dean, "Madman or Martyr? Retired Minister Sets Self on Fire, Dies," *Tyler Morning Telegraph*, July 1, 2014.
20 Castelli, *Martyrdom and Memory*, 184.
21 Watson, *The Martyrs of Columbine*, 24–5.
22 Avalos, *Fighting Words*, 18.
23 Joiner, *Why People Die by Suicide*, 86, 92.
24 Armstrong, *Fields of Blood*, 26, 43.
25 James K. Wellman Jr. and Kyoko Tokuno, "Is Religious Violence Inevitable?," *Journal for the Scientific Study of Religion* 43, no. 3 (2004), 291–6.
26 Ibid., 294.
27 Avalos, *Fighting Words*, 19.
28 Wellman Jr. and Tokuno, "Is Religious Violence Inevitable?," 292.
29 See J. Z. Smith, *Imagining Religion: From Babylon to Jonestown* (Chicago: University of Chicago Press, 1982), ch. 7.
30 Sophia Moskalenko and Clark R. McCauley, *The Marvel of Martyrdom: The Power of Self-Sacrifice in a Selfish World* (New York: Oxford University Press, 2019), 6–10.
31 Costica Bradatan, *Dying for Ideas: The Dangerous Lives of the Philosophers* (New York: Bloomsbury Academic, 2015), 3.
32 Bradatan distinguishes between religious martyrdom and the "philosophical" martyrdom he is primarily exploring on the basis, in part, of the lack of institutionalization in the latter. Ibid., 122.

33 Ibid., 112.
34 O. Wilde, *The Portrait of Mr. W. H.* (New York: M. Kennerley, 1921), 29.
35 Margaret Watkins Tate, "Martyrdom and Integrity," *Philosophia Christi* 9, no. 1 (2007), 101.
36 Ibid., 116.
37 Ibid., 118–19.

Conclusion

1 Daniel Boyarin, *Dying for God: Martyrdom and the Making of Christianity and Judaism* (Stanford, CA: Stanford University Press, 1999), 121.
2 Sophia Moskalenko and Clark R. McCauley, *The Marvel of Martyrdom: The Power of Self-Sacrifice in a Selfish World* (New York: Oxford University Press, 2019), 6.
3 Marvin J. Newell, *A Martyr's Grace: Stories of Those Who Gave All for Christ and His Cause* (Chicago: Moody, 2006), 204.
4 The governor Pliny, whose letter to Trajan about Christians we discussed in Chapter 4, explains that while waiting for the emperor's response on how to punish Christians, he adopted the practice of putting in prison those who persist in their beliefs upon threat of punishment, since "their pertinacity and inflexible obstinacy certainly ought to be punished" (*Letters*, 10.96.3). See also Robert Louis Wilken, *The Christians as the Romans Saw Them* (New Haven, CT: Yale University Press, 2003), 82; Paul Middleton, "Enemies of the (Church and) State: Martyrdom as a Problem for Early Christianity," *Annali di storia dell'esegesi* 29, no. 2 (2012), 167–9.
5 Bart Ehrman's work is a thoughtful example of a recent attempt to assess Christianity's impact dispassionately. Bart D. Ehrman, *The Triumph of Christianity: How a Forbidden Religion Swept the World* (New York: Simon & Schuster), 2017.
6 Andrew L. Seidel, *The Founding Myth: Why Christian Nationalism Is Un-American* (New York: Sterling, 2019), 17.
7 See, for example, John Fea, *Believe Me: The Evangelical Road to Donald Trump* (Grand Rapids, MI: William B. Eerdmans, 2018).
8 See Jason Bruner, *Imagining Persecution: Why American Christians Believe There Is a Global War against Their Faith* (New Brunswick, NJ: Rutgers University Press, 2021); Candida R. Moss, *The Myth of Persecution: How Early Christians Invented a Story of Martyrdom* (New York: HarperOne, 2013).

Bibliography

Armstrong, Karen. "Charter for Compassion." Accessed November 20, 2021. http://charterforcompassion.org/.

Armstrong, Karen. *Fields of Blood: Religion and the History of Violence*. New York: Alfred A. Knopf, 2014.

Asad, Talal. *On Suicide Bombing*. New York: Columbia University Press, 2007.

Ascough, Richard. "Judith Perkins and Christian Identity Formation." *Westar National Meeting* (March 24, 2017): 1–21.

Ashford, Bruce Riley. "Daddy, Where Is God during the Hurricane?" *Fox News* (September 15, 2018): https://www.foxnews.com/opinion/daddy-where-is-god-during-the-hurricane.

Atkinson, J. Maxwell. *Discovering Suicide: Studies in the Social Organization of Sudden Death*. Pittsburgh, PA: University of Pittsburgh Press, 1978.

Avalos, Hector. *Fighting Words: The Origins of Religious Violence*. Amherst, NY: Prometheus Books, 2005.

Avalos, Hector. "Religion and Scarcity: A New Theory for the Role of Religion in Violence." In *The Oxford Handbook of Religion and Violence*, edited by Mark Juergensmeyer, Margo Kitts, and Michael K. Jerryson, 554–70. New York: Oxford University Press, 2013.

Barnes, Timothy David. "Pre-Decian *Acta Martyrum*." *Journal of Theological Studies* 19 (October 1968): 509–31.

Barnes, Timothy David. *Tertullian: A Historical and Literary Study*. Oxford: Clarendon Press, 1971.

Barrett, David B., Todd M. Johnson, Christopher R. Guidry, and Peter F. Crossing. *World Christian Trends AD 30–AD 2200*. Pasadena, CA: William Carey Library, 2001.

Barton, Carlin A. "Savage Miracles: The Redemption of Lost Honor in Roman Society and the Sacrament of the Gladiator and the Martyr." *Representations* 45 (Winter 1994): 41–71.

Basu, Moni. "15 Years after 9/11, Sikhs Still Victims of Anti-Muslim Hate Crimes." *CNN* (September 15, 2016): https://www.cnn.com/2016/09/15/us/sikh-hate-crime-victims/index.html.

Bataille, Georges. *Death and Sensuality: A Study of Eroticism and the Taboo*. New York: Walker, 1962.

Becker, Ernest. *The Denial of Death*. New York: Free Press, 1973.

Becker, Ernest. *Escape from Evil*. New York: Free Press, 1975.

Bélanger, Jocelyn J., Julie Caouette, Keren Sharvit, and Michelle Dugas. "The Psychology of Martyrdom: Making the Ultimate Sacrifice in the Name of a Cause." *Journal of Personality and Social Psychology* 107, no. 3 (2014): 494–515.

Bernard, Larry C., Michael Mills, Leland Swenson, and R. Patricia Walsh. "An Evolutionary Theory of Human Motivation." *Genetic, Social, and General Psychology Monographs* 131, no. 2 (May 1, 2005): 129–84.

Bisbee, Gary A. *Pre-Decian Acts of Martyrs and Commentarii*. Philadelphia, PA: Fortress Press, 1988.

Bowersock, G. W. *Martyrdom and Rome*. New York: Cambridge University Press, 1995.

Boyarin, Daniel. *Dying for God: Martyrdom and the Making of Christianity and Judaism*. Stanford, CA: Stanford University Press, 1999.

Bradatan, Costica. *Dying for Ideas: The Dangerous Lives of the Philosophers*. New York: Bloomsbury Academic, 2015.

Bradford, David T. "Early Christian Martyrdom and the Psychology of Depression, Suicide, and Bodily Mutilation." *Psychotherapy: Theory, Research, Practice, Training* 27, no. 1 (1990): 30.

Brent, Allen. "Ignatius of Antioch and the Imperial Cult." *Vigiliae Christianae* 52, no. 1 (1998): 30–58.

Brimlow, Robert W. *What about Hitler?: Wrestling with Jesus's Call to Nonviolence in an Evil World*. Grand Rapids, MI: Brazos Press, 2006.

Brown, Peter. "Review: Approaches to the Religious Crisis of the Third Century A.D." *English Historical Review* 83, no. 328 (July 1968): 542–58.

Brown, Peter Robert Lamont. *The Cult of the Saints: Its Rise and Function in Latin Christianity*. Chicago: University of Chicago Press, 1981.

Brubaker, Rogers, and Frederick Cooper. "Beyond 'Identity.'" *Theory and Society* 29, no. 1 (February 2000): 1–47.

Bruner, Jason. *Imagining Persecution: Why American Christians Believe There Is a Global War against Their Faith*. New Brunswick, NJ: Rutgers University Press, 2021.

Buck, P. Lorraine. "Voluntary Martyrdom Revisited." *Journal of Theological Studies* 63, no. 1 (April 2012): 125–35.

Byman, Seymour. "Guilt and Martyrdom: The Case of John Bradford." *Harvard Theological Review* 68, nos. 3/4 (1975): 305–31.

Cabezon, Jose, and Sheila Greeve Davaney. *Identity and the Politics of Scholarship in the Study of Religion*. New York: Routledge, 2004.

Castelli, Elizabeth A. *Martyrdom and Memory: Early Christian Culture Making*. New York: Columbia University Press, 2004.

Cavanaugh, William T. *The Myth of Religious Violence: Secular Ideology and the Roots of Modern Conflict*. Oxford: Oxford University Press, 2009.

Chesnut, Glenn F. *The First Christian Histories: Eusebius, Socrates, Sozomen, Theodoret, and Evagrius*. Macon, GA: Mercer University Press, 1986.

Clarke, G. W. *The Letters of St. Cyprian of Carthage*. New York: Newman Press, 1984.

Clarke, Steve. *The Justification of Religious Violence*. Chichester: Wiley-Blackwell, 2014.

Conroy, J. Oliver. "The Life and Death of John Chau, the Man Who Tried to Convert His Killers." *Guardian* (February 3, 2019): https://www.theguardian.com/world/2019/feb/03/john-chau-christian-missionary-death-sentinelese.

"Costs of War." *Watson Institute for International and Public Affairs at Brown University*. Accessed October 15, 2021. https://watson.brown.edu/costsofwar/.

"CPJ Condemns Murder of US Journalist Steven Sotloff." *Committee to Protect Journalists* (September 2, 2014): https://cpj.org/2014/09/cpj-condemns-murder-of-us-journalist-steven-sotlof/.

Cullen, Dave. "Inside the Columbine High Investigation." *Salon* (September 23, 1999): Accessed January 25, 2014. http://www.salon.com/1999/09/23/columbine_4/.

Curtin, Deane W., and Robert Litke. *Institutional Violence*. Atlanta, GA: Rodopi, 1999.

Daube, David. "The Linguistics of Suicide." *Philosophy and Public Affairs* 1, no. 4 (Summer 1972): 387–437.

Dean, Kenneth. "Madman or Martyr? Retired Minister Sets Self on Fire, Dies." *Tyler Morning Telegraph*, July 1, 2014.

Delehaye, Hippolyte. *The Work of the Bollandists through Three Centuries, 1615–1915*. Princeton, NJ: Princeton University Press, 1922.

Dodds, E. R. *Pagan and Christian in an Age of Anxiety: Some Aspects of Religious Experience from Marcus Aurelius to Constantine*. Cambridge: Cambridge University Press, 1990.

Drake, H. A. *Constantine and the Bishops: The Politics of Intolerance*. Baltimore, MD: Johns Hopkins University Press, 2000.

Drake, H. A. "Intolerance, Religious Violence, and Political Legitimacy in Late Antiquity." *Journal of the American Academy of Religion* 79, no. 1 (March 2011): 193–235.

Dreyfus, Hubert L., and Mark A. Wrathall. *A Companion to Heidegger*. Malden, MA: Blackwell, 2008.

Droge, Arthur J., and James D. Tabor. *A Noble Death: Suicide and Martyrdom among Christians and Jews in Antiquity*. San Francisco, CA: HarperSanFrancisco, 1992.

Dunn, Geoffrey D. *Tertullian*. New York: Routledge, 2004.

Durkheim, Émile. *Suicide: A Study in Sociology*. Translated by John A. Spaulding and George Simpson. New York: Free Press, 1979.

Ehrman, Bart D. *Lost Christianities: The Battles for Scripture and the Faiths We Never Knew*. New York: Oxford University Press, 2005.

Ehrman, Bart D. *The Triumph of Christianity: How a Forbidden Religion Swept the World*. New York: Simon & Schuster, 2017.

Fea, John. *Believe Me: The Evangelical Road to Donald Trump*. Grand Rapids, MI: William B. Eerdmans, 2018.

Fields, Karen E., and Barbara Jeanne Fields. *Racecraft: The Soul of Inequality in American Life*. New York: Verso, 2012.

Fletcher, Dan. "Why Is Pat Robertson Blaming Haiti?" *Time*. Accessed October 30, 2021. http://content.time.com/time/specials/packages/article/0,28804,1953379_1953494_1953674,00.html.

Foucault, Michel. *Discipline and Punish: The Birth of the Prison*. New York: Vintage Books, 1995.

Franz, Marie-Luise von, and Daryl Sharp. *The Passion of Perpetua: A Psychological Interpretation of Her Visions*. Toronto: Inner City Books, 2004.

Frend, W. H. C. *Martyrdom and Persecution in the Early Church: A Study of a Conflict from the Maccabees to Donatus*. Garden City, NY: Anchor Books, 1967.

Freud, Sigmund. *On the History of the Psycho-Analytic Movement: Papers on Metapsychology, and Other Works*. London: Hogarth Press, 1957.

Friedland, Roger. "Institution, Practice, and Ontology: Toward a Religious Sociology." In *Institutions and Ideology*, edited by Renate E. Meyer, Kerstin Sahlin, Marc J. Ventresca, and Peter Walgenbach, 45–84. Bingley: Emerald Group, 2009.

Gaddis, Michael. *There Is No Crime for Those Who Have Christ: Religious Violence in the Christian Roman Empire*. Berkeley: University of California Press, 2005.

Gebhart, Oskar Leopold von. *Acta Martyrum Selecta*. Berlin: A. Duncker, 1902.

Gettleman, Jeffrey, Kai Schultz, AyeshaVenkataraman, and Hari Kumar. "John Chau Aced Missionary Boot Camp: Reality Proved a Harsher Test." *New York Times* (November 30, 2018): https://www.nytimes.com/2018/11/30/world/asia/john-chau-andaman-missionary.html.

Gibbon, Edward. *The History of the Decline and Fall of the Roman Empire: Constantine and the Christian Empire*. London: Folio Society, 1995.

Greene, J., and J. Haidt. "How (and Where) Does Moral Judgment Work?" *Trends in Cognitive Sciences* 6, no. 12 (2002): 517–23.

Greene, Joshua David. *Moral Tribes: Emotion, Reason, and the Gap between Us and Them*. New York: Penguin Books, 2013.

Gregory, Brad S. *Salvation at Stake: Christian Martyrdom in Early Modern Europe*. Cambridge, MA: Harvard University Press, 1999.

Grig, Lucy. *Making Martyrs in Late Antiquity*. London: Duckworth, 2004.

Griswold, Eliza. "John Chau's Death on North Sentinel Island Roils the Missionary World." *New Yorker* (December 8, 2018): https://www.newyorker.com/news/on-religion/john-chaus-death-roils-the-missionary-world.

Haidt, J. "The Emotional Dog and Its Rational Tail: A Social Intuitionist Approach to Moral Judgment." *Psychological Review* 108, no. 4 (2001): 814–34.

Hall, Michael. "Man on Fire." *Texas Monthly* (December 2014). Accessed May 19, 2016. http://www.texasmonthly.com/articles/man-on-fire/.

Haslam, Nick. "Concept Creep: Psychology's Expanding Concepts of Harm and Pathology." *Psychological Inquiry* 27, no. 1 (2016): 1–17.

Heidegger, Martin. *Being and Time*. Translated by John Macquarrie and Edward Robinson. New York: Harper, 1962.

Hill, Lamar M., and E. Mansell Pattison. "Communications." *American Historical Review* 84, no. 4 (1979): 1229–40.

Hood, Jeff. "Pushing into the Flames: Rev. Charles Moore and the Struggle against Racism." *Fellowship of Reconciliation* (June 23, 2015). Accessed May 19, 2016. http://forusa.org/blogs/jeff-hood/pushing-into-flames-rev-charles-moore-struggle-against-racism/13205.

Hopkins, Keith. "Christian Number and Its Implications." *Journal of Early Christian Studies* 6, no. 2 (1998): 185–226.

Horner, Thad R., Daniel D. Isgrigg, Angela Sample, Jane B. Malcolm, Sally J. Shelton, and Roger Rydin. "The John Allen Chau Archive: Citations to Primary Sources, Major News Reports & Commentary" (2018): https://digitalshowcase.oru.edu/chau/14/.

Innaiah, N. *Forced into Faith: How Religion Abuses Children's Rights*. Amherst, NY: Prometheus Books, 2009.

Joiner, Thomas. *Why People Die by Suicide*. Cambridge, MA: Harvard University Press, 2007.

Jong, Jonathan. *Death, Anxiety, and Religious Belief: An Existential Psychology of Religion*. New York: Bloomsbury, 2016.

Jong, Jonathan, and Jamin Halberstadt. "Death Anxiety and Religious Belief: Responses to Commentaries." *Religion, Brain & Behavior* 9, no. 2 (2019): 207–18.

Kaplan, Howard. "The Rule of Law and Civil Disobedience: The Case behind King's Letter from a Birmingham Jail." *Social Education* 77, no. 3 (2013): 117–21.

Kelley, Nicole. "Philosophy as Training for Death: Reading the Ancient Christian Martyr Acts as Spiritual Exercises." *Church History: Studies in Christianity and Culture* 75, no. 4 (2006): 723–47.

Khazarzar, Ruslan. "Son of Man." Accessed October 2021. http://khazarzar.skeptik.net/pgm/PG_Migne/.

Kirkpatrick, Lee A., and Carlos David Navarrete. "Reports of My Death Anxiety Have Been Greatly Exaggerated: A Critique of Terror Management Theory from an Evolutionary Perspective." *Psychological Inquiry* 17, no. 4 (2006): 288–98.

Laine, James W. *Meta-Religion: Religion and Power in World History*. Berkeley: University of California Press, 2014.

Lankford, Adam. *The Myth of Martyrdom: What Really Drives Suicide Bombers, Rampage Shooters, and Other Self-Destructive Killers*. New York: Palgrave Macmillan, 2013.

Lankford, Adam. "Précis of the Myth of Martyrdom: What Really Drives Suicide Bombers, Rampage Shooters, and Other Self-Destructive Killers." *Behavioral and Brain Sciences* 37, no. 4 (2014): 351–62.

Leemans, Johan. *"Let Us Die That We May Live": Greek Homilies on Christian Martyrs from Asia Minor, Palestine, and Syria (c. 350–c. 450 AD)*. London: Routledge, 2003.

Leemans, Johan. *More Than a Memory: The Discourse of Martyrdom and the Construction of Christian Identity in the History of Christianity*. Leuven: Peeters, 2005.

Lefkowitz, Mary R. "The Motivations for St. Perpetua's Martyrdom." *Journal of the American Academy of Religion* 44, no. 3 (1976): 417–21.

Lehtipuu, Outi. "'What Harm Is There for You to Say Caesar Is Lord?' Emperors and the Imperial Cult in Early Christian Stories of Martyrdom." *Collegium* 20 (2016): 98–118.

Lieberoth, Andreas. "The Evolution of Martyrdom? Considerations in the Study of Religious Self-Sacrifice." In *Human Characteristics: Evolutionary Perspectives on Human Mind and Kind*, edited by Henrik Høgh-Olesen, Jan Tønnesvang, and Preben Bertelsen, 274–95. Cambridge: Cambridge Scholars, January 23, 2009.

Lieu, Judith. *Christian Identity in the Jewish and Graeco-Roman World*. Oxford: Oxford University Press, 2004.

Lieu, Judith. *Neither Jew nor Greek?: Constructing Christian Identity*. London: Bloomsbury T&T Clark, 2016.

Lieu, Judith M. "The Forging of Christian Identity." *Mediterranean Archaeology* 11 (1998): 71–82.

Markus, R. A. *The End of Ancient Christianity*. Cambridge: Cambridge University Press, 1990.

Markus, R. A. "The Problem of Self-Definition: From Sect to Church." In *The Shaping of Christianity in the Second and Third Centuries*, edited by E. P. Sanders, Albert I. Baumgarten, and Alan Mendelson, 1–15. London: SCM Press, 1980.

Martin, Jeffery, Jessica M. LaCroix, Laura A. Novak, and Marjan Ghahramanlou-Holloway. "Typologies of Suicide: A Critical Literature Review." *Archives of Suicide Research* 24, no. 1 (2020): S25–S40.

Martin, Leonard L., and Kees Van den Bos. "Beyond Terror: Towards a Paradigm Shift in the Study of Threat and Culture." *European Review of Social Psychology* 25, no. 1 (2014): 32–70.

Massey, Alana. "Must James Foley and Steven Sotloff Be Martyrs to Not Have Died in Vain?" *Religion Dispatches* (September 9, 2014): http://religiondispatches.org/must-james-foley-and-steven-sotloff-be-martyrs-in-order-to-have-not-died-in-vain/.

Matthews, Shelly. "The Need for the Stoning of Stephen." In *Violence in the New Testament*, edited by E. Leigh Gibson and Shelly Matthews, 124–39. New York: T&T Clark, 2005.

Matthews, Shelly. *Perfect Martyr: The Stoning of Stephen and the Construction of Christian Identity*. New York: Oxford University Press, 2010.

McGregor, Ian. "Offensive Defensiveness: Toward an Integrative Neuroscience of Compensatory Zeal after Mortality Salience, Personal Uncertainty, and Other Poignant Self-Threats." *Psychological Inquiry* 17, no. 4 (2006): 299–308.

McIntyre, Alison. "Doctrine of Double Effect." *Stanford Encyclopedia of Philosophy* (Winter 2014): http://plato.stanford.edu/archives/win2014/entries/double-effect/.

McIntyre, Drew B. "Heroism, Martyrdom and Suicide: Thoughts on Self-Immolation." *United Methodist Insight* (July 17, 2014). Accessed May 19, 2016. http://um-insight.net/perspectives/heroism,-martyrdom-and-suicide%3A-thoughts-on-self-immolation/.

Meeks, Wayne A. *The First Urban Christians: The Social World of the Apostle Paul*. New Haven, CT: Yale University Press, 1983.

Mendels, Doron. *The Media Revolution of Early Christianity: An Essay on Eusebius's Ecclesiastical History*. Grand Rapids, MI: William B. Eerdmans, 1999.

Merari, Ariel, Ilan Diamant, Arie Bibi, Yoav Broshi, and Giora Zakin. "Personality Characteristics of 'Self Martyrs'/'Suicide Bombers' and Organizers of Suicide Attacks." *Terrorism and Political Violence* 22, no. 1 (December 22, 2009): 87–101.

Mercier, Brett, Stephanie R. Kramer, and Azim F. Shariff. "Belief in God: Why People Believe, and Why They Don't." *Current Directions in Psychological Science* 27, no. 4 (2018): 263–8.

Metzl, Jonathan M., and Kenneth T. MacLeish. "Mental Illness, Mass Shootings, and the Politics of American Firearms." *American Journal of Public Health* 105, no. 2 (December 12, 2014): 240–9.

Middleton, Paul. "Early Christian Voluntary Martyrdom: A Statement for the Defence." *Journal of Theological Studies* 64, no. 2 (October 2013): 556–73.

Middleton, Paul. "Enemies of the (Church and) State: Martyrdom as a Problem for Early Christianity." *Annali di storia dell'esegesi* 29, no. 2 (2012): 161–81.

Middleton, Paul. *Radical Martyrdom and Cosmic Conflict in Early Christianity*. London: T&T Clark, 2006.

Middleton, Paul. "What Is Martyrdom?" *Mortality* 19, no. 2 (2014): 117–33.

Migne, J.-P. *Patrologiae Cursus Completus: Series Graeca*. Paris: J.P. Migne, 1857.

Minton, Gretchen E. "'The Same Cause and Like Quarell': Eusebius, John Foxe, and the Evolution of Ecclesiastical History." *Church History* 71, no. 4 (2002): 715–42.

Mitchell, Jolyon. *Martyrdom: A Very Short Introduction*. Oxford: Oxford University Press, 2012.

Moskalenko, Sophia, and Clark R. McCauley. *The Marvel of Martyrdom: The Power of Self-Sacrifice in a Selfish World*. New York: Oxford University Press, 2019.

Moss, Candida R. *Ancient Christian Martyrdom: Diverse Practices, Theologies, and Traditions*. New Haven, CT: Yale University Press, 2012.

Moss, Candida R. "The Discourse of Voluntary Martyrdom: Ancient and Modern." *Church History* 81, no. 3 (September 2012): 531–51.

Moss, Candida R. *The Myth of Persecution: How Early Christians Invented a Story of Martyrdom*. New York: HarperOne, 2013.

Moss, Candida R. "Notions of Orthodoxy in Early Christian Martyrdom Literature." In *The Other Side: Apocryphal Perspectives on Ancient Christian "Orthodoxies,"* edited by Tobias Nicklas, Candida R. Moss, Christopher Tuckett, and Joseph Verheyden, 165–76. Göttingen: Vandenhoeck & Ruprecht, July 17, 2017.

Moss, Candida R. *The Other Christs: Imitating Jesus in Ancient Christian Ideologies of Martyrdom*. New York: Oxford University Press, 2010.

Musurillo, Herbert. *The Acts of the Christian Martyrs*. Oxford: Clarendon Press, 1972.

Newell, Marvin J. *A Martyr's Grace: Stories of Those Who Gave All for Christ and His Cause*. Chicago: Moody, 2006.

Newman, Jay. "The Motivation of Martyrs: A Philosophical Perspective." *Thomist* 35, no. 4 (October 1971): 581–600.

Nietzsche, Friedrich Wilhelm. "Twilight of the Idols or, How One Philosophizes with a Hammer." In *The Portable Nietzsche*, edited by Walter Arnold Kaufmann, 463–564. New York: Penguin Books, 1982.

Odahl, Charles M. *Constantine and the Christian Empire*. London: Routledge, 2004.

Okure, Teresa, Jon Sobrino, and Felix Wilfreld. *Rethinking Martyrdom*. London: SCM Press, 2003.

Parke, Caleb. "US Missionary Killed by Remote Island Tribe Inspires Others to Join Mission Field" (November 15, 2019). Accessed February 10, 2021. https://www.foxnews.com/faith-values/missionary-john-chau-christian-inspiration.

Parry, Marc. "Death Denial: Does Our Terror of Dying Drive Almost Everything We Do?" *Chronicle Review* (May 22, 2015): https://www.chronicle.com/article/death-denial/.

Pearse, Roger. "The Tertullian Project." Accessed November 5, 2021. https://www.tertullian.org.

Perkins, Judith. "The Apocryphal Acts of the Apostles and the Early Christian Martyrdom." *Arethusa* 18, no. 2 (1985): 211–30.

Perkins, Judith. "Perpetua's Vas: Asserting Christian Identity." In *Group Identity and Religious Individuality in Late Antiquity*, edited by Éric Rebillard and Jörg Rüpke, 129–64. Washington, DC: Catholic University of America Press, 2015.

Perkins, Judith. *The Suffering Self: Pain and Narrative Representation in the Early Christian Era*. London: Routledge, 1995.

Perry, Alex. "The Last Days of John Allen Chau." *Outside* (July 26, 2019): https://www.outsideonline.com/2400030/john-allen-chau-life-death-north-sentinel.

Pilpel, Avital, and Lawrence Amsel. "What Is Wrong with Rational Suicide." *Philosophia* 39, no. 1 (2011): 111–23.

Pliny. *Letters, and Panegyricus*. Translated by Betty Radice. Cambridge, MA: Harvard University Press, 1972.

Post, Jerrold M., Farhana Ali, Schuyler W. Henderson, Steven Shanfield, Jeff Victoroff, and Stevan Weine. "The Psychology of Suicide Terrorism." *Psychiatry: Interpersonal and Biological Processes* 72, no. 1 (March 1, 2009): 13–31.

Potter, David. "Martyrdom as Spectacle." In *Theater and Society in the Classical World*, edited by Ruth Scodel, 53–88. Ann Arbor: University of Michigan Press, 1993.

Rebillard, Éric. *Christians and Their Many Identities in Late Antiquity, North Africa, 200–450 CE*. Ithaca, NY: Cornell University Press, 2012.

Rebillard, Éric, and Jörg Rüpke, eds. *Group Identity and Religious Individuality in Late Antiquity*. Washington, DC: Catholic University of America Press, 2015.

Recla, Matthew. "Autothanatos: The Martyr's Self-Formation." *Journal of the American Academy of Religion* 82, no. 2 (2014): 472–94.

Recla, Matthew. "*Homo Profanus*: The Christian Martyr and the Violence of Meaning-Making." *Critical Research on Religion* 2, no. 2 (2014): 147–64.

Recla, Matthew. "Martyrdom and the Creation of Christian Identity." In *The Wiley-Blackwell Concise Companion to Christian Martyrdom*, edited by Paul Middleton, 199–214. Hoboken, NJ: Wiley-Blackwell, 2018.

Recla, Matthew (Matt) J. "Pathology, Identity, or Both? Making Meaning from Early Christian Martyrdom." *Mortality* 27, no. 1 (2020): 1–15.

Riddle, Donald W. *The Martyrs: A Study in Social Control*. Chicago: University of Chicago Press, 1931.

Rollins, Peter. *The Fidelity of Betrayal: Towards a Church beyond Belief*. Brewster, MA: Paraclete Press, 2008.

Ronsse, Erin. "Rhetoric of Martyrs: Listening to Saints Perpetua and Felicitas." *Journal of Early Christian Studies* 14, no. 3 (Fall 2006): 283–327.

Sapolsky, Robert M. *Behave: The Biology of Humans at Our Best and Worst*. New York: Penguin Press, 2017.

Sartre, Jean-Paul, John Kulka, and Arlette Elkaïm-Sartre. *Existentialism Is a Humanism = (L'Existentialisme Est Un Humanisme); Including, a Commentary on the Stranger (Explication De L'Étranger)*. Translated by Carol Macomber. New Haven, CT: Yale University Press, 2007.

Scarry, Elaine. *The Body in Pain: The Making and Unmaking of the World*. New York: Oxford University Press, 1987.

Schaff, Philip, and Henry Wace, eds. *Eusebius: Church History, Constantine the Great, and Oration in the Praise of Constantine*. Edinburgh: T&T Clark, 1997.

Schweitzer, Albert. *The Quest of the Historical Jesus: A Critical Study of Its Progress from Reimarus to Wrede*. Translated by W. Montgomery. New York: Macmillan, 1956.

Scott, W. R. *Institutions and Organizations: Ideas and Interests*. Los Angeles, CA: Sage, 2008.

Seidel, Andrew L. *The Founding Myth: Why Christian Nationalism Is Un-American*. New York: Sterling, 2019.

Sizgorich, Thomas. *Violence and Belief in Late Antiquity: Militant Devotion in Christianity and Islam*. Philadelphia: University of Pennsylvania Press, 2009.

Smilansky, Saul. "A Puzzle about Self-Sacrificing Altruism." *Journal of Controversial Ideas* 1, no. 1 (April 25, 2021): 1–14.

Smith, J. Z. *Drudgery Divine: On the Comparison of Early Christianities and the Religions of Late Antiquity*. Chicago: University of Chicago Press, 1990.

Smith, J. Z. *Imagining Religion: From Babylon to Jonestown*. Chicago: University of Chicago Press, 1982.

Smith, J. Z. "Religion, Religions, Religious." In *Critical Terms for Religious Studies*, edited by Mark C. Taylor, 269–84. Chicago: University of Chicago Press, 1998.

Smith, Lacey Baldwin. *Fools, Martyrs, Traitors: The Story of Martyrdom in the Western World*. Evanston, IL: Northwestern University Press, 1999.

Solomon, Sheldon, Jeff Greenberg, and Thomas A. Pyszczynski. *The Worm at the Core: On the Role of Death in Life*. New York: Random House, 2015.

Stark, Rodney. *The Rise of Christianity: A Sociologist Reconsiders History*. Princeton, NJ: Princeton University Press, 1996.

Ste. Croix, G. E. M. de. "Aspects of the 'Great' Persecution." *Harvard Theological Review* 47, no. 2 (April 1954): 75–113.

Ste. Croix, G. E. M. de. *Christian Persecution, Martyrdom, and Orthodoxy*. Oxford: Oxford University Press, 2006.

Ste. Croix, G. E. M. de. "Why Were the Early Christians Persecuted?" *Past and Present* 26 (November 1963): 6–38.

Stoops, Robert F., Jr. "If I Suffer ... Epistolary Authority in Ignatius of Antioch." *Harvard Theological Review* 80, no. 2 (1987): 161–78.

Strauss, David Friedrich. *The Life of Jesus*. Translated by George Eliot. New York: C. Blanchard, 1860.

Talk, D. C., and Voice of the Martyrs. *Jesus Freaks: Stories of Those Who Stood for Jesus, the Ultimate Jesus Freaks*. Tulsa, OK: Albury, 1999.

Tate, Margaret Watkins. "Martyrdom and Integrity." *Philosophia Christi* 9, no. 1 (2007): 101–20.

The Center for Public Integrity. "False Premise for Going to War" (December 10, 2008): https://publicintegrity.org/politics/false-premise-for-going-to-war/.

"The Last Night." *Friends of Flight 93 National Memorial*. Accessed October 15, 2021. https://www.flight93friends.org/learning-center/crime-scene-investigation/the-last-night-document.

"Thích Quảng Đức." *Wikipedia*. Accessed October 22, 2021. https://en.wikipedia.org/wiki/Th%C3%ADch_Quảng_Đức.

Tilley, Maureen A. "The Ascetic Body and the (Un)making of the World of the Martyr." *Journal of the American Academy of Religion* 59, no. 3 (Autumn 1991): 467–79.

Tite, Philip L. "Voluntary Martyrdom and Gnosticism." *Journal of Early Christian Studies* 23, no. 1 (Spring 2015): 27–54.

Vardoulakis, Dimitris. *Sovereignty and Its Other: Toward the Dejustification of Violence*. New York: Fordham University Press, 2013.

Watson, Justin. *The Martyrs of Columbine: Faith and the Politics of Tragedy*. New York: Palgrave Macmillan, 2002.

Weber, Max. *From Max Weber: Essays in Sociology*. New York: Oxford University Press, 1946.

Weiner, Eugene, and Anita Weiner. *The Martyr's Conviction: A Sociological Analysis.* Atlanta, GA: Scholars Press, 1990.

Wellman Jr., James K., and Kyoko Tokuno. "Is Religious Violence Inevitable?" *Journal for the Scientific Study of Religion* 43, no. 3 (2004): 291–6.

Wicker, Brian. *Witnesses to Faith?: Martyrdom in Christianity and Islam.* Aldershot: Ashgate, 2006.

Wilde, O. *The Portrait of Mr. W. H.* New York: M. Kennerley, 1921.

Wilken, Robert Louis. *The Christians as the Romans Saw Them.* New Haven, CT: Yale University Press, 2003.

Young, Robin Darling. *In Procession before the World Martyrdom as Public Liturgy in Early Christianity.* Milwaukee, WI: Marquette University Press, 2001.

Zilboorg, Gregory. "Fear of Death." *Psychoanalytic Quarterly* 12, no. 4 (1943): 465–75.

Žižek, Slavoj. *Violence: Six Sideways Reflections.* London: Profile, 2008.

Index

abnormal(ity)
   death wish 126, 166
   and evolution 35–6, 152
   and John Chau 9–11
   psychological 13, 115, 124–5, 131, 139
affiliation
   Christian 75, 88, 97, 115, 147
   group 146, 150, 152–4, 158–9, 163
Agamben, Giorgio 44, 178 n.19
agency (of the martyr)
   absence or removal 14, 21, 100, 129
   conveying or returning 26, 75
Allah 142
anagke 100. *See also* divine compulsion
anxiety
   about death 11, 39, 49, 75, 159
   existential 24, 28, 30–2
apostasy 65, 68, 76, 85, 87
Aquinas, Thomas 98
Armstrong, Karen 53–4
Ascough, Richard 130
Augustine (bishop) 96, 111, 134, 164
autonomy
   of the martyr 46, 90
   of violence 43, 47
   of willing suicide 11, 36, 58, 69, 117, 164
Avalos, Hector 15, 140–1, 143, 149, 153

Barnes, T. D. 59, 72, 186 n.43
Bataille, Georges 42–3
Becker, Ernest 34–7, 42, 48–51, 132
Being and Time. See Heidegger
belongingness 108–10
Benjamin, Walter 44
Bernall, Cassie 144–8, 166
biological
   imperative for survival 35, 37, 105, 148–9, 152, 161
blame
   for martyrdom 7, 78, 80–1, 97, 155
   for violence 53–4

blood
   and Cyprian 78
   and faith 71
   and the institution 6, 52, 74, 167
   and Jesus 156
   of the martyr 68, 137
   of Polycarp 64
   Tertullian's phrase 57, 90, 122, 163
Bowersock, G. W. 70, 72, 77
Boyarin, Daniel 165, 184 n.28
Bradatan, Costica 158–9
Bradford, John 126
Branch Davidians 102
Brimlow, Robert 133
Brown, Peter 127
Brubaker, Rogers and Frederick Cooper 128–9
Bruner, Jason 136
Buck, P. Lorraine 96–102, 104
burdensomeness 108–10
Bush, George W. 93
Byman, Seymour 126–7

certificate (of sacrifice) 78, 80–2
Chau, John Allen 1–10
   and evil forces 48
   and martyrdom 93, 116
   sincere 163
   and social interaction 148
   and willing suicide 16, 110
Christ
   affirmation of 59–60, 71–2, 146. *See also* Jesus
   death of 19, 21
   as end of martyrdom 31, 61
   imitation of 64–6, 68, 82, 122
Christian
   as us 44
   defining a martyr 23, 25–6, 104
   as identity 6–7, 114–16, 129–33
   as institution 6, 55, 72, 167–8
   narrative 59, 118, 124, 164

persecuted 128, 147–8, 166
training 119–23
triumph 12, 48, 59, 87–8, 90
as voluntary 75, 95
civil rights movement 47
Clement (bishop) 70–7
collateral damage 42, 97, 99, 140
Columbine 144, 147, 166
confessor 68, 78–83, 85, 151
Constantine 57–9, 68, 117, 124
Cyprian (bishop) 58, 77–86, 94

Dasein 27–36
death
  anxiety about 11
  aversion to 20–2
  being-towards 26–3
  control of 83–4
  criterion of martyrdom 143–51
  defiance 50
  as element of martyrdom 6, 16, 21–2
  fear/terror of 35–40, 49–50
  institutional use of 41, 47, 84, 104, 116, 150–1
  intentional 22–3
  justification of 14
  and meaning 5–7, 10–11, 38–40, 51, 146–8
  morality of 153–61
  training for 119–23
  voluntary 97, 99–103
  wish for 70, 74, 96, 111, 125–8, 166
democracy 16, 45, 51, 142, 168
Denial of Death. See Becker, Ernest
Derrida, Jacques 44
devil 64, 68, 71
Dionysius (bishop) 70, 85–6
divine compulsion 94, 99–100, 133–4, 155
Dodds, E. R. 101, 111, 184 n.30
Donatist 68, 111
double effect 98
Droge, Arthur 100
Durkheim, Emile 2–3, 107

early Christian(ity) 13
  history 23
  identity 114–15, 123
  martyrdoms 15–16, 19, 22

Ecclesiastical History. See Eusebius
Ehrman, Bart 127, 190 n.29
empirical
  difference between suicide and martyrdom 112
  divine compulsion 134
  and religious violence 149, 153–5
  Terror Management 36–9
Escape from Evil. See Becker, Ernest
Eusebius (bishop)
  critique of 125
  triumphant paradigm of 57–8, 61, 87–8
evil. *See* Becker, Ernest
evolution
  and cooperation 99
  and death 35, 37, 84, 134, 161
  and immortality 49

finality (of death) 23–4, 30, 37, 87, 133, 164
Foucault, Michel 44, 84, 134
Foxe, John 124
Frend, W. H. C. 58–9, 101

genetic
  factors in suicide 108, 135–6, 167
Gibbon, Edward 15, 89, 125
gospel 9
"Great Persecution" 59, 86, 88, 95, 118
Greene, Joshua 98–9, 141–2, 176 n.45
Gregory, Brad 125–7

Heaven's Gate 102
Heidegger, Martin 11, 26–8, 30–8, 164
Henning, Alan 145–7
heretic
  in Augustine 111
  in Clement 71–3
  in Gibbon 125
  Tertullian 70
  violence against 89–90
hero
  in Becker 50–1
  contrasted to the martyr 106, 127, 158
  and Rome 75

identity
  "approach" 128–30
  Christian 12, 104, 106, 131–4

discourse 114–16, 119, 124, 149, 165–6
formation 6
martyrdom and 6–7, 12–14, 16, 19, 70
religious/institutional 23–5
suffering 122
ideology
   as component of martyrdom 2–3, 12–13, 25, 40, 166
   insufficient for suicide 117
   scholarly 96, 102–4, 136
   triumph of Christianity 90
Ignatius (martyr) 61–2, 121, 126–7
imitatio Christi (imitation of Christ) 64–8, 82, 117, 120, 122
immoral
   martyrdom 15
   violence 15
immortality 35, 39, 75, 152, 156–7
   projects 49–51
imperialism 114, 137
inherent (violence in religion) 153–4
institution(ality)
   Christianity 3, 6, 9
   claim of martyrdom 48, 144–52, 155, 158, 161, 166–7
   and control 13, 36, 94, 179 n.22
   core of 17
   definition of 6, 43, 180 n.30
   explanation of martyrdom 10, 47
   self-promotion 160–1
   and violence 41, 43
   as virus 156
intention(ality)
   of Chau's death 5
   of death 22
   of martyrs 20, 23, 96–7

Jesus
   and argument against martyrdom 73
   death of 132, 136. *See also* Christ
   model of martyrdom 22, 100, 116, 156–7
Jews
   and Montanism 69
   in Polycarp 65
   and voluntary martyrdom 100
Joiner, Thomas 108–9, 111, 135
Jonestown 157
justification
   of martyrdom 5, 14, 145, 148
   of suicide 160
   of violence 44–7, 52, 139–41, 154
Justin Martyr 61–2, 183 n.16, 184 n.25

Kelley, Nicole 121–2
Kierkegaard, Soren 36
King, Jr., Martin Luther 166, 179 n.21

lapsed 78–86, 94, 101
Late Antiquity 89, 94, 119, 128
law 8
Leemans, Johan 133
Lehtipuu, Outi 123
Lieu, Judith 119, 129
love
   in Clement 71–2
   and desire for salvation 63, 66
   and Divine Command Theory 156
   "in love with death" 96, 111
   motivation for martyrdom 20–1
   in Thich Quang Duc 145
Lyons and Vienne (martyrs of) 58, 61, 67–9, 78

Marcus Aurelius (emperor) 68, 126
Markus, Robert 128
martyr(s)
   Christian 19
   motivation of 20–1
   small number of 15, 26, 36, 104, 132, 156
   texts 12–13
   "true" 64–5, 72, 76. *See also* martyrdom
martyrdom
   as aberrant 21, 100, 118, 131
   and authenticity 29–34
   for the Church 81–2
   criteria for 143–53
   definition 2–3
   difference from suicide 25, 70, 105–12
   meaning to the martyr 22–3
   moral implications of 14–15, 154–62
   as orthodox 58, 107, 113, 117, 127, 131, 134, 155
   as pathology 115, 118–19, 125–8, 131
   and persecution 89–91, 166–9
   research on 15–16, 26
   training 119–23

and violence 42, 46–8, 53–4, 136–7
voluntary 93–105, 131
Martyrs of Palestine 86, 95–6, 187 n.66
Middleton, Paul 190 n.33
Montanism 69–70, 86
and Tertullian 71, 76
Moore, Charles 93, 104, 107, 112, 145–6, 148
moral(ity)
calculus 152
institutional 15
interpretation of martyr actions 97–8, 136
of John Chau 4
of martyrdom 9, 14
of unintentional harm 99
of suicide 148
of violence 41–2
Moss, Candida 120, 129–31, 181 n.42
murder
contrast to martyr 71, 167
mass 124, 147
prohibited 43, 45
Musurillo, Herbert 15, 66

Newman, Jay 19–20, 24
Nietzsche, Friedrich Wilhelm 176 n.52
9/11 (event) 52, 139, 142
nonreligious 3, 14, 143
nonviolence 34, 47–8, 154

Obama, Barack 142
orthodox(y)
Christianity 102, 114, 117
and Eusebius 87
and martyrdom 58, 61–2, 107, 113, 127, 131, 134, 155
and Tertullian 71–2, 76

passive (martyrdom) 23, 84, 87, 120, 173 n.15
pathology. *See* martyrdom
Paul (apostle) 60, 62, 64, 71
Perkins, Judith 122, 128, 130
Perpetua (martyr) 83–4, 122–3
persecution
by Christianity 89–90, 124
of Christians 59, 95
component of martyrdom 146–8

doctrine of 125
emphasis on 128–30
Eusebius's use 67–8, 85–8, 164
flight from 76–7
and Polycarp 61
responsibility for 154, 168
role in martyrdom 102–3, 117–19
sporadic 123
Peter (apostle) 60, 62
phenomenon
discrete religion 53
existential 32–3, 116
of martyrdom 1–6, 16–17, 22–3, 46, 127, 163–5
masochism 125
"suicide-by-cop" 110
violence as 43
of willing suicide 41
Plato 70, 158
Pliny (the Younger) 60–1, 64, 67, 182 n.10–12, 199 n.4
Polycarp (martyr) 58, 61–8, 70–1, 118, 121, 134
potentiality
and authenticity 37
of death 23–4, 131, 133
for-being 27–31, 33, 35
Potter, David 84–5
power
of Christianity 58, 114, 117
of death 72, 84
deviation 134
institutional 8, 11, 40, 44, 84, 139
of martyrdom 22, 75, 79, 122, 161
of violence 43, 154
of willing suicide 82, 112
punishment
function of 46, 48
Roman 60–1, 64, 84, 86, 96–7
of Socrates 158

Rank, Otto 50
Rebillard, Éric and Jörg Rüpke 129
religion
and death 36–9
the study of 10, 13, 104, 114–15
and violence 52–5, 139–43, 153–4, 164, 166
Riddle, Donald 119–20, 125–6

Roman
  culture 71
  Empire 57-9, 77, 89, 125
  religion 74. *See also* persecution
Rome (city) 61, 78, 80-1
Romero, Oscar 166

sacrifice 5, 11, 16
  certificate of 78
  in contrast to martyrdom 23-5, 68
  defining martyrdom 19-22, 32, 38, 144
  to Rome 64-5, 81-2, 85, 95
  willingness to 135
salvation
  result of martyrdom 82
scarce resources 117, 149
self-harm 10, 108-10, 161
self-interest
  and harm 109
  institutional 17, 153
  of the martyr 20-1, 53, 106, 155
self-preservation 4, 35, 45
sin
  and death 71
  of suicide 94
Smith, Lacey Baldwin 127, 181 n.41
Socrates 100, 127, 158-9
sovereign(ty) 12, 43
  and democracy 45. *See also*
    institution(ality)
Ste. Croix, G. E. M. de
  on Christian persecution 89-90, 94-7,
    103, 121, 188 n.68
  and pathology 100-1, 126, 182 n.13
Stephen (protomartyr) 60, 62, 68
stigma (of suicide) 9, 13, 112, 118, 143
  of martyrdom 127, 131, 136
Streeter, Joseph 89-90
suicide
  as aberrant 30, 105
  anti-institutional nature of 23, 94
  by-cop 25, 110
  definition 2-3
  morality of institutional use 139,
    143, 162
  morality of 159. *See also* stigma
  perceived distinction from
    martyrdom 13, 25-6, 94, 105-13,
    127, 148

  prohibitions of 46
  propensity for 136
  terrorism 135
survival 7. *See also* self-preservation

Tabor, James 100
Tate, Margaret Watkins 161-2
Terror Management Theory 36-9, 132
Tertullian 58, 64, 70-7, 84, 186 n.43
  and "blood is seed" 57, 90, 122,
    132, 163
theology
  understanding of martyrdom 2, 7,
    19-21, 115, 124, 133
Thich Quang Duc 145-6, 148
Tilley, Maureen 120
tolerance 89-90
Trolley Problem 98

unverifiable
  beliefs 157
  institutions 154-5, 162
  Jesus 156
  legitimacy of religious violence 15,
    141, 143
  legitimacy of martyrdom 94, 100, 103,
    153, 158
  religion 140, 142, 149, 151, 154, 159
utilitarian 14-15

Vardoulakis, Dimitris 44-5, 51
veneration 66, 90, 120, 166
victim
  blaming 7
  Christian 95
  and innocence 52
  martyr as 84, 155, 158, 167
  of suicide 2, 107, 160, 168
  Trolley Problem 98
  of violence 47, 113, 154
violence
  exposure to 109
  institutional control of 11-13, 25, 36,
    41, 43-8, 164
  justifiability 51-2, 149, 159, 161
  and morality 41-3, 139-43
  relation to religion 52-5, 139, 153-4
  religious 15
  and suicide 26, 94

willingness to participate in 136
voluntary martyr(dom) 13, 62–3,
    84, 94–6
  opposition to 96–105
  as suicide 134, 155
  unnatural 131

well-being 24, 124, 143, 152, 154–9
willing suicide
  agency of 75
  anti-institutional nature of 11,
    45, 48, 90
  blaming religion for 53–4
  and choice 14
  in Clement 71
  defiance of death 50
  as defining martyrdom 2–3, 25
  as a gamble 160

  as inauthentic 30–2
  and the institution 8, 46–7, 51, 164
  power of 82, 84
  and religious commitment 127
  telos of 90
  violence of 76–7
  as voluntary 95, 103, 134
willingness
  criterion for martyrdom 144
witness
  in Clement 71–2
  and martyrdom 60, 76–7
  and Polycarp 64–6

Young, Robin Darling 120–1

Žižek, Slavoj 178 n.19

www.ingramcontent.com/pod-product-compliance
Lightning Source LLC
Chambersburg PA
CBHW062222300426
44115CB00012BA/2174